A New Birth of
FREEDOM

A New Birth of
FREEDOM

The Effect of the Civil War and Reconstruction on Ohio Law

W. Thomas Minahan

ARCHWAY
PUBLISHING

Archway Publishing books may be ordered through booksellers or by contacting:

Archway Publishing
1663 Liberty Drive
Bloomington, IN 47403
www.archwaypublishing.com
1 (888) 242-5904

ISBN: 978-1-4808-5425-3 (sc)
ISBN: 978-1-4808-5424-6 (e)

Library of Congress Control Number: 2017917581

Print information available on the last page.

Archway Publishing rev. date: 12/14/2017

Contents

Chapter 1

Why Study Ohio?

Mrs. Powel, confronting Benjamin Franklin after he signed the Constitution: "Well, Doctor, what have we got—a republic or a monarchy?"

Benjamin Franklin: "A republic, Madam, if you can keep it."

The Republic, sir, is in the hands of its friends, and its only safety is in the hands of its friends.

—John A. Bingham, 1866

I. Introduction

The American Civil War was by far the most traumatic event in this nation's history. Because of a great number of factors, the country became divided against itself. Tension between the sections had been brewing for many years, but a number of events occurred in the 1850s that created the explosive atmosphere that led to the Civil War: a more stringent Fugitive Slave Act, which was enacted by Congress as part of the Compromise of 1850; arguments regarding whether the vast territories acquired as a result of the war against Mexico should be open to slavery; the regional bloodshed that occurred as a result of the Kansas-Nebraska Act; the decision of the

US Supreme Court in the case of *Dred Scott vs. Sandford;* and last, but certainly not least, the publication of the antislavery novel *Uncle Tom's Cabin.*[1]

While *Uncle Tom's Cabin* may be the literary piece that foreshadowed the Civil War, President Lincoln was the political force that pushed the country to the breaking point. Lincoln, an antislavery Republican, was elected as president in 1860. Within two months of Lincoln's victory, seven states seceded from the Union and established the Confederate States of America. The fighting began when the Confederate Army opened fire on Fort Sumter, a federal installation located in Charleston Harbor, South Carolina, on April 12, 1861. A four-year struggle ensued that cost more than six hundred thousand lives.

President Lincoln resorted to extraordinary measures to win the war and preserve the Union, including calling forth the state militias, suspending habeas corpus, and declaring a naval blockade of all Southern ports. Lincoln assumed near-dictatorial powers that strained the Constitution in ways never seen before or since.[2] Did Lincoln usurp the powers of Congress and the courts when performing these actions? Probably.[3] Did he trample on the Bill of Rights and the rule of law to preserve the Union? Unquestionably.[4]

Although Lincoln had no personal ties to Ohio, the state still played a key role in the American Civil War, both politically and logistically. In the 1840s and '50s, Ohio emerged as an intellectual leader and provided both political leadership and Western idealism. By 1860, Ohio was the third most populous state in the Union, with 2,339,000 residents. Ohio was the fourth most industrialized state in the nation and a leader in agriculture. Ohio provided over three hundred thousand troops to the Union Army during the Civil War—the third largest number of troops to come from any Union state. More than thirty-five thousand Ohioans, or one out of every ten who served, died as a result of the war. Several of the Union's leading

---

[1]   For an excellent discussion of the struggle between nationalism and sectionalism in the 1850s, see David M. Potter, *The Impending Crisis: America before the Civil War, 1848–1861* (New York: Harper Perennial, 2011).

[2]   Justin Ewers, "Revoking Civil Liberties: Lincoln's Constitutional Dilemma," *US News and World Report*, February 10, 2009, accessed May 18, 2017, http://www.usnews.com/news/history/articles/2009/02/10/revoking-civil-liberties-lincolns-constitutional-dilemma.

[3]   Ibid.

[4]   Ibid.

generals—including Ulysses S. Grant, William Tecumseh Sherman, and Phillip H. Sheridan—hailed from Ohio. Many leading politicians—such as Secretary of War Edwin Stanton, Treasury Secretary and later Chief Justice Salmon P. Chase, Senators Benjamin Wade and John Sherman, and Congressmen Clement Vallandigham, George Pendleton, John Bingham, and James A. Garfield—called Ohio home. Finally, five Ohio-born Union Army officers later served as president of the United States: Ulysses S. Grant, Rutherford B. Hayes, James A. Garfield, Benjamin Harrison, and William McKinley.

Even though Ohio played such an influential role in the war, its citizens paid a high price. Ohio and the other Union states were required to cede an enormous amount of power to the federal government to win the war. Ohioans were also forced to endure the curtailment of many of their individual rights as guaranteed by the US and Ohio Constitutions. Professor Daniel Farber discussed in detail infringements on individual rights that occurred during this era—most notably the suspension of habeas corpus, arrests without trials, trials of civilians by military commissions, and infringements on free speech.

Farber writes that at least thirteen thousand civilians were held under military arrest during the Civil War. Some of the arrestees, particularly draft dodgers, deserters, and blockade runners, were arguably under military jurisdiction. Others—most notably citizens of the Confederacy, those Northern citizens caught trading with the Confederacy, and individuals accused of disloyal speech—were often denied their constitutional right to jury trial and other protections.[5]

Thus, because of the infringements on individual rights, the original goal of this study was to examine and discuss the changes in Ohio law that occurred because of the Civil War. The individual human rights (generally referred to as civil rights or political rights at that time) abuses listed previously are certainly issues ripe for further examination. However, it soon became clear that the abuses that occurred because of the Civil War were merely temporary measures enacted to win the war. Yet the power shift that occurred between the states and the federal government became a lasting paradigm via the Reconstruction era (1863–77). This shift was necessary to abolish slavery, but there were many collateral effects as well.

---

[5]   Daniel Farber, *Lincoln's Constitution* (Chicago: University of Chicago Press, 2003), 144–46.

II. The Thirty-Ninth Congress

Those responsible for leading the country out of the war had to deal with managing the shift in power to a more centralized federal government that was required to guarantee individual rights. Among them was Ohio congressman John Bingham, a member of the Thirty-Ninth Congress, which was in session from March 4, 1865, to March 4, 1867. Bingham and his colleagues faced three major challenges: (1) the loss of life and property in the war; (2) the uncertainty about whether the war was really over; and (3) the enormity of the task of economic and political reconstruction. By denying seats to the congressmen and senators elected to represent the former Confederate states at the end of the war, the Thirty-Ninth Congress held a Republican majority of 77 percent in the House and 79 percent in the Senate. This majority gained for the Republicans not only a veto-proof Congress but also the supermajority necessary to enact constitutional amendments (three-quarters of the states still had to ratify amendments). Their majority allowed the Congress to ignore veto threats from President Andrew Johnson, who succeeded to the presidency after Lincoln's assassination, and it also provided very little incentive for them to negotiate with the Democrats.

The Thirty-Ninth Congress passed 714 pieces of legislation during its term, more than any Congress had passed up to that time. Included in the legislation enacted by this Congress was: (1) the Civil Rights Act of 1866; (2) the extension of the Freedmen's Bureau for another two years; and (3) the Fourteenth Amendment (which was ratified in 1868). Congressman Bingham, a freshman legislator from Cadiz, Ohio, was the principal author of section 1 of the amendment. Bingham and his colleagues knew that such an amendment, even though it was proposed to address abuses within the former Confederate states, could seriously affect the Northern states as well. For this reason, the terms of the amendment were far more lenient than those proposed by the states in the North and East, who desired a far more stringent reconstruction policy.

III. Historical Theories of Reconstruction

Professor Laura Edwards explains several of the historical theories that have attempted to explain the Civil War era and Reconstruction. The Dunning School, named for its most vocal advocate,[6] had its roots in the direct aftermath of the war. Professor Dunning and his disciples believed that Reconstruction was a failure and that the enactment of the Thirteenth, Fourteenth, and Fifteenth Amendments was merely a power grab by the federal government at the expense of the states. They also claimed that the Civil War was started by abolitionist elements in the North and was avoidable. Openly racist in their beliefs, these historians blamed a radical minority for granting rights to African American males who were incapable of exercising them. Although it was in vogue for many years, most modern scholars have rejected the Dunning theory.

In 1881, former Confederate president Jefferson Davis published a two-volume memoir entitled *The Rise and Fall of the Confederate Government*. Davis denied that the peculiar institution was the primary cause of the war, and Douglas Egerton notes that Davis considered the reforms caused by Reconstruction as the "imposing [of] an oppressive peace on honorable men who had laid down their arms."[7]

W. E. B. DuBois published his work *Black Reconstruction in America* in 1935. DuBois conducted an extensive analysis of the economies of the former Confederate states, the composition of their legislatures, and their state budgets. Highlighting the accomplishments, rather than the failures, of the era, DuBois wrote that the Reconstruction governments established public education in the South, invested in public infrastructure, and established public health agencies to combat the spread of disease. Any economic or political unrest during this era was primarily the result of the white planter class and paramilitary groups attempting to suppress the votes of the freedmen.[8]

Later theories, Edwards writes, arose in the wake of *Brown v. Board of Education* and the civil rights era. These theorists believe that the conflicts between the various sections of the country made the Civil War inevitable. The weaknesses of the original Constitution, particularly the lack of authority at the federal level,

---

[6]   *The Cambridge History of Law in America: Volume II, The Long Nineteenth Century (1789–1920)*, eds. Michael Grossberg & Christopher Tomlins, 313–14; William A. Dunning, *Reconstruction, Political and Economic, 1865–1877* (New York: Harper & Brothers, 1907).

[7]   Jefferson Davis, *The Rise and Fall of the Confederate Government* (Cambridge, MA: DeCapo Press, 1990); Douglas R. Egerton, *The Wars of Reconstruction, the Brief, Violent History of America's Most Progressive Era* (New York: Bloomberry Press, 2014), 325–26.

[8]   W. E. B. DuBois, *Black Reconstruction in America* (New York: Free Press, 1998).

prevented the development of a central government strong enough to prevent the war. Reconstruction, rather than war, was to them the primary vehicle of change.[9]

Foremost among those vehicles of change were the Fourteenth and Fifteenth Amendments. These two amendments and their enabling legislation not only changed the legal status of every American, but they also transferred the issue of civil and political rights from the states to the federal government. These amendments granted civil and political rights to African Americans not only in Arkansas but in Ohio as well. During this era, Congress also shifted the authority to enforce civil and political rights from the states to the federal courts. Congress passed a series of enactments, beginning with the Habeas Corpus Act of 1863 and culminating with the Removal Act of 1875, to accomplish this purpose.

One modern school of thought focuses on the failure of Reconstruction. White former Confederates quickly regained control of the Southern governments through a process known as redemption, ignored federal law, and created a segregated culture that did not differ markedly from slavery. Corporations and railroads used their power and influence to hijack the provisions of the Fourteenth Amendment to serve their own purposes. Even the courts did not enforce the mandates of Reconstruction in the manner intended.[10]

Another modern school of thought has a more positive view of Reconstruction. Reconstruction, particularly the Fourteenth Amendment, ushered in a "Second American Revolution" with the hope of fulfilling the promises of the first one. Although progress was glacial, by the mid-twentieth century, its effects culminated with the decisions of the *Warren* Court and the Civil Rights Act of 1964.[11]

Edwards also writes that most of the legal research in this era concentrated on the events that occurred at the national level, particularly the changes that occurred in the executive, legislative, and judicial branches of the federal government. These effects of these changes were then followed to the states and then to the local level.[12]

More recently, Edwards writes, works that examine the changes to the law that occurred at the state and local level during this era have been written. This recent

---

[9]   II The Cambridge History of Law, *supra* note 6, 315.

[10]   The Cambridge History of Law, *supra* note 6, 314.

[11]   Ibid.

[12]   Ibid., 315.

trend not only concerns itself with legal history but also examines women's issues, African American issues, as well as social, cultural, and economic changes that occurred.[13] Examining those changes from the perspective of Ohio and its citizens should contribute significantly to the existing literature in this area.

IV. Amar

In his book entitled *The Bill of Rights: Creation and Reconstruction,*[14] Professor Akhil Reed Amar challenges the conventional thinking regarding the origins and the original intent of the bill.[15] It is Amar's hypothesis that, contrary to popular belief, the Bill of Rights was not originally constructed to protect minorities against oppression by the majority but rather to protect the rights of the majority from a distant and tyrannical (a.k.a., federal) government.[16] The notion that incorporation of the Bill of Rights against the individual states through the due process clause of the Fourteenth Amendment did not take hold until the Reconstruction Era following the Civil War.[17]

Amar's divided his book into two parts. In part I, Amar analyzes the bill as it was originally conceived.[18] Amar carefully examines the original Bill of Rights clause by clause, to show its inherent anti-federalist character. For example, Amar

---

[13] Ibid.

[14] Akhil Reed Amar. *The Bill of Rights: Creation and Reconstruction.* (New Haven, CT: Yale University Press, 2000).

[15] During the time the bill was being debated and ratified (1789–1791), the French Revolution (1789–1799) was in its early stages. During the Reign of Terror (1793–94), it is estimated that as many as forty thousand prisoners were executed without trial or died awaiting trial. Donald Greer, *The Incidence of the Terror During the French Revolution: A Statistical Interpretation,* Cambridge, MA: Harvard University Press, 1935.

[16] Akhil Reed Amar, *The Bill Of Rights: Creation And Reconstruction.* (New Haven, CT: Yale University Press, 1980). Reviewed by John M. Scheb II, Department of Political Science, University of Tennessee, Knoxville. From *The Law and Politics Book Review,* Vol. 9, No. 1 (January 1998), 1–2.

[17] For a history of the US Supreme Court's decisions regarding incorporation, see Justice Black's dissent in *Adamson v. California,* 332 U.S. 46 (1947).

[18] Twelve amendments were originally proposed.

characterizes the role of free speech and assembly, and a well-regulated militia, as populist checks on the (federal) government.[19] Amar further divided the Bill into its two component parts—*structure* (of the government) and (individual) *rights*—and explains the origins and evolution of each category. Amar also discusses why the various clauses are lumped together and how they interrelate. He explains the themes that connect the amendments and how the original Constitution and the bill are linked together.

Amar then discusses the history of the Fourteenth Amendment and notes that the speeches Bingham had given before Congress in 1866, while arguing for the amendment, closely mirror the speeches he gave in 1859 in response to the holding in *Dred Scott*. Bingham blasted the *Scott* court, which he claimed went too far in limiting certain rights, such as due process, that are guaranteed to all persons, not just citizens. Seven years later, Bingham acknowledged that the bill did not extend to the states and that his amendment would specifically overrule *Barron*.

Amar then points out the similarities between the Constitution and the Fourteenth Amendment. Both the convention and the joint committee debates were shrouded in secrecy, and Americans anxiously awaited both final products. Partisan feelings were at a high level during both ratification periods, and the ratification process for both documents ran much longer than the authors had hoped.[20]

Democrats and other critics of the amendment argued that most of the states, including Ohio, had written specific provisions protecting individual rights and freedoms into their state constitutions. While that is true, many of the Southern states ignored these provisions when dealing with "the peculiar institution." Despite this, Democrats argued that the responsibility for guarding and preserving civil and political rights should remain with the states.[21]

Finally, the proponents wondered how the courts would interpret the amendment. Although the Supreme Court had used the doctrine of judicial review to strike several state statutes in the era before the Civil War, they had only invoked the Bill of Rights once against Congress, invalidating the provision of the Missouri Compromise that prohibited slavery above the line of 36° 30'. Bingham argued that

---

[19]   Amar, *supra* note 870, 21.

[20]   Amar, *supra* note 14, 204.

[21]   Ibid., 205.

the Supreme Court could neither interfere with the ratification of the amendment nor strike it down. In the event the court did interfere, the House could "sweep away their appellate jurisdiction in all cases," and annihilate "the usurpers in the abolition of the tribunal."[22]

In part II, Amar shows how Reconstruction and the ratification of the Fourteenth Amendment transformed the nature of the bill into what we recognize today.[23] Amar carefully discusses whether the Fourteenth Amendment incorporates the Bill of Rights against the states and how it does so. He analyzes the three conventional approaches to incorporation, Justice Black's "total incorporation" theory, Justice Brennan's "selective incorporation" model, and Justice Frankfurter's "fundamental fairness" doctrine. Amar finds the fatal flaw in each of these arguments and instead proposes a "refined incorporation" model, using a combination of the three theories.[24] Amar finds that refined incorporation helped adapt amendments that were originally designed to empower majorities into rules that protect individual and minority rights.

V. Goals.

This work will focus on the Reconstruction Era and the influence Ohio politicians had in the shaping of the Fourteenth Amendment by carefully examining the theories put forth by Professor Akhil Reed Amar in his book entitled: *The Bill of Rights: Creation and Reconstruction.* Amar discusses the paradigm shift that occurred in the relationship between the federal and state governments, to the point where today the federal, rather than state, government is the primary guarantor of the individual rights of its citizens and residents. Because Congress expanded the jurisdiction of the federal courts and allowed the removal of state cases to federal courts, the courts have assumed the role as the primary protector of individual rights.

---

[22] Gerard N. Magliocca, *American Founding Son: John Bingham and the Invention of the Fourteenth Amendment.* (New York: NYU Press, 2013), 134–135.

[23] Professor Amar also stresses that when analyzing cases involving the Fourteenth Amendment, the courts must determine the intent of Congress in 1868, when the amendment was ratified, and not 1791, when the Bill of Rights was adopted.

[24] Amar, *supra* note 14, 140.

In the former Confederacy, that power shift was quick to occur and easily recognizable. Four of the five paragraphs of the Fourteenth Amendment were directed primarily toward abuses that had occurred in the southern states. While such abuses occurred to a much more limited extent in the northern states, they still occurred. This work will examine that power shift as it occurred in Ohio during this era.

Early chapters will follow the development of the legal system in Ohio, including the legal system in the Northwest Territory, Ohio's Constitution of 1802, Ohio Law in the age of Jackson, Ohio's Constitution of 1851 and the discordant decade that followed, and the state of relations between Ohio and the federal government during each era. The human rights abuses (an anachronistic term) that occurred during the Civil War, as described by Farber, will be discussed in some detail. However, the primary emphasis will be on Ohio's role in the drafting and ratification of the Fourteenth Amendment, and the changes brought on by that text, which has been called the most important amendment to the US Constitution.

Summary

The Civil War began on April 12, 1861, and by the time it ended four years later, over six hundred thousand American lives were lost. President Lincoln resorted to extraordinary measures to win the war and preserve the Union. Many of Lincoln's actions infringed on the rights granted to all citizens by the first ten Amendments to the US Constitution and by most state constitutions.

Most of the changes that occurred because of the war were temporary, and almost all of them ended at the war's conclusion. The real change to federal-state relations, particularly the dramatic increase in federal power, occurred during the Reconstruction Era (1863–1877), and because of the enactment and ratification of the Thirteenth, Fourteenth, and Fifteenth Amendments.

The state of Ohio played a critical role in this era. Its military leaders won the war, and its political leaders set the course for Reconstruction. Most of the Reconstruction policies were designed for moderate states, like Ohio, striking a balance between the support of President Johnson and his followers, who felt that no Reconstruction policy was necessary, and the Radical Republicans, who desired a stricter and more punitive Reconstruction policy.

The goal of this work is to examine the changes that occurred in Ohio and its laws because of the Civil War and Reconstruction, using the criteria described by Professor Akhil Reed Amar in his book *The Bill of Rights: Creation and Reconstruction*.

Chapter 2

Antecedents: Ohio Law in the Prestatehood Era

I am George Rogers Clark. You have just become a prisoner of the Commonwealth of Virginia.

—George Rogers Clark, 1779

I. Introduction

In 1984, the Ohio Division of Travel and Tourism adopted the slogan "Ohio, the heart of it all." The new slogan appeared on all official publications of the division, as well as on highway signs welcoming people to the state. Ohio's boundaries form the rough shape of a heart,[25] but many other thoughts were behind the slogan.

Ohio has long been at the center of the nation's population, geography, and economic activity. The same can be said of Ohio's past. Ohio was the first state admitted from the Northwest Territory, and its admission set the precedent for the admission of other states. Ohio's western frontier was the center of warfare between white settlers and the Native American (Indian) tribes in the 1780s and 1790s and was a main theatre of conflict during the War of 1812. Ohio's northern border faced the British and the Canadians. Its southern border faced the slaveholding states. Ohio also served as the gateway from the industrial states in the mid-Atlantic region to the agricultural states to the West.

Known as a "swing state" since the 1980s, one in which no single candidate has overwhelming support, the last time Ohio voters declared for the losing presidential

---

25   Ohio History Central, available at: http://ohiohistorycentral.org/w/Ohio's_State_Tourism_Slogans.

candidate was in the 1960 election. Also known as a home rule state, the Ohio Constitution grants certain powers, such as police powers, ownership of public utilities, and local self-government to municipal corporations that the General Assembly cannot amend by simple majority vote.[26]

A. Early Ohio

In colonial times, the Ohio country was at the center of a "world war" among the empires of France, Great Britain, and Spain. The French were the first to lay claim to Ohio, after an exploration conducted by Robert de LaSalle in 1669. The French later established trading posts throughout the area to control the fur trade with the Native Americans.[27]

By the mid-1750s, several Native American tribes had relocated to the Ohio country. Delaware and Shawnee arrived the from east, the Wyandot and the Ottawa came from the north, and the Miami migrated into western Ohio and Eastern Indiana. The Mingos were made up of Iroquois tribes that had relocated to Ohio from New York State, combined with the remnants of several other tribes pushed west by colonists along the eastern seaboard.[28] The struggle between the British and French for control of the fur trade in the Ohio country reached its zenith during the Seven Years' War (1756–63), better known in the colonies as the French and Indian War. While Great Britain fought with Spain and France over control of their respective American colonies, several other nations, including Prussia, Austria,

---

[26]   128 *Ohio Legislative Service Commission*, Issue 8. Municipal Home Rule. January 26, 2010. Available at: http://www.lsc.state.oh.us/membersonly/128municipalhomerule.pdf

[27]   The French solidified their claim to the area in the summer of 1749, when a French expedition led by Celeron de Blainville traveled downstream from the Upper Allegheny River to the Ohio. Celeron buried lead plates at each important river confluence, claiming the region for France. Once he reached the confluence with the Great Miami River, he traveled upstream to the Miami Indian village of Pickawillany, and finally to Detroit. George W. Knepper, *Ohio and Its People* (Kent State University Press, 1989).

[28]   R. Douglas Hurt, *The Ohio Frontier: Crucible of the Old Northwest* (Bloomington, IN: Indiana University Press, 1998), 19–21.

Portugal, Sweden, Saxony, and the Russian Empire, fought one another as part of a continuing series of wars that had been raging since the 1680s.[29]

Great Britain eventually prevailed, and because of the 1763 Treaty of Paris, it gained control of the bulk of Eastern Canada, Spanish Florida, several islands in the Caribbean and the West Indies, the colony of Senegal on the West Coast of Africa, and the French trading posts located on the Indian subcontinent. The British also gained control of the Ohio Country, but the Native American tribes residing there were excluded from the peace negotiations. Their dissatisfaction with British policies resulted in Pontiac's rebellion (1763–66), named after the most prominent of the Native American leaders involved.[30]

During the American Revolution, in an effort to defend white Kentucky settlements against Native American raids, troops led by Virginia[31] Major George Rogers Clark crossed the Ohio River and captured the British outposts of Kaskaskia, Cahokia, and Vincennes. Although Clark's conquest of the Illinois Country[32] was considered by some to be only a temporary occupation, his campaign significantly reduced the British influence in the area. The resulting power vacuum led Great Britain to cede the entire territory to the United States as part of the 1783 Treaty of Paris.[33]

---

[29]   Knepper, supra note 27, 26.

[30]   Pontiac (c. 1720–1769) was an Ottawa leader who sided with the French during the French and Indian War. Dissatisfied with the trading practices of the victorious British, Pontiac and his followers attempted to capture Ft. Detroit in 1763. While they failed to take Detroit, the war soon spread throughout the Great Lakes region. Enjoying some local successes, Pontiac's followers, suffering from smallpox and short on powder and lead, withdrew to the Illinois country. Pontiac continued to encourage resistance to British rule, but he eventually agreed to stop fighting in 1766. He was killed by a Peoria Indian near Cahokia in 1769. David Dixon, *Never Come to Peace Again: Pontiac's Uprising and the Fate of the British Empire in North America* (Norman, OK: University of Oklahoma Press, 2005).

[31]   Virginia created Fincastle County, Virginia, from the Kentucky settlements in 1772.

[32]   The lands located west of Pennsylvania, north of the Ohio River, south of the Great Lakes and east of the Mississippi River are referred to as the Ohio Country, the Northwest Territory, and the Illinois Country at various times.

[33]   David Schoenbrun, *Triumph in Paris: The Exploits of Benjamin Franklin* (New York: Harper & Row, 1976).

At the war's conclusion, the new country faced many problems, including an enormous national debt. The United States owed over $12 million to foreigners, mostly the French. The national government owed $40 million and the state governments owed $25 million to Americans who sold food, horses, and other supplies to the American Army during the course of the war.[34]

Toward the end of the war, to combat the continued issue of paper currency that had become largely worthless, Congress and the states began to issue land grants to officers and soldiers who had served during the war but had not yet been paid. Many of the states, including Virginia and Connecticut, set aside lands in the new territory to use as payment to their citizens who served during the Revolution.

B. Ordinances of 1784, 1785, and 1787

In order to establish procedures for the settlement and the political incorporation of these new lands,[35] prevent illegal settlement by squatters, and provide a defense against Indian raids, the Confederation Congress enacted the Ordinances of 1784, 1785, and 1787. The first of these, drafted by Thomas Jefferson and passed by Congress, divided the Trans-Appalachian region into seventeen roughly rectangular, self-governing districts, with ten of these districts located in the Northwest Territory. When the population of a district reached twenty thousand, a representative from the district could be sent to Congress. A district would become eligible for statehood when its population equaled that of the least-populous state then in existence. One article, prohibiting slavery and involuntary servitude, was rejected by delegates from the southern states. Critics of this plan stressed that the many smaller states proposed by Jefferson in this ordinance would dilute the power of the original thirteen states in Congress. Because of those and other concerns, most of the provisions of this ordinance were eventually superseded by other laws.

The Ordinance of 1785 provided for a scientific survey and the systematic subdivision of the new lands. Since the Confederation Congress lacked the power to tax, legislators saw the sale of land to raise money to operate the country and repay

---

[34]   Joseph J. Ellis, *His Excellency: George Washington,* (New York: Alfred A. Knopf, 2004), 204.

[35]   Specifically, the Northwest Territory consisted of that part of the American frontier lying west of Pennsylvania, north of the Ohio River, east of the Mississippi River, and South of the Great Lakes.

war debts. The basic unit of land was to be the township, a tract of land measuring six miles on each side. The townships were divided into sections, and to fund education, one section in each township was reserved for schools. The procedures established in this ordinance, called the Public Lands Survey System,[36] were to guide American land use policies until Congress enacted the Homestead Act in 1862.[37]

The final and most important of these three acts was the Ordinance of 1787. Passed by the Confederation Congress in July 1787, the ordinance established government in the Northwest Territory, provided a means for the admission of its constituent parts as states, equal in stature to the original thirteen, and superseded parts of the 1784 ordinance. The ordinance also provided that no fewer than three or more than five states could be carved from the territory.

C. Establishing a Government

Ohioans have always guarded their rights dearly. When the first settlers arrived at Marietta in 1788, well ahead of any organized government, they created a temporary legal code and posted it to a tree trunk.[38] The Confederation Congress enacted the Northwest Ordinance in 1787,[39] but before the governmental functions were established in the new territory, settlers in the Miami area framed a temporary legal code, established a court, and appointed a judge and a sheriff.[40]

---

[36] Staff (May 29, 2012). "The Public Land Survey System (PLSS)." *National Atlas of the United States. U.S. Department of the Interior.* Retrieved April 9, 2014.

[37] C. Albert White, *A History of the Rectangular Survey System* (Bureau of Land Management, 1983).

[38] Walter Havingshurst, *Ohio: A History* (New York: W.W. Norton, 1976; repr. Urbana: University of Illinois Press, 2001), 32.

[39] The newly created US Congress reaffirmed the ordinance in 1789.

[40] 31 Robert E. Chaddock, *Ohio Before 1850: A Study of the Early Influence of Pennsylvania and the Southern Populations in Ohio, Studies in History, Economics and Public Law,* faculty of Political Science of Columbia University eds. (New York: Columbia University Press, 1908), 51–52.

Under the Northwest Ordinance,[41] Congress appointed a governor, a secretary to act in the absence of the governor, and three territorial judges, whose terms ran during "good behavior." The path to statehood consisted of three stages. During Stage 1, the governor and the judges shared the legislative and judicial functions. The governor occupied the most powerful post in the territorial government. In addition to his legislative and judicial authority, he commanded the militia and appointed all militia officers below the rank of general officer. He was also tasked with creating new counties, organizing their governments, dealing with the Native American tribes, and appointing magistrates and other local officials.[42] Congress authorized the governor and judges to adopt any law then in force in any of the original states.[43]

Stage 2 began when the population was large enough (five thousand free males). At that time a territorial legislature,[44] consisting of a lower house elected by the citizens and an upper house chosen by the lower house, would be empaneled. The legislature was empowered to alter any of the original territorial laws as they saw fit. One (nonvoting) delegate to Congress would be selected. When a portion of the territory reached a population of sixty thousand, it could apply for statehood (Stage 3).[45]

The Ordinance of 1787 reflected the then-prevailing notion of republican government. Section 13 declared that "fundamental principles of civil government

---

[41]   The Northwest Ordinance (officially known as And Ordinance for the Government of the Territory of the United States, North–West of the River Ohio) was enacted by the Congress of the Confederation of the United States on July 13, 1787. Congress reaffirmed the ordinance, with several modifications, in 1789 after the adoption of the US Constitution.

[42]   *The History of Ohio Law* (Michael Les Benedict & John F. Winkler eds., Ohio University Press, 2003) (quoting Andrew R. L. Cayton, *Law and Authority in the Northwest Territory*), 18–19.

[43]   The judges also wanted the ability to *adapt* laws from the original states and the common law, arguing that the territory needed laws not found in the codes of the original states. *The History of Ohio Law, supra* note 16, 30 (quoting Andrew R. L. Cayton, *Law and Authority in the Northwest Territory*).

[44]   Northwest Ordinance, art.6.

[45]   In 1796 the governor and judges published *Laws of the Territory of the United States North-West of the Ohio*, more commonly known as *Maxwell's Code*, named after its publisher. *Maxwell's Code* was the first civil and criminal code for the new American frontier, as well as the first book published in the Northwest Territory. *Maxwell's Code*, available at www.ohiohistorycentral.org/w/Maxwell's_Code?rec=1470

and religious liberty … form the basis whereupon these republics, their laws and [their] constitutions are either directed."

Section 14 of the ordinance described key principles, including religious freedom, writs of habeas corpus, trial by jury, and bail. Fines were to be moderate, cruel and unusual punishment was prohibited, and one could be deprived of liberty or property only by judgment of one's peers or by the law of the land. A taking of private property required full compensation, and no law could interfere with bona fide private contracts previously made. Other articles mandated the encouragement of education, promoted religion, morality, and knowledge, promoted good faith toward Native Americans, and banned slavery.[46]

The Confederation Congress appointed Arthur St. Clair of Pennsylvania as governor of the new territory. Seconding St. Clair as secretary was Winthrop Sargent of Massachusetts. Both appointments were confirmed by the Congress that had been established following the adoption of the new constitution.[47]

D. Ohio's Early Leaders

Arthur St. Clair (1736–1818) was an American soldier and politician. Born in Scotland, St. Clair attended the University of Edinburgh and served as a junior officer in the British Army during the French and Indian War under Generals Jeffrey Amherst and James Wolfe. After the war, he settled in western Pennsylvania and served as a judge. In 1775 Congress appointed him as a colonel in the Continental Army. St. Clair participated in the Quebec Invasion and fought at the Battles of Trenton and Princeton. His retreat from Fort Ticonderoga in 1777 led to his

---

[46] See, Arthur Zilversmit, *The First Emancipation: The Abolition of Slavery in the North* (Chicago: University of Chicago Press, 1967); Richard S. Newman, *The Transformation of American Abolitionism: Fighting Slavery in the Early Republic* (Chapel Hill, NC: University of North Carolina Press, 2002).

[47] The Northwest Ordinance contained many of the provisions of the Bill of Rights that were eventually adopted as amendments to our US Constitution. Arguably these applied to the states before the adoption of the Fourteenth Amendment. *Concurring Opinions. The Northwest Ordinance of 1787 and the Bill of Rights.* Available at: http://concurringopinions. com/archives/2011/11/the-northwest-ordinance-of-1787-and-the-bill-of-rights.html

court-martial. Although exonerated, St. Clair never held another field command in the war.[48]

By the war's end, St. Clair was Washington's aide-de-camp, with the rank of major general. In 1785, he was elected to the Continental Congress from Pennsylvania, and Congress appointed him as the first governor of the Northwest Territory in 1787. A Federalist, St. Clair frequently clashed with the territorial judges and actively opposed Ohio's admission as a state.[49] After denouncing the Enabling Act, which established the mechanism for Ohio's admission as a state, President Jefferson removed St. Clair from office in 1802.[50]

Arthur St. Clair, 1736-1818.
(Image courtesy of the Ohio History Connection).

---

[48] 1 & 2 William Henry Smith, ed., *The Life and Public Services of Arthur St. Clair* (Cincinnati, OH: Robert Clarke & Company, 1882).

[49] Ohio History Central. Arthur St. Clair. Located at: http://www.ohiohistorycentral.org/w/ Arthur_St._Clair

[50] Hurt, *supra* note 28, 272–283.

The new territorial secretary, Winthrop Sargent, was born in Massachusetts and graduated from Harvard College. He served during the American Revolution with Henry Knox's Regiment of Artillery, ending the war as a brevet major. He served with his regiment at the Battles of Long Island, White Plains, Trenton, Monmouth, and Brandywine Creek. He also served during the winter encampment at Valley Forge. After the war, Sargent became a land speculator, surveyed the Seven Ranges tract in southern Ohio, and was one of the founders of the Ohio Company.

Sargent participated in the Northwest Indian Wars of the 1790s and eventually became Colonel and adjutant general. Sargent's position was critical to the new territory, since he acted in the place of the governor during his absences, and St. Clair was frequently absent. Sargent, like St. Clair, clashed with the judges and local officials over their respective spheres of influence. President Adams appointed Sargent as governor of the Mississippi Territory in 1798. Adams appointed William Henry Harrison to replace Sargent as secretary in 1798. Sargent was dismissed as governor of the Mississippi Territory when Thomas Jefferson assumed the office of president in 1801.[51]

Harrison was born into the Virginia aristocracy. Harrison's father, Benjamin, signed the Declaration of Independence and served as governor of Virginia. William was studying medicine in Philadelphia when his father died, leaving him without the funds to continue his studies. Harrison joined the army, was commissioned as an officer, and joined his regiment at Fort Washington, just outside Cincinnati.

Harrison served throughout the Northwest Indian Wars of the 1790s and eventually became aide-de-camp to commanding General Anthony Wayne. Harrison was at Wayne's side during the Battle of Fallen Timbers, and he later signed the Treaty of Greenville. President Adams appointed Harrison as secretary of the Northwest Territory, and he was later elected as that territory's nonvoting delegate to Congress.

President Adams appointed Harrison as governor of the new Indiana Territory in 1800, and he served in that capacity until 1812. He led the American forces against the Seven (Indian) Nations at the Battle of Tippecanoe and led the Army of the

---

[51]   *Encyclopedia of Alabama*. Winthrop Sargent. Located at: http://www.encyclopediaofalabama.org/face/Article.jsp?id=h-2371

Northwest during the War of 1812. Harrison ran unsuccessfully for the presidency in 1836 and later was elected in 1840. He died after thirty-one days in office.[52]

Charles Willing Byrd served both as the final governor and the final secretary of the Northwest Territory. Born into a wealthy family in Virginia, Byrd studied law in Philadelphia and gained admission to the bar in 1794. Appointed as territorial secretary by President Adams in 1800, he served in that capacity until Ohio became a state on March 1, 1803. Appointed as governor after St. Clair's firing in 1802, he served until he was replaced by the newly elected Ohio governor, Edward Tiffin, on March 3, 1803. Byrd was a member of Ohio's first constitutional convention and is considered by many to be the principal author of that document. President Jefferson named Byrd as the first judge of the US District Court for the District of Ohio on March 3, 1803, and he served in that post until his death in 1828.

Congress selected John Armstrong, Samuel Holden Parsons, and James Mitchell Varnum as the first judges of the territorial court. Congress also established the original courts for the territory on August 23, 1788. A general or circuit court was established for the entire territory, which could be presided over by all three judges, any two, or one alone. The court met annually at Marietta in October, at Cincinnati in March, and at Detroit, Vincennes, and Kaskaskia, whenever one of the judges could reach those places.[53]

John Armstrong was born in Carlisle, Pennsylvania, and studied at the College of New Jersey (now Princeton University). Armstrong joined a Pennsylvania militia regiment in 1775, and he served as aide-de-camp to General Hugh Mercer at the Battle of Princeton. Armstrong served throughout the war, ending as a major. Armstrong was also at the center of a group of officers that met to discuss back pay and other grievances. Washington managed to defuse this "protest," and he took no official action against Armstrong for his role.

In 1787 and 1788 Armstrong served as a Pennsylvania delegate to the Continental Congress. Congress appointed him as chief justice of the new Northwest Territory, but he declined this appointment as well as several other public offices over the next few years. Armstrong was later elected senator from New York and was selected as minister to France and Spain. At the outbreak of the War of 1812, President Madison

---

[52]   A.J. Langguth, *Union 1812: The Americans Who Fought in the Second War of Independence* (New York: Simon & Schuster, 2006).

[53]   Indiana Commission on Public Records. *The Judicial Structure in Indiana: Northwest Territory Period*, 1787–1800. Available at: http://www.in.gov/icpr/2750.htm.

appointed him first as brigadier general in the regular army and later as secretary of war. Madison dismissed him from the latter office after the British captured, and then burned, Washington in 1814.[54]

Parsons was born in Lyme, Connecticut, and graduated from Harvard College in 1756. Parsons read law with his uncle and was admitted to the bar in 1759. He was elected to the Connecticut General Assembly, and he supported resistance to British rule in the days before the American Revolution.

Congress commissioned him as a colonel in the Continental Army in 1775; he served continuously until the end of that conflict, ending the war as a major general. Parsons participated in the Battle of Bunker Hill and the battles around New York City and was a member of the board of officers that tried and convicted Major John Andre of espionage.[55]

After the war, Parsons became a director of the Ohio Company and was a member of the Connecticut Convention for adopting the US Constitution. Congress appointed him as chief justice of the Northwest Territory in 1788. Assuming his judicial duties in the new territory, Parsons also surveyed the Ohio Company's lands and the Connecticut Western Reserve. Parsons drowned while surveying government lands in Pennsylvania in November 1789.

Perhaps the most renowned of the original judges of the territory was James Mitchell Varnum. Born in Massachusetts, Varnum attended Harvard College and graduated from the English Colony of Rhode Island and the Providence Plantations (later renamed Brown College) at age twenty.

Varnum served in the Continental Army as a brigadier general until 1779. After his resignation, he was appointed major general in the Rhode Island volunteer militia. Varnum fought at the siege of Boston, the battles on Long Island, at White Plains and Red Bank, and the winter encampment at Valley Forge. After the war, Varnum was a founding member of the Society of Cincinnati and later served as its president.[56]

---

[54] Carl E. Skeen, *John Armstrong, Jr., 1758–1843: A Biography* (Syracuse, NY: Syracuse University Press, 1982).

[55] Charles S. Hall, *Life and Letters of Samuel Holden Parsons: Major General in the Continental Army and Chief Judge of the Northwestern Territory, 1737–1789* (Binghamton, NY: Otseningo Publishing Co., 1905). Available at: https://archive.org/details/lifelettersofsam00hall

[56] *General James Mitchell Varnum, The Man and His Times.* Located at: http://www.varnumcontinentals.org/about.htm

After the war, Varnum worked as an attorney in Rhode Island and successfully represented the defendant in the case of *Trevett v. Weeden,* one of the first cases in which a court declared an act of the legislature void as unconstitutional.[57] Varnum served as a delegate to the Continental Congress and was appointed to the Court of the Northwest Territory. He died at Marietta in 1789 at the age of forty.[58]

Congress selected John Cleaves Symmes of New Jersey to take Armstrong's place in February 1788. Symmes was born on Long Island, educated as an attorney, and relocated to Morristown, New Jersey. During the American Revolution, he served as a colonel in the New Jersey militia and on the New Jersey Legislative Council. Symmes served on the New Jersey Supreme Court in 1777 and 1778 and represented New Jersey in the Continental Congress from 1785 to 1786. In 1788, Symmes purchased 311,682 acres in the Northwest Territory from Congress. Known as the Symmes Purchase, the tract was later reduced to 248,250 acres. Symmes settled in North Bend, Ohio, and served as a judge of the Territorial Court from 1788 until Ohio became a state in 1803.[59] He was the father-in-law of President William Henry Harrison and the great-grandfather of President Benjamin Harrison.

Although most of the territorial judges were well educated and legally trained, historian Andrew Cayton wrote that none would be likely to survive the close scrutiny or congressional hearings that today's federal judges must endure. Most of them were major land speculators who would earn huge amounts of money once a stable government was established. Moreover, most of these judges would not be sympathetic to the interests of small landowners or squatters.[60]

Setting aside ethical considerations and possible conflicts of interest, the most

57   William E. Nelson, *Marbury v. Madison: The Origins and Legacy of Judicial Review* (University Press of Kansas, 2000), 37.

58   James Mitchell Varnum, *A Sketch of the Life and Public Services of James Mitchell Varnum of Rhode Island, Brigadier – General of the Continental Army; Member of the Continental Congress; Judge U.S. Supreme Court, N. W. Territory; Major – General Rhode Island Volunteer Militia* (Boston: David Clapp &, Son, Printers, 1906). Available at: https://archive. org/stream/sketchoflifepubl00varn#page/n9/mode/2up

59   *Ohio History Central.* John C. Symmes. Available at: http://www.ohiohistorycentral.org/w/ John_C._Symmes

60   The History of Ohio Law, *supra* note 42, 20–21 (quoting Andrew R. L. Cayton, *Law and Authority in the Northwest Territory*).

important trait Congress sought in the new judges was reliability. Were they loyal to the federal government? Did they pledge their private fortunes to ensure the success of the new country? Could they adequately represent the interests of the federal government on the far-flung frontier? Congress ensured that its early appointees met these criteria. The governor and judges largely followed these standards when appointing local officials as well.[61]

Once the portion of the territory that would become Ohio reached the threshold of five thousand free male settlers, a territorial legislature was created. This bicameral legislature consisted of a House of Representatives, elected by the citizens, and a council, nominated by the House and appointed by Congress. Locked in a power struggle with the governor, the legislature selected William Henry Harrison as the delegate to Congress, narrowly defeating the governor's son, Arthur St. Clair Jr.

William McMillan was elected as delegate to replace Harrison in 1800. McMillan was born in Virginia and graduated from the College of William and Mary. He moved to Cincinnati and was admitted to the bar in 1788. McMillan served as a local judge and Hamilton County commissioner before being elected as delegate. He declined renomination in 1800.

Paul Fearing was the last delegate to serve prior to statehood. Born in Massachusetts, he graduated from Harvard College and was admitted to the bar in 1787. He relocated to Marietta shortly thereafter and became the first practicing attorney in the Northwest Territory. Fearing served as probate judge and member of the territorial legislature prior to his election as delegate. After his term as delegate ended, Fearing practiced law and was appointed as common pleas judge in 1810. He served one seven-year terms and died in 1822.

In addition to gaining the population necessary to apply for statehood, several other conflicts had to be resolved. Among these were: the conflict between settlers and the Native Americans; the conflict between legitimate settlers and squatters; the conflict between the federal government and the British; the conflict between territorial and local control; and finally, the conflict between Governor St. Clair and the territorial judges, and later with the territorial legislature.

---

[61]   Ibid.

II. Trouble with the Tribes (1775–1795)

A. The Militia

Conflicts between the Americans and the Native American tribes began soon after Daniel Boone led the first settlers into Kentucky via the Wilderness Road in 1775. At first the tribes raided isolated outposts and settlements, but in 1777, the Native Americans, aided by British regulars and Canadian militia, conducted a largely unsuccessful campaign to drive the remaining settlers from Kentucky. When the American Revolution ended in 1783, the Allied tribes were again not consulted or represented. As a result, the fighting on the frontier continued, with the primary targets being flatboats of settlers floating down the Ohio River.

George Rogers Clark led punitive expeditions against the tribes in 1780, 1782, and 1786, but these were largely ineffective. Instead of cowing the Native Americans as intended, these attacks served only to further incite the tribes and increase the depredations along the Ohio River.[62]

B. The US Army Takes Charge

The new federal government, installed in 1789, had no better luck quelling the tribes. US forces launched three major expeditions against the principal Miami villages located at Kekionga, today's Fort Wayne, Indiana, in 1790, 1791, and 1794.[63] The first two of these, led by Generals Harmar and St. Clair, were wildly unsuccessful.

---

[62] About.com Military History. *American Revolution: Brigadier General George Rogers Clark.* Located at: http://militaryhistory.about.com/od/americanrevolutio1/p/American-Revolution-Brigadier-General-George-Rogers-Clark.htm

[63] The conflict between the Americans and the Indian Confederation for control of the Northwest Territory was known by several names, including the Northwest Indian War, Little Turtle's War, the Ohio War, the Ohio Indian War, the War for the Ohio River Boundary, the Miami Confederacy War, and the Miami Campaign. Some scholars consider this war to be part of a larger struggle that began with the Braddock Expedition in 1755 and did not end until the conclusion of the War of 1812. *See, e.g., The Sixty Years' War for the Great Lakes, 1754–1814,* David Curtis Skaggs & Larry L. Nelson eds. (East Lansing, MI: Michigan State University Press, 2001).

C. Harmar's Defeat

The first expedition was led by General Josiah Harmar and consisted of almost fifteen hundred men, mostly untrained militia and levees. Harmar's force left Fort Washington (Cincinnati) in early October 1790, and by October 19 the force was within striking distance of Kekionga. Over the next three days, Harmar sent out several small detachments, which burned several abandoned villages. Each detachment was defeated by the Native Americans and driven back to Harmar's main force.[64]

Harmar then determined that because of his high number of casualties (over two hundred killed and wounded by some accounts), the approaching winter, the lack of supplies and forage, and the desertion of some of the militia, he was unable to attack with his full army. Harmar then marched his force back to Cincinnati, declared victory, and promptly resigned his army commission.[65]

D. Massacre Along the Wabash

President Washington, incensed at Harmar's defeat and the escalating violence against the settlements, ordered St. Clair to mount another expedition the next year. Because of shortages of men, horses, and supplies, St. Clair, like Harmar, was unable to start the expedition until early October. St. Clair's Army consisted of about twenty-three hundred men, including most of the strength of the Regular US Army, augmented by six-month levees from Virginia and Pennsylvania, and militia from Kentucky. St. Clair built two stockades, Forts Hamilton and Jefferson, as supply depots along his line of march. From the start his expedition was desperately short on supplies, forage, and pack animals.[66] Morale among the troops was low to nonexistent.

Plagued by desertions among the levees and the militia, the army reached the headwaters of the Wabash, near today's Fort Recovery, Ohio, on November 3 with less than twelve hundred men and camp followers. Early on November 4, a thousand warriors led by Little Turtle and Blue Jacket attacked St. Clair's encampment. The allied tribes quickly surrounded St. Clair's army, inflicting devastating casualties.

---

[64]   For a more in-depth discussion of Harmar's Campaign, see, Wiley Sword, *President Washington's Indian War: The Struggle for the Old Northwest, 1790–1795* (Norman, OK: University of Oklahoma Press, 1985), 96–124.

[65]   Hurt, *supra* note 28, 105–111.

[66]   For an excellent discussion of the Campaign of 1791, see, Sword, *supra* note 64, 160–195.

After several hours of fighting, the survivors, led by St. Clair, broke out of the encirclement and retreated toward Fort Jefferson, twenty-nine miles to the south. The retreat quickly turned into a rout, which then turned into headlong flight. The Americans lost over eight hundred soldiers and camp followers.[67]

Exasperated by this second defeat, Washington set aside any concerns about a large standing[68] army and appointed his former lieutenant, Anthony Wayne, as major general and commander of the Legion of the United States. The legion was to be a professional force, recruited and trained in the Pittsburgh area. It consisted of four sub-legions, each with two battalions of infantry, a battalion of riflemen, a battery of artillery, and a troop of dragoons. Given sufficient time to assemble and train his force, Wayne moved the Legion to Fort Washington in April 1793.

E. Anthony Wayne and Victory

In 1794, General "Mad" Anthony Wayne constructed a series of forts in the heart of hostile country, repelled a siege against Fort Recovery,[69] and defeated the Seven Nations at the Battle of Fallen Timbers.[70] After the battle, Wayne ordered that all the

---

[67]   Hurt, *supra* note 28, 111–119.

[68]   The Continental Army was disbanded by Congress after the American Revolution in 1783. On June 3, 1784, Congress reestablished the Regular Army as the First American Regiment. Congress added the Second Regiment in 1791, after Harmar's Defeat, and both regiments were reconstituted as sub-legions in 1792. Department of the Army: Lineage and Honors. Available at: http://www.history.army.mil/html/forcestruc/lineages/branches/inf/0003in.htm

[69]   Wayne built Fort Recovery at the site of St. Clair's defeat in 1793.

[70]   Just before the battle, the Miami chief Little Turtle addressed his colleagues and said: "We have beaten the enemy twice under separate commanders. We cannot expect the same good fortune always to attend us. The Americans are now led by a chief who never sleeps; the night and the day are alike to him and during all the time that he has been marching upon our village notwithstanding the watchfulness of our young men we have never been able to surprise him. Think well of it. There is something whispers to me, it would be prudent to listen to his offers of peace." History Center Notes & Queries. *Our Stories* From Ft. Wayne & Allen County, Indiana. Located at: http://historycenterfw.blogspot.com/2012/07/remembering-little-turtle.html *See, also,* Calvin M Young, Little Turtle (Me-she-kin-no-quah*): The Great Chief of the Miami Indian Nation; Being a Sketch of His Life, Together with that of William Wells and Some Noted Descendants* (Sentinel Ptg. Company, 1917), 82.

Native American villages and their crops within a fifty-mile radius be destroyed. Wayne's forces also threatened the British post of Fort Miami,[71] located just down the Maumee River from the battle site. The warring parties met the next year at Fort Greenville and signed the Treaty of Greenville on August 20, 1795. By its terms, the tribes ceded almost all of Ohio to the United States, allowing settlement to resume at an accelerated pace. This treaty also ushered in an era of friendly relations between the white settlers and the tribes that lasted almost fifteen years.[72]

III. The Jay Treaty

Once the Seven Nations were defeated, Great Britain saw the need to make peace with the Americans, particularly in light of the fact that it had been at war with France since 1792. President Washington sent Chief Justice John Jay to London to negotiate a treaty. Among the issues were: normalizing relations and trade between the two countries; the return of or compensation for, several hundred American merchant vessels seized by the British Navy; evacuation of military posts the British had built on American soil;[73] and finally, determining the border between the United States and Canada.

Although bitterly opposed by the Jeffersonians, the US Senate ratified the Jay Treaty in August 1795. The treaty terms were to be effective on February 29, 1796. By its terms, the British agreed to evacuate all posts on American soil by June 1796.

---

[71] Although they ceded the entirety of the Northwest Territory to the United States in the Treaty of Paris (1783), the British continued to garrison several posts in the area, including Fort Miami and Detroit.

[72] Alan D. Gaff, Bayonets in the *Wilderness: Anthony Wayne's Legion in the Old Northwest* (Norman, OK: University of Oklahoma Press, 2004). *See, also,* John F. Winkler, *Fallen Timbers 1794: The US Army's First Victory* (Campaign) (Oxford: Osprey Publishing; 1st ed. 2013).

[73] These posts included Forts Detroit and Mackinac in modern-day Michigan, Fort Miami in modern-day Ohio, and Forts Niagara and Oswego in modern-day New York State.

The British also agreed to compensate American ship owners for their losses, and in return, the Americans agreed to most of the British anti-French maritime policies.[74]

IV. Squatters

As noted previously, the Land Ordinance of 1785 established procedures for the survey and sale of the lands ceded by the British. Some prospective settlers decided not to wait for the survey to be completed. Following the theory that vacant land should be free for the taking, these settlers crossed the Ohio River, settled on public lands, and dared the rightful owners to evict them. Legitimate land purchasers were incensed by the effrontery of these settlers and demanded that the government act against them.

The first squatters arrived in the Ohio country soon after the start of the American Revolution. Their illegal settlements posed a danger to legitimate settlers by encroaching on Indian lands and inciting them to violence. Even General Washington was affected by these illegal settlers. When he traveled to Pennsylvania in 1784 to survey the lands awarded to him by the British for his service in the French and Indian War, he discovered that several Scotch-Irish families had already cleared the land, erected cabins and fences, and begun growing crops and raising cattle.[75] These squatters claimed that by clearing and planting the land, they had a moral and legal claim of ownership greater than that of an absentee landlord, who simply had a paper title to the property. The circuit court held in favor of the general, and rather than pay him rent or purchase the land outright, the settlers simply abandoned their homesteads and settled elsewhere.

The British and later the American governments took steps to address the

---

[74]   Sword, *supra* note 64, 314–315. The British granted the United States "most favored nation" trading status. The issues of seizures of American ships and impressments of American sailors on the high seas were to be resolved by arbitration. US Department of State, Office of the Historian. Milestones 1784–1800. Available at: http://history.state.gov/milestones/1784-1800/jay-treaty

[75]   ExplorePAhistory.com: George Washington, Covenanter squatters Historical Marker. Located at: http://explorepahistorry.com/hmarker.php?markerId+1-A-28F See, also, Charles H. Ambler, *George Washington and the West* (Chapel Hill, NC: University of North Carolina Press, 1936).

problem of squatters. Following their victory in the French and Indian War, the British issued the Proclamation of 1763. This act prohibited the English colonists from settling on lands west of the Appalachian Mountains. The Americans largely ignored this act, and the migration west continued.

At the end of the American Revolution, the Confederation Congress prohibited settlement of the lands in the Ohio country, but the squatters ignored this law as well. Beginning in 1785, the Army attempted to remove illegal settlers from their holdings, but aside from burning their cabins and destroying their crops, the army's efforts were mostly ineffective.[76] The language of the Fort McIntosh Treaty, signed in 1785, provided that squatters residing on land reserved to the Indians would not be protected by the army and that the Indians "may punish [them] as they pleased."[77] It eventually became clear that the army was too small, the country too big, and the squatters too plentiful for the government to curtail the practice of squatting.

V. Turf Wars

Congress appointed Arthur St. Clair as governor of the new territory and tasked him with forming local governments and establishing peace, security, and prosperity there. While Congress was authorized to veto any of St. Clair's actions, it very rarely did so. St. Clair arrived in Marietta on July 15, 1788, appointed as a proconsul from afar. One of his first acts was to establish Washington County, with Marietta as the county seat, on July 27. Almost from the moment he arrived, a struggle ensued between St. Clair and the territorial judges over their respective authority.

A. Creating Laws

The ordinance required the governor and judges "to adopt and publish ... such laws of the original states, criminal and civil, as may be necessary, and best suited to the needs of the district."[78] St. Clair interpreted this provision to mean that they must

---

[76] Ohio History Central: Squatters. Located at: http://www.ohiohistorycentral.org/w/Squatters

[77] Hurt, *supra* note 28, 146.

[78] Northwest Ordinance, July 13, 1787, section 5.

adopt laws *only* from the original thirteen states. He also believed that any law must be approved by him, even if all three judges favored it.[79]

Conversely, the judges argued for a liberal reading of this provision, believing that the conditions in the Northwest Territory were unlike that of any existing state and therefore required a set of laws specifically designed for the territory. In addition, the judges attacked the common law as the last vestige of a monarchical (British) government.[80] They acknowledged that the common law should be used when there was no alternative, but they also believed that the law should be flexible, particularly in cases where the common law did not apply.[81]

In the end, the governor and the judges compromised. Taking a pragmatic approach to the problem, they agreed that the laws of the several states could be combined, and that the supposedly static common law could be adjusted to meet the unique conditions of the frontier.[82]

In the summer and fall of 1788, the governor and judges created a code of laws for the territory.[83] These laws provided for a militia, setting minimum ages from marriage, statutes of limitations on civil and criminal actions, and the administration of county governments. They adapted laws from Pennsylvania and the common law and established a list of crimes and punishments. Noting that the governor and the judges were former army officers, historian Theodore Pease noted that the laws read "more like general orders … than laws."[84]

---

[79]   Hurt, *supra* note 28, 273–74.

[80]   *See, generally*, William E. Nelson, *Americanization of the Common Law: The Impact of Legal Change on Massachusetts Society, 1760–1830* (Cambridge, MA: Harvard University Press, 1975).

[81]   *The History of Ohio Law, supra* note 42, 24–25.

[82]   *The History of Ohio Law, supra* note 42, 22–23.

[83]   The full text of this code is available at: *Full Text of the Laws of the Northwest Territory.* Available at: http://archive.org/stream/lawsofnorthwestt17nort/lawsofnorthwestt17nort_djvu.txt

[84]   Theodore Calvin Pease, *The Laws of the Northwest Territory, 1788–1800* (Springfield, IL: Trustees of the Illinois State Historical Library, 1925). Available at: http://www.historykat.com/TNWRO/statutes/theodore-calvin-pease-laws-northwest-territory-1788-1800-springfield-ill-trustees-illinois.html

As might have been expected judges did strange things. Especially was this true in Illinois. John Reynolds has left on record the story of the court at Prairie du Rocher that tried a man for the murder of a hog. Another court in the Illinois paraded a man through the street with his face to his horse's tail, his wife leading the horse. August 16, 1794, a man was adjudged 16 stripes for nonpayment of a debt. In 1799 an Illinois court entertained the indictment of a man as a common nuisance for living with another man's wife. The legislation of the Northwest Territory can be picked full of defects, but it is a question whether the scattered communities for which it was made would not generally have governed themselves in about the way they actually did whatever the legislation provided for them.[85]

Prior to the signing of the Treaty of Greenville, most of the white settlements in the Northwest Territory were located close to the Ohio River. Once a treaty was signed with the Native American tribes and peace was established, settlements were founded farther up the Ohio River tributaries, and the population grew exponentially. Because cash was in short supply, speculators began to sell their lands on time installments or by granting credit. The Harrison Frontier Land Act, passed by Congress on May 10, 1800, allowed prospective sellers to purchase public lands on credit, spurring additional settlement.[86]

Once peace was established throughout the territory, government officials began the process of civil administration of the territory and the growing population. Before 1795, the governor and the judges could enact laws that were contrary to the procedures (to only adopt laws from the original thirteen states) previously established by the Northwest Ordinance. Governor St. Clair knew the judges were exceeding their statutory authority, but he largely overlooked this issue.

---

[85] 2 Bateman and Selby, *Historical Encyclopedia of Illinois and History of St. Clair County*, 698–701, found in: http://archive.org/stream/lawsofnorthwestt17nort/lawsofnorthwestt17nort_djvu.txt

[86] Hurt, *supra* note 28, 171–174. See, also, hermitsdoor. *Great American Documents: The Harrison Land Act of 1800*. Available at: http://hermitsdoor.wordpress.com/2012/05/16/great-american-documents-the-harrison-land-act-of-1800/

B. Slavery

Article VI of the Northwest Ordinance decreed:

> There shall be neither slavery nor involuntary servitude in the said
> territory, otherwise than in the punishment of crimes whereof the
> party shall have been duly convicted: Provided, Always, any person
> escaping into the same, from whom labor or service is lawfully
> claimed in any one of the original States, such fugitive may be
> lawfully reclaimed and conveyed to the person claiming his or her
> labor or service as aforesaid.[87]

French settlers in the region had owned slaves long before the American
government was established. Governor St. Clair, under pressure from French-
speaking individuals in the area, chose to interpret the provision to prohibit the
future introduction of slavery but not to disturb the peculiar institution in areas
where it already existed.[88] Settlers moving into the Virginia Military District twice
petitioned the territorial legislature for permission to bring their slaves with them.
Both requests were rejected.[89]

C. Maxwell's Code

By 1795, however, the federal government began closer scrutiny of the situation in
the territory, and congressional debates began. The federal House of Representatives
debated and eventually rejected several of the laws passed by St. Clair and the judges.
The US Senate failed to concur, and the "arbitrary" laws remained in place.

Perhaps in response this congressional scrutiny, in the summer of 1795 the
governor and judges met at Cincinnati to prepare a more comprehensive civil
and criminal code. This work became known as Maxwell's Code, named after its
publisher. Twenty-five of the thirty-seven laws that were proposed were taken from
the Pennsylvania Code, while the remaining laws were taken from the laws of other

---

[87]   An Ordinance for the government of the Territory of the United States Northwest of the
        River Ohio. Article VI.

[88]   *The History of Ohio Law, supra* note 42, 27.

[89]   Knepper, *supra* note 27, 85.

states. Maxwell's Code established the English common law, restructured certain court practices, prohibited excessive taxation, and imposed a variety of regulations.

Three years later, the acting governor and the judges adopted eleven more laws, including four taken from Kentucky. The latter laws were created despite the requirement of the Northwest Ordinance that any laws be adopted from the *original* thirteen states. The acting governor and the judges justified their actions by declaring that the conditions in Kentucky, which was admitted as a state in 1792, were similar to the conditions in the Northwest Territory.[90]

VI. Stage 2

By the summer of 1798, Governor St. Clair, having realized that there were now "5000 free male inhabitants of full age" in the territory, called for a census to establish the second stage of territorial government. The governor didn't wait for the results of the census and on October 29, 1798, declared that the requisite number of eligible males had been reached. He set the third Monday in December as the date for choosing delegates to the territorial legislature.

A. The Territorial Assembly

In February 1799, the twenty-two members of the new lower house met and nominated ten persons for the five seats in the upper house or Legislative Council. Members of the lower house were required to own at least two hundred acres, and members of the upper house were required to own at least five hundred acres. The members chose Edward Tiffin as president of the House of Representatives.

The new territorial assembly dealt with the issue of slavery in the new territory, streamlined election laws, enacted laws dealing with personal conduct and criminal actions, and levied taxes.

B. Congress Forms the Indiana Territory

While the settlers living east of the Great Miami River looked anxiously toward statehood, the settlers west of that river (today's states of Indiana and Illinois) wanted to return to the first stage of territorial government, which they believed served their

---

[90]   Knepper, *supra* note 27, 82–83.

interests better. Governor St. Clair, on the other hand, wanted to postpone statehood and divide his enemies, located in the valley of the Scioto River, from his supporters, centered east of the Scioto River near Marietta.

Congress sided with the settlers located west of the Great Miami River and created the Indiana Territory on May 7, 1800. The Northwest Territory was divided along a line running north from the mouth of the Kentucky River, through Fort Recovery, and north to Canada. Cincinnati was named as the capital of the territory east of the border, and Vincennes was designated as the capital of the territory west of the border. President Adams appointed William Henry Harrison as governor, and the new territory reverted to Stage 1 of territorial government until 1809.[91]

C. Jefferson Elected as President

Meanwhile, on the national level, Democratic-Republican Thomas Jefferson was elected president in 1800, sweeping the Federalist majority from power. Prior to leaving office, however, the lame duck President John Adams appointed St. Clair to another term as governor.

The Ohio Republicans, led by Nathaniel Massie and Thomas Worthington, preferred local control of the government. The Republicans wanted statehood and opposed the Bank of the United States and the fiscal policies of Alexander Hamilton. They believed that the sixty thousand inhabitants necessary for statehood would be reached in the 1800 census. Their center of power was Chillicothe.

The Federalists, led by Governor St. Clair, believed in a strong national government. They believed that men of property should control the government. The Federalists opposed statehood and wanted to further divide the territory along the Scioto River. They supported a large standing army and navy and backed the Bank of the United States. The Cincinnati and Marietta areas were their centers of power.

To retain power, St. Clair persuaded the territorial assembly to pass the Division Act of 1801. His purpose was to establish the western border of Ohio at the Scioto River. By dividing Ohio as St. Clair suggested, neither area would possess the sixty thousand inhabitants necessary for statehood, thus allowing St. Clair and the Federalists to remain in office. In January 1802, Congress overwhelmingly rejected the Division Act, greatly increasing Ohio's chances for statehood in the near term.

---

[91]   Knepper, *supra* note 27, 87.

Summary

The new United States of America gained control of the Ohio Country at the close of the American Revolution. The Confederation Congress hoped to raise money to repay war debts through the sale of these lands to the public. Congress also granted lands to war veterans as a reward for their service.

Congress enacted the Ordinances of 1784, 1785, and 1787, which established procedures for the settlement of the new lands. Initially, the governmental powers were divided between the governor, a secretary to act in the governor's absence, and three territorial judges. Once the population of a specific area reached five thousand free males, a territorial legislature would be elected. Once an area gained a population of sixty thousand, it could apply for statehood.

The Native American population residing in the area bitterly contested white settlement. The Confederation, known as the Seven Nations, humiliated federal forces on two occasions until they were defeated by General Anthony Wayne at the Battle of Fallen Timbers in August 1794. The Treaty of Greenville, signed in 1795, opened the Ohio Country to settlement.

Ohio's population increased exponentially, and by 1800 there were enough settlers to elect a legislature. The legislature clashed frequently with the governor and the judges over their respective spheres of influence. The territorial governor, Arthur St. Clair, actively opposed statehood for Ohio, but by 1802 the area reached a population of sixty thousand and clamored for statehood.

Chapter 3

Ohio's 1802 Constitution and Statehood

A Bill of Rights is what the people are entitled to against every government on earth, general or particular; and what no just government should refuse, or rest on inferences.

—Thomas Jefferson, 1787

I. Introduction.

Once Congress rejected the Division Act, Ohio Republicans[92] set their eyes on statehood. They felt certain that the new president and the newly elected Republican Congress supported their agenda. The US House of Representatives appointed a committee to report on Ohio's prospects for statehood. Although the 1800 census revealed that Ohio only had 45,365 residents, the committee determined that the region would soon have the 60,000 residents required for statehood. They issued a report proposing that the steps be established for Ohio's statehood.[93] Although Paul Fearing,[94] the nonvoting delegate, opposed the committee's findings, Congress accepted the committee's report.

---

[92]   The political party referred to here is at various times known as the Democratic–Republican Party, the Republican Party, or the Jeffersonian Republicans. This party was organized in 1791, primarily to oppose the programs of Secretary of the Treasury Alexander Hamilton. Because of the presidential election of 1824, this party eventually split into four factions.

[93]   Knepper. *supra* note 27, 90.

[94]   Fearing was an ally of Governor St. Clair and opposed statehood for Ohio.

A. Enabling Act of 1802

On April 30, 1802, Congress passed the Enabling Act of 1802.[95] Section 1 of the Act read:

> That the inhabitants of the Eastern division of the territory northwest of the river Ohio, be and they are hereby, authorized to form for themselves a constitution and State government, and to assume such name as they shall deem proper, and the said State, when formed, shall be admitted to the Union upon the same footing with the original States in all respects whatever.

The Enabling Act described Ohio's new boundaries[96] and set November 1, 1802 as the date for a constitutional convention. The new constitution was to be "Republican, and not repugnant to the Ordinance of 13 July 1787, between the original States and the people and States of the territory northwest of the River Ohio."[97]

The voters would elect thirty-five delegates, or one delegate for each twelve hundred[98] people. While the Northwest Ordinance limited the vote to men who owned a "freehold in 50 acres," the Enabling Act included "all male citizens of the United States, who have arrived at full age, and resided within the said territory at least one year previous to the day of election, and shall have paid a territorial or County tax ..." However, noncitizens who owned at least fifty acres could also vote

---

[95] The full text of the Enabling Act of 1802 is available at: *Ohio History Central: Enabling Act Of 1802*. Available at: http://www.ohiohistorycentral.org/w/ Enabling_Act_of_1802_(Transcript)

[96] The state boundaries were established at the Pennsylvania line, the Ohio River to the mouth of the Great Miami, the meridian northward to its intersection with a line projected due east from the southern tip of Lake Michigan, then along that line to the international boundary.

[97] Enabling Act of 1802, § 5.

[98] Enabling Act of 1802, § 4.

since the Enabling Act allowed the electors who had qualified under the Northwest Ordinance to vote for convention delegates.[99]

Like the Northwest Ordinance, the Enabling Act permitted most male residents to vote. The prior laws allowed voting only at the county courthouses, but since the original counties were so large, voting was encouraged by establishing polling places at the township level.[100] The result was a large voter turnout, with most precincts reporting a doubling or tripling of voters compared to earlier territorial elections.[101]

The Enabling Act also provided that the new state would be allowed one member of the House of Representatives until the time of the next census.[102] Finally, the act provided that the federal government would control public lands within the new state, and the state agreed to allocate one-twentieth of the net proceeds of land sales in Ohio for building roads. Specifically, the one-twentieth portion should "be applied to the laying out and making public roads, leading from the navigable waters emptying into the Atlantic, to the Ohio, to the said State, and through the same, such roads to be laid out under the authority of Congress, with the consent of the several States through which the road shall pass."[103]

B. Ohio's First Constitutional Convention

On November 1, 1802, the thirty-five delegates assembled at Chillicothe. Twenty-six of the delegates supported of the platform of the Democratic-Republican Party. Seven of the delegates identified themselves as Federalists, and two were independents.[104] The Democratic–Republicans favored a small government of limited powers, and they believed that the legislative branch should control most of the powers that

---

[99]   Steven H. Steinglass & Gino J. Scarselli, *The Ohio State Constitution* (Westport, CT: Oxford University press, 2011), 212.

[100] *The History of Ohio Law*, *supra* note 42, 42.

[101] Barbara A. Terzian, *Symposium: The Ohio Constitution—Then and Now: An Examination of the Law and History of the Ohio Constitution on the Occasion of Its Bicentennial: Ohio's Constitutions: An Historical Perspective*, 51 Clev. St. L. Rev. 357, 360 (2004).

[102] Enabling Act of 1802, § 6.

[103] Enabling Act of 1802, § 7.

[104] Phillip R. Shriver & Clarence E. Wunderlin Jr., *Documentary Heritage of Ohio* (Athens, OH: Ohio Bicentennial Series) 99 (Ohio University Press, 1st ed. 2001).

the government possessed. Conversely, the Federalists believed in a stronger, more centralized government structure.[105] The delegates only voted on a straight party-line basis once, when the Democratic–Republicans defeated a Federalist-backed proposal to submit the proposed constitution to the voters for approval.[106]

During the delegate campaign, the Federalists accused the Democratic–Republican candidates of proslavery leanings, while the latter candidates claimed that they were falsely accused to defeat their candidacies. While there may have been some support in committee for a limited form of slavery in the new state,[107] most likely from the delegates originally from Kentucky or Virginia, none of these views were presented to the entire convention.[108]

The delegates quickly elected officers, including Edward Tiffin[109] as president, validated the delegates' credentials, established rules, and formed committees. Governor St. Clair addressed the delegates on the third day and urged them to ignore the Enabling Act and retain the current government structure. On November 22, 1802, President Jefferson learned the details of St. Clair's speech and promptly dismissed him as governor. The delegates ignored St. Clair's advice and recommended that the convention draft a constitution and form a state government.[110] The delegates agreed to form a state, and drafted the constitution of 1802.

---

[105]   Ohio History Central. Ohio Constitutional Convention of 1802. Available at: http://www.ohiohistorycentral.org/w/Ohio_Constitutional_Convention_of_1802?rec=523

[106]   History of Ohio Law, *supra* note 42, 363.

[107]   Ibid., 360.

[108]   Ibid., 47.

[109]   Edward Tiffin was born in Carlisle, England, and studied medicine before emigrating to Virginia in 1784. He moved to Chillicothe in 1796 to practice medicine. Tiffin served as speaker of the Territorial House of Representatives; president of the Ohio Constitutional Convention; first governor of Ohio; US senator; and finally, surveyor general of the United States. Tiffin died in Chillicothe in 1829. Biographical Directory of the United States Congress. Edward Tiffin (1766–1829). Available at: http://bioguide.congress.gov/scripts/biodisplay.pl?index=T000268

[110]   Enabling Act of 1802, § 5.

Edward Tiffin, 1766-1829.
(Image courtesy of the Ohio History Connection).

In crafting Ohio's new constitution, the delegates relied on several recently written or rewritten constitutions from other states. During the American Revolution, patriots from the original thirteen colonies had overthrown their colonial governments. To provide governance, the colonies needed to prepare new constitutions to supersede the royal charters then in existence. While New Hampshire, Virginia, South Carolina, and New Jersey created new constitutions before July 4, 1776, Rhode Island and Connecticut simply deleted all references to the Crown in their existing royal charters.

C. Drafting Issues

Two different types of constitutions were drafted during this era, depending on whether the wealthy or the less affluent had control of the process.[111] In the more

---

[111]   Jack P. Greene & J.R. Pole, eds., *A Companion to the American Revolution* (Hoboken, NJ: Wiley-Blackwell, 2003).

affluent states, such as Maryland, Virginia, Delaware, New York, and Massachusetts, the new constitutions included the following:

- substantial property qualifications for voting and elected office;
- bicameral legislatures, with an upper house as a check on the lower (democratically elected) house;
- strong governors, with veto power and substantial appointment authority;
- few or no restraints on individuals holding multiple government offices;
- state-established religion.

In the states where the less-affluent individuals held power, particularly Pennsylvania, New Jersey, and New Hampshire, the new constitutions embodied the following factors:

- universal white male suffrage, with no or minimum property requirements for voting or holding office;
- strong, unicameral legislatures;
- weak governors, lacking veto powers and little appointment authority.

Ohio's first constitution was perhaps the most democratic state constitution yet adopted.[112] Cognizant of the authoritarian rule of King George III and later Governor St. Clair,[113] the first Ohio Constitution vested nearly all the state's power in a bicameral legislature, with elections every two years for state senators and annually for state representatives. Representation for both houses was based on the

---

[112] Shriver & Wunderlin, *supra* note 104, 99.

[113] Arthur St. Clair (1736–1818) was an American soldier and politician. Born in Scotland, St. Clair served as a junior officer in the British Army during the French and Indian War. After the war, he settled in western Pennsylvania and served as a judge. In 1775 Congress appointed him as a colonel in the Continental Army. He served throughout the war and attained the rank of major general. In 1785, he was elected to the Continental Congress from Pennsylvania and was appointed as the first governor of the Northwest Territory in 1787. A Federalist, St. Clair frequently clashed with the territorial judges and actively opposed Ohio's admission as a state. After denouncing the Enabling Act, setting up the mechanism for Ohio's admission as a state, President Jefferson removed St. Clair from office in 1802. Hurt, *supra* note 28, 272–283.

number of white male inhabitants over the age of twenty-one.[114] Bills could originate in either house, subject to alteration, amendment, or rejection by the other house. The governor was to be "elected" by the voters, but all other state officials as well as the judiciary[115] were elected by the legislature.

II. The General Assembly

The delegates to Ohio's first constitutional convention met with goals to 1) curb the power of the governor, and 2) create a General Assembly that was the dominant branch of state government. As a result, the authority of the governor was severely limited, while the General Assembly was granted wide-ranging powers. Although the framers of Ohio's first constitution separated the governmental powers into three distinct branches, the legislature was by far the recipient of most of those government powers. Checks on the General Assembly came not from the other two branches but from the voters, acting through frequent elections.

The delegates determined that governmental power sprang from the will of the people. Many of the state constitutions written during this era were very democratic, allowing white male suffrage, frequent elections, dominant legislatures, and weak executives.[116] Ohio was no exception.

The preamble of the 1802 constitution began with "We, the people." The first section of the Bill of Rights recognized that "every free Republican government" was founded on the "sole authority" of the people, who had a right "at times … To alter, reform, or abolish their government."[117] The constitution attempted to restrict legislative power by explicitly retaining in the people "all powers, not hereby delegated."[118]

---

[114]   Ohio Const. of 1802, art. I, § 2,5.

[115]   Justices of the peace were also elected locally. Les Benedict and Wheeler, *supra* note 42, 364.

[116]   Allen Nevins, *The American States During and After the Revolution, 1775–1789* (New York: Macmillan, 1924; repr. New York: Augustus M. Kelly, 1969), 139–205; Richard B. Morris, *The Forging of the Union, 1781–1789,* (New York: Harper and Row, 1987), 111–129.

[117]   Ohio Const. of 1802, art. VIII, § 1.

[118]   Ohio Const. of 1802, art. VIII, § 28.

The General Assembly would appoint the secretary of state,[119] the state treasurer and auditor,[120] the judges of the supreme and common pleas courts,[121] and major generals and quartermasters of the militia.[122] The General Assembly was also authorized to impeach the governor and all other civil officers.[123] The constitution gave the General Assembly appointment power over the judiciary but remained silent on the issue of judicial checks on legislative power. The US Supreme Court issued its ruling on *Marbury v. Madison*[124] in the same year that Ohio was admitted as a state, but the doctrine of judicial review was not mentioned.[125]

III. The Governor

Territorial Governor Arthur St. Clair ruled the Northwest Territory with an iron fist during his fourteen years in authority. He could convene or dissolve the territorial legislature at will, appoint nearly all local public officials, establish new counties and draw county lines, and administer territorial law. No act of the territorial legislature could become law without his approval, even if approved by the territorial judges. He held the power of veto and did not hesitate to use it.

Frustrated by St. Clair's use (or abuse) of his veto powers, the delegates intended to strip the chief executive of nearly all the power that the territorial governor had exercised. Charles Willing Byrd, Hamilton County's delegate, wanted the delegates to adopt provisions from the Tennessee Constitution of 1796,[126] which sharply limited the power exercised by the executive.

The delegates wrote Article II, which vested the "supreme executive power of the state" in the office of the governor, who would have responsibility to "take care

---

[119]   Ohio Const. of 1802, art. II, § 6.

[120]   Ohio Const. of 1802, art. VI, § 2.

[121]   Ohio Const. of 1802, art. III, § 8.

[122]   Ohio Const. of 1802, art. V, § 5.

[123]   Ohio Const. of 1802, art. I, § 24.

[124]   5 U.S. 37 (1803).

[125]   The subject of judicial review in Ohio is discussed in chapter 4.

[126]   The full text of the Tennessee Constitution of 1796 is available at: http://www.tn.gov/tsla/founding_docs/33633_Transcript.pdf

that the laws shall be faithfully executed."[127] However, in constitutional terms, the term *power* is an exaggeration.

While the governor had the authority to make recess appointments when the General Assembly was not in session, he had little real power. The governor had no veto, a provision that the delegates included clearly in reaction to the veto power St. Clair had frequently exercised as territorial governor. The governor under the new constitution could only recommend measures to the legislature. He was commander of the state's army, navy, and militia forces, but was subject to term limits of "no more than six years and any term of eight years." Historian Barbara Terzian suggested that the delegates wanted the governor to represent the state but not control it.[128]

The governor's term of office was set at "two years, and until another governor shall be elected and qualified."[129] The governor was chosen by popular vote, but the General Assembly had the authority to intervene in the event of "[c]ontested elections."[130] There was no lieutenant-governor; in the event of the death, impeachment, resignation or removal of the governor, the speaker of the Senate was first in line to exercise the office. If the Senate leader was unavailable to serve, then the speaker of the House would fill the vacancy.[131]

Finally, the delegates established strict eligibility requirements for the office of governor. The governor's term was two years, with a limit of six years in an eight-year period,[132] a minimum age requirement of thirty years, and a citizenship requirement of twelve years in the United States and four years in the state preceding his election.[133] Members of Congress and any person holding any office under the United States, or the state were ineligible, and compensation was capped at $1,000 annually.[134]

---

[127]   Ohio Const. of 1802, art.II, §§ 1,7.

[128]   The History of Ohio Law, *supra* note 42, 46.

[129]   Ohio Const. of 1802, art. II, § 3.

[130]   Ohio Const. of 1802, art. II, § 2.

[131]   Ohio Const. of 1802, art. II, § 12.

[132]   Ohio Const. of 1802, art. II, § 3.

[133]   Ohio Const. of 1802, art. II, § 3.

[134]   Ohio Const. of 1802, art. I, § 19.

Although important as a ceremonial position, with its lack of real power, the office of the governor was not a great job. Of the sixteen persons who held the position under the 1802 constitution, four (Edward Tiffin, Return J. Meigs Jr., Ethan Allen Brown, and Wilson Shannon) resigned in the middle of their terms to accept another appointed or elected position. Only one, Alan Trimble, served long enough to be disqualified from the office by term limits.[135] Governor Thomas Worthington wrote of the office that "[t]he extraordinary increase of population in the state has increased in the same proportion as the duties of the office of Governor and makes it necessary he should spend much of his time at the seat of Government."[136] Clearly, the governor's office was a full-time job with part-time pay.

IV. The Judiciary

The Northwest Ordinance, passed by Congress in 1787, provided for, among other things, a judicial system for the Northwest Territory. Congress appointed the judges initially, then after the adoption of the US Constitution, the president appointed and the Senate confirmed the territorial judges pursuant to Article III. The highest court in the territory was the three-judge general court. Below the general court were county courts of common pleas, a general court of quarter sessions of the peace, and various specialized courts.

Under the new Ohio Constitution, Article III provided for common pleas courts in each county. The state was divided into three circuits, and each circuit would have a court "president." Each county in the circuit would have no fewer than two or more than three associate judges. Three judges constituted a quorum. Initially, only the court "president" was legally trained, while the two associate judges were laymen. A vote of the two associate justices could "overrule" the court's president. Each judge would be elected to a seven-year term.

The Supreme Court consisted of a Chief Justice and two Associate Justices, "elected" by the General Assembly to a term of seven years "so long as they behave well."[137] Two justices would constitute a quorum. The General Assembly was

---

[135]   The History of Ohio Law, *supra* note 42, 145.

[136]   Frank Theodore Cole. Thomas Worthington. *Ohio Archaeological and Historical Quarterly* 12, 365 (October 1903).

[137]   Ohio Const. of 1802, art. III, § 8.

authorized to add another Justice to the Court after five years, at which time the court could divide the state into two circuits, with two justices sitting each circuit.[138] After much debate, and to keep the administration of justice at the local level, the Supreme Court was required to meet in each county every year.[139]

In some states in the colonial and postcolonial eras, there appears to have been support for an elected judiciary, but this support did not occur in Ohio.[140] In its constitutional convention, Ohio delegates wanted the judiciary to be controlled by the legislature. And since the constitution was not presented to the electorate for approval, there were no ratification debates to worry about.

The other court established by the constitution was the justice of the peace court, established at the township level, and again reflecting the delegates' desire to keep the administration of justice local. The justices of the peace would be elected by township and would serve three-year terms.[141] The problems associated with a judiciary "selected" by the legislature would soon be demonstrated.

V. Other Provisions

A. Ohio's Bill of Rights

Ohio's first constitution also included a Bill of Rights,[142] adopted just eleven years after the federal Bill of Rights. Ohio's Bill of Rights consisted of twenty-eight sections and was substantially like its federal counterpart. However, the Ohio Constitution's Bill of Rights included the right to alter, reform, or abolish government,[143] a prohibition against slavery and involuntary servitude,[144] rights of conscience[145] and

---

[138]   Ohio Const. of 1802, art. III, §§ 2,10.

[139]   Ohio Const. of 1802, art. III, § 10.

[140]   Steven P. Crowley. *The Majoritarian Difficulty: Elected Judiciaries and the Rule of Law*, 62 U. Chi. L. Rev. 689, 714 716 (Spring 1995).

[141]   Ohio Const. of 1802, art. III, § 8.

[142]   Ohio Const. of 1802, art. VIII.

[143]   Ohio Const. of 1802, art. VIII, § 1.

[144]   Ohio Const. of 1802, art. VIII, § 2.

[145]   Ohio Const. of 1802, art. VIII, § 3

education,[146] rights for victims of crime,[147] a prohibition on imprisonment for debt,[148] and a declaration that all powers not otherwise delegated are to remain with the people.[149] Section 12 provided that the writ of habeas corpus shall not be suspended, "unless when the case of rebellion or invasion, the public safety may require it."[150]

B. Slavery/Suffrage

Although the delegates intended that Ohio be a free state, and had originally approved a proposal granting suffrage to African American men, they reconsidered this proposition and voted against African American suffrage. Suffrage for women was also voted down. The constitution required voters to reside in the state for at least one year and pay a state or county tax. The tax requirement had the effect of limiting the vote to property owners, since the only state and county taxes at that time were real property taxes.[151] However, a temperance provision barring the state from licensing the sale of alcohol was presented to the voters as a separate amendment and passed by a vote of 113,237 to 104,255.[152] Finally, there was a provision that if two-thirds of the General Assembly found it necessary to amend or change the constitution, they would so recommend to the electorate. If a majority of the electors agreed, a convention would be called to revise, amend, or change the constitution.[153]

C. Only White Men May Participate

Historian Barbara Terzian wrote that Ohio's new constitution was designed primarily to benefit white men. After one year's residency, his right to vote was guaranteed

[146] Ohio Const. of 1802, art. VIII, § 25.

[147] Ohio Const. of 1802, art. VIII, § 7.

[148] Ohio Const. of 1802, art. VIII, § 15.

[149] Ohio Const. of 1802, art. VIII, § 28.

[150] Ohio Const. of 1802, art. VIII, § 12.

[151] Steven H. Steinglass & Gino J. Scarselli, *The Ohio State Constitution* (Westport, CT: Oxford University press, 2011), 212.

[152] *The History of Ohio Law, supra* note 42, 60.

[153] Ohio Const. of 1802, art. VII, § 5.

by either paying a state or county tax or by working on local roads. He could elect his state representatives and could easily replace them because elections were held annually. He could vote for a governor, who could be easily replaced by election or impeachment if he ignored local issues or became corrupt. The legislature chose his judges, but he could still elect justices of the peace, who handled local civil and criminal matters. He could elect all county and township officials, and if he was a member of the militia, he could elect his own officers.

If accused of a crime, his right to jury trial was "inviolate." If prosecuted, he had a right to be informed of any charges against him, he could testify in his own defense and could face witnesses testifying against him, he could compel witnesses to testify, and he was entitled to a speedy trial. He had a right to speak, to assemble, and to petition the government. He had a right to bear arms and to rely on contracts, and he had full access to the courts. The state provided schools to educate his children, and he could not be imprisoned for debts.[154] Conversely, African Americans and women were regarded as second-class citizens.[155]

The convention completed its work on November 29, 1802, and then adjourned. Unlike most of the state constitutions rewritten after 1776, Ohio's proposed constitution was not submitted to the voters for ratification.[156] The Ross County delegate, Thomas Worthington, presented the proposed constitution to President Jefferson on December 20 and to Congress on December 22.[157]

---

[154] Terzian, *supra* note 73, 368–369.

[155] At the time Ohio's Constitution was drafted, there were about 337 African Americans living in the Northwest Territory, with most of these in Detroit. Knepper, *supra* note 3, 93. Under the state's new constitution, voting was limited to "white male inhabitants above the age of twenty-one years." Some of the rights detailed in Ohio's Bill of Rights, such as enjoying liberty, acquiring, possessing, and protecting property, and the right to worship are specifically reserved to "all men." Others, such as the right to be free from warrantless searches and seizures, the right to answer to criminal charges, the right to bail, the right to peaceably assemble, and several others, are reserved to "all persons." Ohio Const. of 1802, art. VIII.

[156] Robert D. Geise, *American History to 1877 (Barron's EZ 101 Study Keys)* (Barron's Educational Series, February 19, 1992), 37.

[157] Shriver & Wunderlin Jr, *supra* note 76, 99

D. Congress Approves

Congress approved several alterations that the delegates suggested to the requirements contained in the Enabling Act. The delegates proposed reserving public lands for educational purposes in the Virginia Military District, the US Military District, the Connecticut Reserve, and Indian lands not ceded. A college township was to be located within the Symmes purchase, and 3 percent (instead of the 5 percent specified in the Enabling Act) of the receipts from the sale of public lands were to be used for public roads in the state. The state also agreed to refrain from taxing federal lands for five years. A provision slightly altering Ohio's northern border was not addressed.[158]

Statewide elections were held in January 1803, even though statehood had not yet been formally approved. The voters elected Edward Tiffin as governor and Jeremiah Morrow as representative. The legislature elected Thomas Worthington and James Smith to the US Senate.[159] A bill passed Congress on February 19, 1803, officially recognizing Ohio as a state. The General Assembly first met on March 1, 1803, and that date is recognized as Ohio's official date of admission to the Union.[160]

Summary

Congress passed the Enabling Act in April 1802. This legislation empowered the citizens of the Eastern division of the lands northwest of the Ohio River to draft a constitution, form a state government, and apply for statehood. All male citizens (including free African Americans) who had reached full age, lived in the area for one year, and paid a county tax were eligible to vote for one of the thirty-five convention delegates. Noncitizens who owned at least fifty acres were also eligible to vote.

On November 1, 1802, the delegates met in Chillicothe. Twenty-six of the delegates were Democratic–Republicans, seven were Federalists, and two were

---

[158] The failure of Congress to act on this provision was one of the primary causes for the Toledo War, discussed in chapter 3. A map of the reserved and purchased land in Ohio is available at: http://upload.wikimedia.org/wikipedia/commons/thumb/1/1e/Ohio_Lands.svg/240px-Ohio_Lands.svg.png

[159] Hurt, *supra* note 28, 282–283.

[160] Knepper, *supra* note 27, 93.

independents. The Democratic–Republicans favored a small government with limited powers, whereas the Federalists favored a stronger, more centralized government. The delegates elected Edward Tiffin to preside.

The new constitution vested nearly all the governmental powers in a bicameral legislature, while the governor had limited powers and no veto. The General Assembly appointed most of the state officials, including those of the executive branch and the judiciary. Elections were held every two years for the Senate and the governor, and annually for the House. Checks and balances on the General Assembly came not from the other two branches, but from the citizens using frequent elections. Suffrage was limited to white males over the age of twenty-one years, striking male African Americans from the voting rolls.

The convention adjourned on November 30, 1802, and the final product was presented to Congress the next month. Congress approved several modifications from the requirements listed in the Enabling Act, and a problem with Ohio's northern border was not addressed. Congress passed a bill officially recognizing the new state of Ohio on February 19, 1803. Ohio's official date of admission was March 1, 1803.

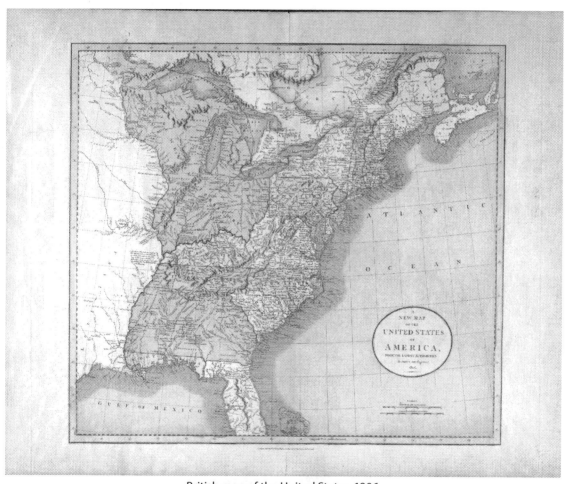

British map of the United States, 1806.
(Image courtesy of the Ohio History Connection).

Chapter 4

Between the Constitutions: Ohio Law in the Age of Jackson

If the Union is once severed, the line of separation will grow wider and wider, and the controversies which are now debated and settled in the halls of legislation will then be tried in fields of battle and determined by the sword.

—Andrew Jackson, 1837

I. Introduction

Once the constitution was drafted and statehood achieved, Ohioans set to the task of governing themselves. With almost all the power of government vested in the General Assembly, problems were bound to occur. From its first constitution in 1803 upon admittance to the Union, to 1851 when a new constitution was drafted and approved, Ohio struggled to enforce its state power in governing its territory and protecting the rights of its citizens

On the national scene, the country endured the War of 1812, enjoyed the Era of Good Feelings, and entered the Age of Jackson. Ohio was a main theater of conflict during the war, and its citizen/soldiers defended the state from invasion by the British and their Native American allies at Forts Meigs and Stephenson.

In most other respects, the war gave a major boost to the state's economy. Ohio's produce helped feed the country's war machine and outfit its soldiers. The removal of the Native Americans after the war helped spur further settlement. In addition, the army built roads throughout the state to transport supplies to its troops. Hard money was scarce in the state, and the resulting barter economy stalled the growth of farms and businesses.[161]

The Era of Good Feelings was a period after the war where the sense of nationalism grew and political and sectional strife declined. The Federalist Party disappeared in the wake of the Hartford Convention, and nearly everyone considered themselves a Republican. The era is roughly defined as synonymous with the administration of James Monroe (1817–1825). The Missouri Compromise and the Monroe Doctrine represented the major political accomplishments during this era.[162]

The Age of Jackson (1828–1850) was an era of tremendous growth of the nation's population, wealth, and economy. Between 1830 and 1850 the population, as well as the number of persons held as slaves, nearly doubled. Seven new states joined the Union during that time frame, and the country acquired a vast tract in the arid southwest because of the war with Mexico.[163]

Ohio also enjoyed a period of increased growth. The completion of the Erie Canal and the National Road led to increased immigration to the northern and central parts of the state. This tremendous growth over a short time period led to growing pains in the state. The increasing reliance on paper money and barter set the stage for the Panic of 1819. Finally, a defect in the original state constitution caused Ohio to flex its political muscle to wrest a disputed area away from its northern neighbor.[164]

During this time, three major constitutional crises occurred within the state: The Sweeping Resolution,[165] the Rebellion of 1820,[166] and the Ohio-Michigan War.[167]

---

[161]   Kevin F. Kern & Gregory S. Wilson, *Ohio: A History of the Buckeye State* (Hoboken, NJ: John Wiley & Sons, Inc., 2014), 162–165.

[162]   George Dangerfield, *The Awakening of American Nationalism: 1815–1828* (New York: Harper & Rowe, 1965), 35.

[163]   Ted Widmer. *The Age of Jackson.* The Gilder Lehrman Institute of American History. Available at: http://www.gilderlehrman.org/history-by-era/jackson-lincoln/essays/age-jackson

[164]   Kern and Wilson, *supra* note 16, 163–165.

[165]   For an in-depth discussion of the Sweeping Resolution, *See,* Donald F. Melhorn Jr., *Lest We Be Marshall'd: Judicial Powers and Politics in Ohio, 1806–1812* (Akron, OH: The University of Akron Press, 2003).

[166]   Called "Ohio's War against the Bank of the United States."

[167]   Sometimes called the Toledo War.

The Sweeping Resolution and the Ohio-Michigan War were a result of defects in the original state constitution, while the Rebellion of 1820 was a major conflict over the issue of state versus federal authority that predated both the Nullification Crisis of 1832 and the Civil War. In addition, the activities of the US District Court in Ohio played a role in ushering in changes to Ohio's Constitution. This chapter will explore the three constitutional crises that occurred in this era. These issues helped shape Ohio's relations with its own government, as well as its relationships with its neighbors and the federal union.

II. The Sweeping Resolutions

A. The Revolution of 1800

In the election of 1800, Republican[168] presidential candidate Thomas Jefferson won an overwhelming victory over incumbent President John Adams, and the Federalist majority in Congress was swept from power. The Federalists, who had controlled the presidency and Congress until that time, had appointed only Federalists to the judiciary. At the end of 1801, Jefferson wrote the following to John Dickinson:

> They [the Federalists] have retired into the judiciary as a stronghold.
> There the remains of Federalism are to be preserved and fed from
> the treasury, and from that battery all the works of Republicanism
> are to be beaten down."[169]

---

[168] The Jeffersonian Republicans of the early 1800s should not be confused with the modern-day Republican Party, which was founded in the 1850s.

[169] Thomas Jefferson, James Madison, John Caldwell Calhoun. The Virginia and Kentucky Resolutions of 1798 and '99: With Jefferson's Original Draught Thereof. Also, Madison's Report, Calhoun's Address, Resolutions of the Several States in Relation to State Rights. With Other Documents in Support of the Jeffersonian Doctrines of '98, Volume 265. Available at: http://books.google.com/books?id=c1c-AAAAYAAJ&dq=thomas+jefferson +quotes+federalists+judiciary&source=gbs_navlinks_s

B. Marbury v. Madison

Every first-year law student is acquainted with the case of *Marbury v. Madison*.[170] In that case, the lame duck Sixth Congress enacted the Judiciary Act of 1801.[171] President Adams signed the bill on February 3, 1801, three weeks before the end of his presidency. The act established ten new federal district courts and increased the number of federal circuit courts from three to six. The act also added additional judges to each circuit and gave the president authority to appoint federal judges and justices of peace to fill the new vacancies. The act gave President John Adams the opportunity to pack the judiciary with federalist appointees before that party lost power. Adams, in pursuit of that goal, appointed William Marbury as a federal justice of the peace just before he left the presidency in 1801. Marbury's commission was signed and sealed but was not delivered to him prior to the expiration of Adams's term.[172] Marbury filed for a writ of mandamus with the US Supreme Court, seeking an order to the new Secretary of State James Madison to deliver his commission.

Madison did not respond to the court and refused to deliver Marbury's commission. Congress, now under the control of the Jeffersonians, passed the Judiciary Act of 1802, which repealed the act passed by the Federalists the previous year, and then suspended the court's 1802 term.[173] The court's prestige, and its very existence as a coequal branch of government, was in serious jeopardy.

Chief Justice John Marshall,[174] facing a major issue involving separation of powers, found that Madison had improperly withheld Marbury's commission.[175]

---

[170] *Marbury v. Madison*, 5 U.S. 137 (1803).

[171] 2 Stat. 89. An act to provide for the more convenient organization of the Courts of the United States. This act was also known as the Midnight Judges Act.

[172] The act also granted to the federal courts jurisdiction over all cases involving federal law, lowered from $500 to $100, the minimum amount required to assert federal jurisdiction, reduced the number of Supreme Court Justices from six to five, and eliminated their circuit riding duties. William E. Nelson. Marbury V. Madison: The Origins and Legacy of Judicial Review (Lawrence, KS: University Press of Kansas, 2000), 37.

[173] Ibid., 57–58.

[174] Ironically, Marshall was serving as secretary of state under Adams and was responsible for Marbury failing to receive his commission before Adams's term expired.

[175] Nelson, *supra* note 172, 60–61.

However, Marshall also held that the court lacked the jurisdiction to grant the relief Marbury requested. By doing so, Marshall declared that Section 13 of the Federal Judiciary Act of 1789, which gave the Court original jurisdiction to issue writs of mandamus, was contrary to the constitution, and thus null and void.[176] This decision infuriated the Jeffersonians, but their only remedy was to give Marbury his commission, which they had no intention of doing. Eventually, the court and the Jeffersonians implicitly agreed to the idea of judicial review.[177] The court did not overturn another congressional statute until 1857, and the president did not challenge the court's authority to do so.

C. Ohio's Courts Adopt Judicial Review

This precedent led state courts to follow suit, and courts in Ohio soon adopted the principle of judicial review.[178] Courts gave themselves the authority to review laws passed by the legislature to determine if they conflicted with the federal or the state constitutions. The involved statute was known as the *50 Dollar Act*, which granted justices of the peace jurisdiction over civil claims not exceeding fifty dollars.[179] In the case of *Rutherford v. McFadden*, (1807, unreported) Justices Tod and Huntington held that the act infringed upon a constitutional right to trial by jury. Relying on *Marbury v. Madison*, the justices struck down the act. The court held that:

> "[a]ny act in violation of the Constitution, or infringing its provisions
> must be void, because the legislature, when they step beyond the
> bounds assigned them, act without authority, and their doings are

---

[176] The US Constitution limited the original jurisdiction of the Supreme Court to certain kinds of cases, and mandamus was not one. US Cons. Art. III. Expanding the Court's jurisdiction to mandamus actions would require a constitutional amendment.

[177] According to the 1817 Pennsylvania case of *Moore v. Houston*, 1817 WL 1787 (Pa. 1817), the concept of judicial review was "well-established by the great mass of opinion, at the bar, on the bench and in legislative assemblies of the United States." Nelson, *supra* note 172, 75.

[178] The term "judicial review" was first used by Professor Edwin S. Corwin. Edwin S. Corwin, *The Rise and Establishment of Judicial Review*," parts 1 and 2, Mich. L. Rev. 9 (December 1910): 102–25; (February 1911): 283–316.

[179] Act of February 12, 1805, 3 Laws of Ohio 21 (1805).

no more than the doings of any other private man." The role of the judiciary was "to expound what the law is."

The court compared the legislative act with the constitution. Since the constitution clearly "[could not] be adjudged void, the judges had no choice but to declare that "any act inconsistent with it [to] be no law."[180]

Circuit Judge Calvin Pease reached a similar conclusion in the case of *E. Wadsworth v. Solomon Braynard, Trumbull County Court of Common Pleas* (1808). These decisions were extremely unpopular at the time, and there was a serious question of whether the doctrine of judicial review could even be asserted under Ohio's 1802 constitution.

D. Impeachment and the Sweeping Resolutions

The members of the Ohio House were so infuriated when their laws were overturned that they brought impeachment charges against Tod and Pease. Huntington, who had recently been elected governor, escaped their wrath. Both Tod and Pease were tried (separately) before the Ohio Senate, and both narrowly avoided conviction.[181]

After failing to remove the justices by impeachment, the General Assembly enacted the Sweeping Resolutions.[182] Under the Ohio Constitution, judges in Ohio were elected to a seven-year term by the General Assembly. The judges who replaced the originally elected judges were under the impression that their seven-year terms began upon their selection, and many of their commissions reflected this fact. The new law provided that current officeholders could not serve beyond the original seven-year term held by their predecessors. This statute would effectively "sweep" all the currently serving judges and justices from office on March 1, 1810. The General Assembly could then elect new Supreme Court Justices and common pleas judges who did not condone the concept of judicial review. Several judges who were

---

[180] Nelson, *supra* note 172, 76. Although there were no official case reporters in Ohio at this time, the state's sixty newspapers occasionally printed important judicial opinions. Columns debating the decisions often followed. *The History of Ohio Law, supra* note 42, 505.

[181] For a more in-depth review of this trial, *See*, Melhorn Jr., *supra* note 134, chapter 8.

[182] Also known as *An act defining the duties of justices of the peace and constables in criminal and civil cases.*

removed under the resolution continued hearing cases, causing an entirely new set of problems.[183]

A group of Federalists and independent Republicans opposed the resolution from the start, but they lacked the votes to repeal the resolutions. The Resolutions were eventually repealed in the 1811–1812 legislative session; the House easily repealed the measure, and despite intense opposition, the Senate repealed the measure by a single vote.[184] Perhaps Thomas Jefferson addressed situation best when he wrote:

> An *elective despotism* was not the government we fought for; but one which should not only be founded on free principles, but in which the powers of government should be so divided and balanced among the several bodies of magistracy, has that no one could transcend their legal limits, without being effectively checked and restrained by the others.[185]

The delegates to Ohio's 1851 constitutional convention, no doubt aware of the problems associated with an "all-powerful" legislature, addressed the checks and balances of power in the new document by restructuring Ohio's judiciary. In addition to dropping the requirement that the Supreme Court meet in each county annually, and creating a new system for the district courts of appeal, all judges would thereafter be elected by popular vote.[186]

While the Sweeping Resolutions were a result of a defect in the original state constitution, the Rebellion of 1820 was a major conflict between federal and state powers in the governance of state territory and protecting individual rights.

---

[183] The judgments in these cases were later set aside by the Ohio Supreme Court. Melhorn Jr., *supra* note 134, 153–55.

[184] *The History of Ohio Law, supra* note 42, 16.

[185] Thomas Jefferson. Notes on the State of Virginia, 122.

[186] Knepper, *supra* note 27, 205.

III. The Rebellion of 1820

A. The Great Bank Robbery

In the early afternoon of September 17, three men burst into the Chillicothe Branch Office of the Bank of the United States.[187] Two of these "ruffians" jumped the counter and entered the bank's vault. The third man, John Harper, prevented the bank's cashier from interfering with the heist. The trio made off with over $120,000 in bank funds, and bank officials were unable to block their escape.

No, the year was not 1933, and the suspects were not John Dillinger and his gang. The year was 1819, and the culprits were Sheriff John Harper and two assistants, acting under a commission from Auditor of State Ralph Osborn, to collect past-due taxes from the bank pursuant to Ohio law. The Bank of the United States sued Osborn and his accomplices for contempt, trespass, and carrying away $100,000[188] "under color and pretense of the laws of Ohio." Just two days before the "robbery," the federal court served State Auditor Osborn with a copy of a petition requesting the injunction and a subpoena to appear before the court in January. However, since no injunction was served upon him, Osborn collected the tax.

Harper deposited the funds in a state-chartered bank in Chillicothe overnight, and the next day, both he and Osborn were served with an injunction that prohibited them from collecting the taxes. Since they had already collected the taxes, both Harper and Osborn claimed that the injunction was moot and ignored it. Osborn deposited the funds in the state treasury, minus a 2 percent fee paid to Harper and his assistants. US marshals arrested Harper, and Osborn was cited for contempt for disregarding the injunction.[189]

---

[187] This branch was known as the Chillicothe Office of Discount and Deposit, one of the two Ohio branches of the Second Bank of the United States. The other branch was located in Cincinnati.

[188] Knepper, *supra* note 27, 137. Some reports claim that Harper seized a total of $120,000 from the bank. The next day he turned the funds over to the state treasurer. Upon discovering the error, the treasurer promptly returned the extra $20,000 to the bank. Ohio History Central: *Osborn v. Bank of the United States.* Available at: http://www.ohiohistorycentral. org/w/Osborn_v._Bank_of_the_United_States.

[189] R. Carlisle Buley, *The Old Northwest: Pioneer Period 1815–1840*, Vol. 1 (Bloomington, IN: Indiana University Press, 1950), 590–592.

B. The Bank of the United States

In the Republic's early years, there was not enough gold or silver available to conduct the nation's business. As a means of expanding available currency, the new nation issued paper money, bank money, and credit. Secretary of the Treasury Alexander Hamilton convinced Congress to charter the First Bank of the United States on February 25, 1791. Hamilton's goal was to furnish a circulating medium and credit system to improve the handling of the financial business of the federal government.

The bank was funded through the sale of $10 million in stock. The US government purchased the first $2 million of stock, while the remaining $8 million in shares was sold to the public. One-quarter of the stock had to be paid in gold or silver, while the remaining balance could be paid with bonds, notes, or government stock. Congress chartered the bank for a period of twenty years, and at the end of that time, Congress could either extend or terminate the bank's charter. Many of the southern states opposed Hamilton's plan. Those states believed that a national bank would primarily serve the interests of the industrial states in the North and East, while they preferred locally chartered banks, which they felt would better serve their largely agricultural interests.[190]

C. Banks on the Frontier

The primary purposes of a bank are: 1) to accept deposits; 2) to make loans; and 3) to issue notes. On the frontier, there is less hard money (specie) available, so the note-issuing function becomes more important.[191] The first bank in Ohio was the Bank of Marietta, chartered by the Ohio legislature in 1808. The Bank of Chillicothe was chartered the same year, and the Bank of Steubenville was chartered in 1809.[192]

Three types of banks were operating in Ohio during this period: The Bank of the United States, state-chartered banks, and unchartered, or wildcat banks. The First Bank of the United States, described above, was in operation from 1791 to 1811, when its charter expired. Five years later, Congress chartered the Second Bank of

---

[190]   Mark R. Wilson, *Law and the American State, From the Revolution to the Civil War: Institutional Growth and Structural Change.* In: *The Cambridge History of Law in America. supra* note 6

[191]   Buley, *supra* note 189, 567.

[192]   Ibid., 568.

the United States, under the same terms, with the government owning 20 percent of the outstanding shares and the public owning the remaining 80 percent. The Second Bank was the largest bank, the largest lender, and the largest business corporation in the United States.[193]

Caught in a wave of prosperity following the War of 1812, Ohio's economy was ready for the expansion of banking services. Ohioans felt that the Second Bank of the United States would help the local economy by providing access to cash and other mediums of exchange essential to conducting the state's business. Further, the bank could issue notes that were secured by US Treasury deposits in Philadelphia.[194] These notes really were "good as gold" and were the preferred medium of exchange in commercial transactions and the payment of debts.

Two different political factions competed for the establishment of a branch office of the bank in their respective communities. William Henry Harrison represented the interests of Ohio's major commercial center, Cincinnati, while Chillicothe, the state's original capital and political center, was represented by Governor Thomas Worthington and Ohio House Speaker Duncan McArthur. To placate the two factions, the bank established a branch in Cincinnati in January 1817, followed by a branch in Chillicothe in October of that year.[195]

The second category consisted of the state-chartered banks. These banks flourished after the First Bank of the United States closed. There were 88 state-chartered banks in Ohio in 1811; there were 208 by the end of 1814.[196] Although these banks issued a huge number of notes, their notes were backed by hard currency and therefore maintained excellent credit.

The third type was the unchartered, or wildcat banks. These banks were most often seriously undercapitalized, some with "the usual assets of a table, chair, or

---

[193]   Kern and Wilson, *supra* note 161, 17–18.

[194]   Knepper, *supra* note 27, 135.

[195]   144 Ohio History 79–104 (R. Douglas Hurt, ed.) (quoting Kevin M. Gannon, The *Political Economy of Nullification: Ohio and the Bank of the United States*, 1818–1824, 81–82).

[196]   Buley, *supra* note 189, 568, (quoting Albert Gallatin, *Considerations on the Currency and Banking Systems of the United States* (Philadelphia, 1831) 45, 49, 53, quoted in annual Report of the Comptroller of the Currency, 1876, US House Executive Documents, 44 Congress, two session, No. 3, XL).

keg of nails with a few coins on top."[197] These banks were accused of distributing nearly worthless currency backed by problematic security. Ohio's wealthiest citizens operated the state-chartered banks, while most wildcat banks were under local control. To stabilize the state's currency, the Ohio legislature outlawed the notes of the unchartered banks after January 1, 1817. Some of these notes were held by state-chartered banks, while others continued to circulate. By the spring of 1817, some of the wildcat bank notes were offered at 80 percent of their face value, and by the next summer most were practically worthless.[198]

D. The Panic of 1819

Rather than providing economic security to the region the founders intended, the Second Bank of the United States, like the state-chartered banks of the day, liberally extended credit. The loan policies of the bank's branch offices actually increased the amount of paper money in the state. Thousands of Ohioans overextended themselves and purchased more land than they could finance. If they couldn't make the payments, they borrowed even more. This excessive borrowing, speculation, and the huge supply of paper money in Ohio was a ticking time bomb ready to explode.[199]

The explosion occurred in the late summer of 1818, when the United States suffered its first economic depression, later known as the Panic of 1819. Because Ohio's economy was built on such a shaky foundation, it and other Western states were hit first and hardest. General causes for the panic included a decrease in the demand for American agricultural products from Europe, the decision of most European countries to return to the gold standard after the Napoleonic Wars, and the British decision to buy cotton from its Indian colonies instead of from the American South.[200]

The Second Bank (Bank) was forced to undertake drastic measures to avoid

---

[197]   W.H. Hunter, *Pathfinders of Jefferson County, Ohio*, Ohio Archaeological and Historical Society Publications, VIII (1900), 195–96.

[198]   Buley, *supra* note 189, 580.

[199]   *Ohio History*, 79–104 (R. Douglas Hurt, ed.) (quoting Kevin M. Gannon, *The Political Economy of Nullification: Ohio and the Bank of the United States, 1818–1824,* 81–82).

[200]   Andrew R. L. Cayton, *Frontier Republic: Ideology and Politics in the Ohio Country, 1780–1825* (Kent, OH: Kent State University Press, 1989) 285–288.

closing. In July 1818, the bank ordered its Cincinnati branch to begin collecting outstanding balances at 20 percent per month. This sudden reversal of their previous policy probably saved the bank from collapse, but it also caused most of the state banks to stop redeeming notes with specie. The bank's actions caused prices to fall rapidly and left worthless bank paper as the primary medium of exchange.[201] The panic became even worse in August when the bank ordered its branches to stop accepting each other's notes.[202]

This economic downturn caused farm prices to crater, and real estate became impossible to sell. The state banks began calling in the loans for the heavily mortgaged properties they had financed in better economic times. Borrowers were unable to repay their loans, and soon the primary real estate transactions in the state became foreclosure actions filed by the bank's Cincinnati office. Several factors were responsible for this economic collapse.[203] However, to most Ohio citizens, the bank was responsible. Most Ohioans felt that the bank's change in policy led directly to the panic.[204]

The bank and the panic became leading issues in the election of 1818. Several members of the bank's board of directors also served in the state government. A great wave of resentment against the state's "elites" soon occurred. Ordinary Ohioans wondered why the bank's policies had changed so quickly, and why the western states were affected by the panic much more than the states of the North and East.[205]

E. The Voters Retaliate

The election of 1818 was a disaster for incumbent officeholders. Governor Worthington was defeated, and Speaker McArthur lost his bid for reelection. Almost

---

[201]   Buley, *supra* note 189, 583.

[202]   Ibid., 583.

[203]   George Dangerfield, *The Awakening of American Nationalism: 1815–1828* (Harper & Rowe, New York, 1965), 179. Among the factors outside of the bank's control were obstruction from private banks, federal regulations, and the European market fluctuations. "If the [Second Bank of the United States] had been wisely managed from the beginning" wrote historian George Dangerfield, "it could not have prevented the panic; it could only have modified its effects."

[204]   Charles Clifford Huntington, A *History of Banking and Currency in Ohio Before the Civil War* (Charleston, SC: BiblioBazaar, 2009), 297–300.

[205]   *Ohio History, supra* note 199 (quoting Gannon, 88).

every politician affiliated with the bank was turned out; most were replaced by anti-bank candidates. The new legislature soon set out to regulate, and possibly tax, the bank's Ohio branches.[206]

The idea of taxing the bank and its branches was not new. In 1817, the General Assembly, concerned about the possibility of unfair competition between the bank of the United States and the state-chartered banks, formed a committee to examine the issue. After all, a tax on the state-chartered banks helped pay Ohio's debt from the War of 1812.

The General Assembly also attempted to regulate wildcat and out-of-state banks after their notes threatened to drive the notes of state-chartered banks out of existence. Why should the National Bank be exempt from regulation and/or taxation, officials asked? After all, the bank was not an entity of the federal government; 80 percent of its shares were privately held. The General Assembly introduced a bill to levy a tax on the bank, but intense lobbying by the bank's directors and bank-friendly politicians led to the bill's eventual defeat.[207]

F. Ohio Taxes the Bank

In the new legislative session, another committee was empaneled, this time stacked with anti-bank men.[208] This committee blamed the bank alone for the recent economic collapse. Ohio was not the only state interested in taxing the bank. Other states including Maryland, Tennessee, Georgia, North Carolina, and Kentucky had enacted laws taxing the branch offices of the bank located in their respective states. In addition, the states of Indiana and Illinois enacted legislation banning the bank within their respective states. Relying on these actions by other states, the committee decided that Ohio could only protect itself by driving the bank out of the state. The committee's final report recommended a tax of $50,000 on any non-state-chartered financial institution doing business in the state.[209]

The new law, entitled: "An act to levy and collect a tax from all banks and

---

[206] William T. Utter, *The Frontier State: 1803–1825* (Columbus, OH: Ohio Historical Society, 1968).

[207] Knepper, *supra* note 27, 136.

[208] Ohio History, *supra* note 199 (quoting Gannon, 87).

[209] Knepper, *supra* note 27, 136.

individuals, and companies, and associations of individuals, that may transact banking business in this state, without being authorized to do so by the laws thereof," also known as the "outlaw" act, became effective on February 8, 1819. The new law would impose a tax on any unauthorized financial institution doing business in the state after September 1, 1819. The tax was due each year on September 15 at a rate of $50,000 per office. The state auditor was empowered to commission agents to collect the tax, and pay the agents a 2 percent commission.[210]

G. McCulloch v. Maryland

About one month after the passage of the act, the US Supreme Court issued its decision in the case of *McCulloch v. Maryland*.[211] The issues were similar to those in Ohio,[212] where the state of Maryland levied a tax on the Baltimore branch of the Bank of the United States. Their ultimate purpose was to drive the bank and its operations from the state. It was soon clear that *McCulloch* involved not only banking issues, but also the larger matter of allocation of state and federal authority. Chief Justice Marshall, writing for a unanimous majority, ruled in favor of the bank. The court held that Maryland's taxation of the bank was unconstitutional, further finding that the federal government possessed implied powers, including the power to charter a bank.

Marshall's assertion of federal sovereignty did not sit well with states' rights advocates. Many Ohioans felt that if they continued their efforts to tax the bank, they would eventually get their day in court, and they could urge the justices to overturn *McCulloch*.[213]

A standoff was inevitable. The bank, relying on the *McCulloch* decision, continued to operate, while the state legislature had no intention of repealing the tax. The auditor felt duty-bound to collect the tax. On September 11, lawyers representing the bank told Auditor Osborne that they intended to file for an injunction in the federal court that would prohibit him from collecting the tax. On September 15, the

---

[210] Knepper, *supra* note 27, 136–137.

[211] *McCulloch v. Maryland,* 17 U.S. 316 (1819).

[212] Many Ohioans rationalized their opposition to *McCulloch* by insisting that the issues in that case were different than the situation in Ohio. Knepper, *supra* note 27, 136–137.

[213] Ohio History, *supra* note 199 (quoting Gannon, 93).

court served Osborn with a copy of the petition and a subpoena to appear before the court. An injunction was not served. Auditor Osborn ignored the documents and commissioned Sheriff Harper to collect the tax, setting the stage for the "robbery" at the Bank's Chillicothe office on September 17. The auditor's actions drew some criticism, but the overwhelming majority of Ohioans approved of his actions.[214]

Eastern newspapers accused the Ohio officials of treason, nullification, and other crimes, and great debates began. Political candidates issued their "Declarations of Independence" against the bank as part of their political platforms. Public opinion mostly supported Ohio's stance. James Wilson,[215] editor of the *Western Herald and Steubenville Gazette*, wrote that for Ohio to submit to the federal judiciary as "dispenser of justice between her and the U.S. bank" would pave the way for some new attack upon state sovereignty.[216]

H. Osborn v. Bank of the United States

The bank quickly filed suit against Osborn, Harper, and Harper's assistants to recover the "stolen" funds. The court jailed Harper and one of his assistants on trespass charges, and Osborn and Harper were summonsed into the circuit court to explain why they ignored the court's injunctions. Chief Justice Marshall then issued a permanent injunction, prohibiting the state from using the ill-gotten funds.

Ohioans celebrated when the bank closed its Cincinnati Office in October 1820. The bank rationalized its decision by stating that Ohio had too many branch offices, but anti-bank feeling in the state certainly had to be a factor.[217]

The General Assembly convened in December 1820 with even greater anti-bank sentiments. The members felt that the bank's actions brought harm to the state. They also felt that the only reason that the federal lawsuit was brought against the state auditor, rather than the state itself, was to avoid the Eleventh Amendment prohibition against suits involving a state as a party. Finally, the legislature was aware of the doctrine of judicial review, discussed above, where the federal courts

---

[214]   Knepper, *supra* note 27, 136–137.

[215]   Newspaper editor James Wilson was the grandfather of future President Woodrow Wilson. Ohio History, *supra* note 199 (quoting Gannon, 92).

[216]   Buley, *supra* note 189, 591–592.

[217]   Ohio History, *supra* note 199 (quoting Gannon, 95–96).

interpret the US Constitution, but they felt that the state, rather than the courts, had the ultimate responsibility to determine the constitutionality of federal actions.[218]

Essentially, the legislature declared that: 1) the Eleventh Amendment prohibited the bank from bringing the action because the state was a party, and 2) even if the bank could bring the action, the states, rather than the federal courts, were the final arbiters of the constitutionality of federal measures. By their actions, the legislature attempted to "nullify" the McCulloch decision.[219]

On January 29, 1821, the General Assembly passed "an act to withdraw from the Bank of the United States the protection and aid of the laws of this state, in certain cases." This law, if rigidly enforced, would have prohibited local courts and law enforcement from assisting the bank in conducting its business activities, and would eventually force the bank to close its doors. In February, the General Assembly offered to suspend the January Act if the bank agreed to be taxed at the same rate as state-chartered banks. The bank, citing the *McCulloch* decision, refused to budge. The act became effective in September 1821.[220]

I. Trial in the Circuit Court

In September 1821, the federal lawsuit was tried in the circuit court before Justice Thomas Todd.[221] Kentucky Senator Henry Clay represented the bank. State Senator Charles Hammond,[222] a leading anti-bank advocate who later served as reporter for

---

[218]   Ohio History, *supra* note 199 (quoting Gannon, 97–980).

[219]   In the 1830s, John C Calhoun tried to explain South Carolina's nullification of federal tariff statutes. The Constitution, he wrote, was a compact among the several states. If one party to the arrangement, namely, the federal government, violated the terms of this compact, the states were free to exercise their rights as parties to that compact and nullify the actions that violated the arrangement. John C. Calhoun, *Exposition and Protest, in Union and Liberty: The Political Philosophy of John C. Calhoun,* Ross M. Lence ed. (Indianapolis, IN: Indianapolis Liberty Fund, 1992), 311–365.

[220]   Buley, *supra* note 189, 593.

[221]   Justice Todd served on the US Supreme Court from 1807 to 1826. Here, Justice Todd was presiding in his capacity of Judge of the Circuit Court.

[222]   Ohio History Central: Charles Hammond. Available at: http://www.ohiohistorycentral. org/w/Charles_Hammond.

the Ohio Supreme Court, represented the state of Ohio. By this time, two injunctions had been issued against the state, one preventing any future collection of taxes from the bank, and the other ordering the return of the funds already seized by the state.

Clay attempted to argue Harper's trespass and centered his case-in-chief on that issue. Hammond, by contrast, argued the larger issue of state sovereignty, or specifically the power of the state to levy a tax against business entities. Hammond then agreed "to an amendment which would raise the actual question-let a verdict pass by consent and take the case on Bill of exceptions to the Supreme Court of the United States."[223] The circuit court ruled in favor of the bank. Federal marshals then arrested the state treasurer, confiscated his keys, and seized a total of $98,000 from state treasury.[224]

J. The US Supreme Court

The case was argued before the US Supreme Court on March 10–11, 1824. Chief Justice Marshall, writing for a 6–1 majority, held for the bank and against Osborn.[225] The court also reviewed and confirmed its prior decision in *McCulloch v. Maryland*, affirmed the jurisdiction of the court to hear the action, upheld the constitutionality of the bank, and prohibited the states from taxing instrumentalities of the federal government. The court also found that, although Osborne was an agent of the state and acting in its behalf, he could not use the state's immunity from suit as a defense.[226]

Once the court announced its decision in *Osborn*, the entire issue died rather quietly. There was neither a public outcry nor fiery editorials in the state's newspapers. Many historians theorized that the state's politicians used the doctrines of states' rights and nullification merely for convenience. When the state's economy improved, the doctrines were easily discarded. In the meantime, the bank closed its Cincinnati office in October 1820 and the activities of the Chillicothe branch were significantly reduced. The bank closed the Chillicothe office at the end 1825, and

---

[223] Clement L. Martzolff, *The Autobiography of Thomas Ewing*, Ohio Archaeological and Historical Society Publications 22 (1913): 171–72.

[224] Kern & Wilson, supra note 161, 201

[225] *Osborn v. Bank of the United States*, 22 U.S. 9 Wheat. 738 (1824).

[226] Ibid.

the General Assembly repealed the "outlaw" act early in 1826. Andrew Jackson, who assumed the presidency in 1829, vetoed the bill providing for the bank's recharter and later removed federal deposits from the bank's coffers.[227]

This line of reasoning regarding Ohio's assertion of state's rights can best be summarized by William Utter, who wrote:

> It seems clear that the argument [of state sovereignty] was developed almost wholly to justify the State's course against the Bank. The very men who drafted the resolutions [asserting state sovereignty] were advocates of national aid in building the Cumberland Road, and in financing the Erie and Ohio canals … Ohio's economic interests were best served by a nationalistic government; in the Bank matter only were economic interests aligned with an opposite theory of government.[228]

Recent historians have put a new spin on this incident. Ohioans felt that the bank was primarily responsible for the Panic of 1819. Ohioans' primary goal was to drive the bank from the state, and they accomplished that goal several years before Jackson vetoed the bank's recharter in 1832. By the time the "outlaw" act was repealed, it was moot.[229]

The court left the larger issues hanging. The issue of the relationship between the states and the federal government was not addressed at all and would continue to percolate over the next forty years. The court left Ohio's states' rights position mostly undisturbed. Further, Marshall resolved the Eleventh Amendment argument very narrowly; since Osborn, not the state of Ohio was the party of record in the suit, the protections of the Eleventh Amendment did not apply.

Finally, the *Osborn* case was simply one in a series of cases that extended federal sovereignty to the detriment of the states. This line of cases started with *Martin v.*

---

[227]   Knepper, *supra* note 27, 137–138.

[228]   Knepper, *supra* note 27, 137–138.

[229]   Ohio History, *supra* note 199 (quoting Gannon, 103–104).

Hunter's Lessee (1816),[230] to *McCulloch*, through *Cohens v. Virginia* (1821),[231] *Osborn* and finally, to *Planter's Bank v. Georgia* (1824).[232] The "war" between the bank and Ohio was not an isolated event; instead it was part of a larger struggle involving federalism and states' rights as well as the economic conflict between the "haves" and "have-nots" in the frontier state. The issues that arose from this "Rebellion" remained hotly contested and would appear again regularly during the prewar period. At the same time, Ohio was fighting to protect its boundary lines in the Ohio-Michigan War.

IV. The Ohio-Michigan War (Toledo War)

Each November, football teams representing the Ohio State University and the University of Michigan gather either at Columbus or Ann Arbor for the annual gridiron classic. This rivalry is one of the most famous in all of college football, but the discord between these two adjoining states does not begin or end with football. The origins of this rivalry are much deeper and more complex.

This "War Between States" occurred thirty years before the American Civil War. Unlike that war, there were no deaths, no grand strategies, and no generals seeking political office. Before it was over, the Toledo War would involve six US presidents, and a future Confederate general.[233] When Ohio's congressional delegation blocked Michigan's application for statehood, the latter state drafted a constitution and

---

[230] *Martin v. Hunter's Lessee*, 14 U.S. 304 (1816). The Supreme Court has jurisdiction over questions of federal law.

[231] *Cohens v. Virginia*, 19 U.S. 264 (1821). The US Supreme Court has the power to review state supreme court decisions in civil law matters when the defendant claims that their constitutional rights have been violated.

[232] *Planter's Bank v. Georgia*, 22 U.S. 904. The circumstance that a state is a member of a private corporation will not give the Supreme Court original jurisdiction of suits where the Corporation is a party.

[233] Andrew Jackson was president and fired Michigan's territorial governor to resolve the dispute. Martin Van Buren served as vice president and would run for president in 1836. James Monroe favored the remarking of the boundary carried out by Captain Andrew Talcott in 1834. Second Lieutenant Robert E. Lee was a member of the survey party. James K. Polk was speaker of the House, and Senator James Buchanan argued against Michigan's claim to the Strip. John Quincy Adams defended Michigan's position in the House of Representatives.

elected state officers in defiance of federal authority. Disputes over the Ohio–Michigan boundary continued into the 1970s.

A. Origins of the Conflict

When Congress enacted the Northwest Ordinance in 1787, one of provisions included as part of the document was a division of the Northwest Territory into not less than three nor more than five states.[234] Section 14, Article 5 of the Northwest Ordinance established boundaries for the "3 to 5 states." This northern boundary of this state (Ohio) would be *an East and West line drawn through the southerly bend or extreme of Lake Michigan* (emphasis added). This northern boundary of the proposed new state would cause trouble in the future.

At the time Congress drafted the ordinance, the most complete map of the Northwest Territory was known as the Mitchell Map, compiled in 1755.[235] According to the Mitchell map, the East-West line referred to in the ordinance intersected Lake Erie near the mouth of the Detroit River. Basing its northern border on that line would give the entire shoreline of Lake Erie west of the Pennsylvania border to Ohio. However, as historian Carl Wittke once observed, "Bad maps produce a lot of history."[236]

B. Ohio's Constitutional Convention

During Ohio's first constitutional convention in November 1802, several members allegedly received reports from a beaver trapper, who disclosed that the southernmost extent of Lake Michigan was much farther south than previously thought or mapped.[237] The delegates believed that Congress's intent in drawing that border

---

[234] An Ordinance for the government of the Territory of the United States Northwest of the River Ohio. § 14, Art. V.

[235] Don Faber, *The Toledo War: The First Michigan–Ohio Rivalry* (Ann Arbor, MI: The University of Michigan Press, 2008). 13.

[236] Carl Wittke, *The Ohio-Michigan Boundary Dispute Re-examined,* Ohio State Archeological and Historical Quarterly (October, 1936).

[237] Knepper, *supra* note 27, 157.

was to place Ohio's northern border north of the mouth of the Maumee River. This would give Ohio access to most or all the Lake Erie shoreline west of Pennsylvania.[238]

To resolve this dilemma, the delegates included a provision in the constitution that if the trapper's report was correct, the boundary line would be angled slightly to the northeast to intersect Lake Erie at the "most northerly cape of the Miami (Maumee) Bay." The delegates realized[239] that if Lake Michigan extended farther south than believed, Ohio would lose a significant amount of territory, and perhaps the entire southern shore of Lake Erie.

When Ohio presented its draft constitution to Congress for approval, the state boundary issue was referred to a committee. The committee reported that the proposed northern boundary was dependent upon "a fact not yet ascertained" (the southernmost extent of Lake Michigan), and the proposed boundary was accepted without further debate.[240] However, when Congress created the Michigan Territory in 1805, they used the northern border described in the Northwest Ordinance instead of the northern border described in Ohio's Constitution of 1802. No one noticed the inconsistency at the time, but it would have serious consequences in a few years.[241]

C. Early Surveys

Residents of the disputed area asked the Ohio government to resolve the border question. Congress approved a request for a survey of the border, but the survey was delayed by the War of 1812. The survey finally began in 1816. The US surveyor general, Edward Tiffin, oversaw the survey. Tiffin,[242] a former Ohio governor, commissioned a survey based on the line described in the Ohio Constitution of 1802, not on the ordinance line. Not surprisingly, the Harris line, named after

---

[238]   Kern & Wilson, *supra* note 161, 204–205.

[239]   Ohio Const. Art. VII., § 6.

[240]   Faber, *supra* note 235, 26–28.

[241]   *See*, Alec R. Gilpin, *The Territory of Michigan (1805–1837)* (Lansing, MI: Michigan State University Press, 2002).

[242]   Tiffin was also the president of the Ohio constitutional convention that redrew Ohio's northern boundary.

surveyor William Harris, placed the Bay of the Maumee River completely within the state of Ohio.[243]

Michigan Governor Lewis Cass was not pleased with the results of Tiffin's survey. Cass believed that the line should be surveyed based on the original Northwest Ordinance line, and he commissioned surveyor John Fulton to survey that line. The Fulton Line showed Ohio's northern boundary south of the mouth of the Maumee River. The disputed region between the Harris Line and the Fulton line became known as the Toledo Strip. The strip was eight miles wide at its intersection with Lake Erie and five miles wide at its intersection with the Indiana border. The strip contained approximately 468 square miles, including the land that would eventually become the city of Toledo. Both Ohio and Michigan claimed ownership of the strip, and neither would compromise.[244]

D. Indiana and Illinois Join In

The dispute became more complicated when Indiana sought admission to the Union in 1816. Indiana wanted frontage on Lake Michigan, and so its constitutional convention placed its northern border ten miles north of the Northwest Ordinance line. Because southwestern Michigan was mostly unpopulated at the time, and because Governor Cass was busy with other duties, Indiana's northern border went unchallenged.[245]

Perhaps emboldened by Indiana's actions, Illinois asked Congress to establish its northern boundary at a line almost sixty miles north of the most southerly end of Lake Michigan, to include Fort Dearborn, now Chicago, and the lead mines surrounding Galena. Congress agreed and a bill adding eighty-five hundred square miles to Illinois,[246] at the expense of the Michigan Territory, was soon passed. Governor Cass argued for strict enforcement of the ordinance line, and asked Congress to examine and modify the borders.

In 1824, the Michigan Territory's population met the five thousand residents

---

[243] Kern & Wilson, *supra* note 161, 204–206.

[244] Faber, *supra* note 235, 30–31.

[245] Faber, *supra* note 235, 32–34.

[246] The Toledo Strip, by contrast, contained approximately 468 square miles.

needed to enter the second stage of territorial government. A Legislative Council was selected[247] consisting of eighteen members and later increased to twenty-six. The completion of the Erie Canal in 1825 caused the population to increase exponentially. By the early 1830s, Michigan had achieved the sixty thousand population necessary to achieve statehood.

E. Ohio Blocks Michigan Statehood

In 1833 Michigan voters sought Congress's approval to hold a constitutional convention, with its southern boundary based on the original Northwest Ordinance (Fulton) Line. Ohio insisted that its northern border was firmly established in its constitution and refused to negotiate. Ohio's congressional delegation[248] convinced several other states to block Michigan's request for statehood.[249]

In January 1835, Michigan's acting governor, Stevens T. Mason,[250] called for a state constitutional convention for May of that year. Congress, at the urging of the Ohio delegation, refused to pass an enabling act that would authorize a constitution. Regardless, the convention met from May 11 to June 24, 1835, and drafted a proposed constitution. In the meantime, the Ohio General Assembly

---

[247] Half of the council was elected by the people and the remainder approved by the president.

[248] Ohio's delegation in the Twenty-Third Congress consisted of 19 representatives and 2 senators in a Congress of 240 representatives and 48 senators.

[249] Indiana and Illinois supported Ohio's position because both of their northern boundaries were moved well to the north of the ordinance line upon their gaining statehood. If Ohio's border was questioned, their own claims might have been challenged. Southern states opposed the admission of another free state unless a slave state was admitted at the same time.

[250] Stevens T. Mason (1811–1843) was the last territorial governor and the first state governor of Michigan. Known as the Boy Governor, Mason was appointed as territorial secretary at age nineteen and acting governor at age twenty-three. Replaced as acting governor by President Jackson in 1835, Mason was elected Michigan's first state governor. He served from 1835 to 1840. For more information on Mason, *See*, Don Faber, *The Boy Governor: Stevens T. Mason and the Birth of Michigan Politics* (Ann Arbor: University of Michigan Press/Regional, 2012).

passed legislation establishing county governments within the strip, including Lucas County, named for Ohio Governor Robert Lucas.[251]

Both sides presented legitimate claims to the strip. Ohio argued, among other things that:

- Congress neither confirmed nor rejected Ohio's revision of its northern boundary. This can be interpreted as implied consent;
- the maps that Congress relied upon in setting the original boundaries were faulty;
- the Northwest Ordinance, unlike the Constitution, can be amended by simple congressional action. Congress has a perfect right to adjust the borders as it sees fit;
- Indiana and Illinois were admitted to the Union after Ohio and Congress accepted their adjusted northern boundaries;
- Ohio was a critical swing state in the upcoming 1836 presidential election, while Michigan was considered safely in the Democratic fold.[252]

Michigan argued the following:

- Congress never consented to a change in the boundary described in the Northwest Ordinance;
- The Northwest Ordinance was not merely an act of Congress, it was a compact between the federal government and the territory; both parties must agree to change the terms of the compact;
- Michigan's boundary claim was based on the Northwest Ordinance and therefore predated the Ohio Constitution;
- Michigan had exercised jurisdiction over the disputed area for the last thirty years. Conversely, the Great Black Swamp served as a natural boundary between the Toledo Strip and the remainder of Ohio;

---

[251] Robert Lucas (1781–1853) served as Ohio's twelfth governor from 1832–1836, and later served as Iowa's first territorial governor from 1838 to 1841. Lucas participated in two border disputes during his terms as governor. The first was the Toledo War between Ohio and Michigan in 1835, and the second was the Honey War, between the state of Missouri and the Iowa Territory in 1837.

[252] Faber, *supra* note 235, 106–110.

- Residents of the Toledo Strip voted in territorial elections and the territorial government was functioning throughout the strip;
- The US attorney general supported Michigan's claim.[253]

F. The Conflict Escalates

The Michigan Legislature enacted the Pains and Penalties Act in February 1835. This act made it a criminal offense for Ohio officials to conduct business within the strip and provided for fines up to $1,000 and five years' imprisonment for violations. Governor Mason appointed Joseph W. Brown to command the state militia and ordered him to move against the Ohio trespassers. Lucas then dispatched a detachment of the Ohio militia to the strip, arriving at Perrysburg, just southwest of Toledo, on March 31, 1835.[254] Mason and Brown arrived shortly thereafter and occupied Toledo with approximately one thousand troops. Lucas, asserting that the dispute was between the state of Ohio and the federal government, refused to deal with Governor Mason or any other territorial officers.

President Andrew Jackson referred the dispute to Attorney General Benjamin Butler for an opinion. Contrary to Jackson's wishes, Butler opined not only that Michigan was entitled to the strip, but also that the Pains and Penalties Act, unless it was overturned by Congress, was valid and enforceable.[255] Because Ohio's had a sizeable congressional delegation and was a crucial swing state in the upcoming presidential election of 1836, Jackson decided that Ohio's claims should win out. He ordered two representatives to the area to negotiate a compromise. While Lucas reluctantly agreed to disband his militia, Mason prepared his troops for a possible armed conflict.

G. Battle

Ohio next conducted elections in the disputed area. On April 8, 1835, the sheriff of Monroe County, Michigan, arrested two Ohio residents and charged them with

---

[253]   Faber, *supra* note 235, 116–119.

[254]   While the Michigan troops had an easy march from Detroit, the Ohio troops were forced to traverse the Great Black Swamp, a vast area of forests, wetlands, and grasslands, approximately one hundred miles long and twenty-five miles wide, located in northwestern Ohio.

[255]   Faber, *supra* note 235, 5.

a violation of the Pains and Penalties Act because they voted in the Ohio election. Lucas sent surveyors to remark the Harris Line, and on April 26, 1835, the surveyors were confronted by a detachment of Michigan militia in what became known as the Battle of Phillips Corners. The surveyors claimed that the attackers fired thirty to fifty shots in their direction and captured nine prisoners.[256] The Michigan troops claimed that they only fired a few shots in the air, with none aimed at the surveyors. This "battle" served to further heighten tensions between the two sides.

Following the "battle," a special session of the Ohio General Assembly established Toledo as the county seat of Lucas County, formed the Common Pleas Court for the county, and appropriated $300,000 to enforce their legislation. Lucas also sent a delegation to Washington to present Ohio's case to President Jackson. Michigan responded by appropriating a similar amount to fund its militia.[257]

In May and June 1835, Michigan officials conducted their own constitutional convention and drafted a state constitution, which provided for a bicameral legislature, a Supreme Court, and other components of state government. Ohio's congressional delegation continued to oppose Michigan's efforts, and Congress again blocked Michigan's bid for statehood. The actions of the Ohio delegation also prevented Michigan from receiving its share of the federal budget surplus that occurred in 1835, which was distributed to the states but not to the territories.[258]

Tensions in the strip remained high throughout the summer of 1835. Arrests of Ohioans by Michigan officials were followed by Ohio officials arresting Michiganders.

---

[256] Mason claimed that, by conducting the survey, the surveyors not only violated the Pains and Penalties Act, but also committed a trespass within Michigan Territory.

[257] Both Governor Lucas and Governor Mason claimed to have ten thousand troops ready for action. Most of these "troops" were unarmed and untrained, and most carried clubs or broomsticks instead of muskets. The *Toledo Gazette,* supporting Ohio's claim, described the Michigan militia as an invading army "composed of the lowest and most miserable dregs of the community—foreigners and aliens, low drunken frequenters of grog shops, who had been hired at a dollar a day." Faber, *supra* note 235, 96–97.

[258] When President Jackson closed the Second Bank of the United States in 1835, the government realized a huge profit on its original investment. The resulting budget surplus of $17.9 million was greater than the government's total expenses for that year. Jackson paid off the remainder of the national debt and returned the surplus to the state governments, many of which were heavily in debt. Bureau of the Public Debt. *Our Country: The 19th Century.* Located at: http://www.publicdebt.treas.gov/history/1800.htm,

Civil suits and criminal prosecutions became commonplace occurrences. Spying parties, organized by both sides, reported on the activities of their counterparts.

The first "casualty" of the war occurred on July 15, 1835. On that date, Monroe County, Michigan, Deputy Sheriff Joseph Wood arrested Major Benjamin Stickney and his three sons in Toledo. During the arrest, Two Stickney,[259] one of Benjamin's sons, stabbed Wood in the leg with a pen knife and fled south to Ohio. Lucas then refused Mason's request to extradite the fugitive.

Mason asked President Jackson to refer the matter to the US Supreme Court.[260] Jackson demurred. Instead, on August 15, 1835, Jackson replaced Mason as secretary and acting governor with John S. (Little Jack) Horner. Before Horner could arrive to assume his duties, Mason ordered his troops to enter Toledo proper and prevent the symbolically important opening session of the Court of Common Pleas. Ohio officials frustrated Mason's efforts by holding a midnight session of the court before returning to Perrysburg the next morning.

Midnight session of the Court of Common Pleas, Lucas County, 1835.
(Image courtesy of the Ohio History Connection).

---

[259]   Not to be confused with his older brother, One Stickney. Kern & Wilson, *supra* note 161, 205.

[260]   Ohio wanted Congress to resolve the dispute because its large congressional delegation and support from other states gave it a decided advantage. In the event Michigan was admitted as a state before the boundary dispute was resolved, the matter would be referred to the US Supreme Court, where the legal arguments would likely favor Michigan's claim.

In October 1835, Michigan held its own elections. The voters approved the proposed constitution and elected Mason as their first governor. However, Congress refused to seat Michigan's duly elected representative and senators. For a time, both federal and state governments competed to govern the territory.

H. President Jackson Takes Charge

In June 1836, President Jackson proposed another compromise. At Jackson's urging, Congress passed the Northern Ohio Boundary Bill.[261] This bill proposed that if Michigan would cede the Toledo Strip, it would receive the Western three-quarters of the Upper Peninsula in exchange.[262] If Michigan agreed with the proposal, it could become a state. At the same time, Congress passed another bill admitting Arkansas to the Union without restrictions. Michiganders were not pleased, and they initially rejected Congress's offer.[263]

Governor Horner favored compromise and wanted to resolve the dispute, but he was very unpopular among Michiganders. On July 3, 1836, Jackson appointed Horner as the territorial secretary for the new Territory of Wisconsin. He soon left to assume his new duties, leaving no federal officials in charge.[264] Michiganders held a convention in September 1836 to consider Jackson's proposal. Because the delegates thought the Upper Peninsula was worthless, they rejected Jackson's proposal.

I. Michigan's Frostbitten Convention and Statehood

By December 1836, the dispute was ready to resolve itself. Because of the funds the territory spent in garrisoning the disputed region, Michigan found itself in a deep financial bind and was nearly bankrupt. On December 14, 1836, another convention, known as the Frostbitten Convention, was held in Ann Arbor. The legislature did not authorize this convention, and Whig delegates boycotted and refused to attend.

---

[261] Michigan.gov. Important Dates in Michigan's Quest for Statehood. Available at: https://www.michigan.gov/formergovernors/0,4584,7-212—79532—,00.html

[262] The eastern half of the Upper Peninsula, that part east of the line drawn north from the mouth Great Miami River, had been part of Michigan since its early days.

[263] Faber, *supra* note 235, 142–144.

[264] Ibid., 167–169.

The delegates voted to approve the compromise proposed by President Jackson, but Michigan voters rejected the compromise. Congress questioned the legality of the convention but accepted its results and admitted Michigan as the twenty-sixth state effective January 26, 1837.[265]

The Upper Peninsula, awarded to Michigan in the compromise, was considered to be a worthless wilderness at the time. However, discoveries of copper and iron led to a mining boom that helped replenish the state's coffers. The harvesting of timber also became a major industry later in the century. Toledo became a great port on Lake Erie, and the opening of the St. Lawrence Seaway in the 1950s increased its value to the state even more. In the end, both states benefited greatly from the compromise, and the only real loser in the deal was the Territory of Wisconsin, which gave up the western three-quarters of the Upper Peninsula and received nothing in return.

Summary

Between the time of Ohio's admission to the Union in 1803 and the ratification of a new constitution in 1851, three major constitutional crises occurred within the state: The Sweeping Resolution, the Rebellion of 1820, and the Ohio-Michigan War. The Sweeping Resolution and the Ohio-Michigan War resulted from defects in Ohio's original constitution, whereas the Rebellion of 1820 was a major conflict over the issue of state versus federal authority that predated both the Nullification Crisis of 1832 and the Civil War.

The Sweeping Resolution occurred because several Ohio judges, following the precedent of the US Supreme Court in the case of *Marbury versus Madison*, invalidated an act of the General Assembly because its terms conflicted with the state constitution. The General Assembly, after failing to remove the judges through impeachment proceedings, passed a resolution that terminated every judicial term in the state effective March 1, 1810. The General Assembly was then able to appoint new judges who did not believe in the concept of judicial review.

Congress chartered the Second Bank of the United States in 1816, and two branch banks were soon established in Ohio. The bank served a vital function on the frontier by providing cash and by issuing notes that were secured by the main

---

[265]   Knepper, *supra* note 27, 157–158.

branch in Philadelphia. The country suffered its first major economic depression in 1818, and Ohioans largely blamed the bank and its policies. The General Assembly levied a tax against the bank and the state-chartered and wildcat banks. The bank refused to pay the tax and filed suit against Ralph Osborn, the state auditor. The Circuit Court found in favor of the bank, and the US Supreme Court affirmed their holding. The court also confirmed its holdings in *McCulloch versus Maryland*, which prohibited the states from taxing instrumentalities of the federal government. Despite the favorable ruling, the bank closed both of its Ohio branches, and after President Andrew Jackson vetoed the bank's recharter, the issue died quietly.

The Northwest Ordinance established Ohio's northern boundary as a line parallel to the southernmost extent of Lake Michigan. During Ohio's original constitutional convention, the delegates received a report that Lake Michigan extended much farther south than was believed, so the delegates wrote a provision into the state constitution altering Ohio's northern boundary. When Congress established the Territory of Michigan in 1805, they used the boundary described in the Northwest Ordinance. When the Michigan Territory sought statehood in the 1830s, the boundary became a major issue. Ohio used its considerable political influence to block Michigan's admission to the Union until the boundary issue was resolved. Both Michigan and Ohio sent troops to the disputed area. President Andrew Jackson needed Ohio's support in the upcoming presidential election, so he attempted to resolve the issue by granting the disputed area to Ohio, and, in exchange, Michigan would be awarded the Upper Peninsula. Michiganders originally rejected the compromise, but they later accepted the compromise and were admitted to the Union in 1837.

These three episodes demonstrated the growing pains that Ohio exhibited during this period, the growing influence of Ohio in the federal Union, and the need for change as Ohio has outgrown its original governing structure.

Chapter 5

A Time for Change: Ohio's Constitution of 1851

> Every constitution, then, and every law, naturally expires at the end of nineteen years. If it be enforced longer, it is an act of force, and not of right.

> —Thomas Jefferson, 1789

I. Introduction

By 1851, Ohio was ready to make some much-needed changes to its constitution. The influence for change was not solely driven by Ohio citizens. The federal courts were rapidly changing, and the Ohio state courts had too much to handle. Some of the changes in the 1851 constitution were reflective of the activities of the newly added federal district courts. Additionally, the 1851 constitution would address: 1) solidifying Ohio's need to protect individual rights via the Bill of Rights; 2) balancing the power between the three branches of government: The General Assembly, the governor, and the judiciary; and, 3) social reform issues of the times.

II. The US District Court

Article III of the US Constitution provides: "The judicial Power of the United States shall be vested in one supreme Court, and in such inferior Courts as the Congress may from time to time ordain and establish."[266] Under that power, Congress established two local federal trial courts by the Judiciary Act of 1789. The District

---

[266] U.S. Const. Art. III.

Court had jurisdiction over maritime cases, suits brought by the United States, and minor civil and criminal cases. The Circuit Court served as an appellate court for District Court cases, and as a trial court for major civil and criminal matters.[267]

Congress created the US District Court for the district of Ohio upon Ohio's admission to the Union in 1803.[268] President Jefferson appointed Charles Willing Byrd as the first judge of the new court, and Byrd served as judge until his death in 1828. At first, the court served as both a District Court and a Circuit Court, but in 1807 Congress established the Seventh Circuit, encompassing the states of Ohio, Kentucky, and Tennessee. One Supreme Court justice and one District Court judge presided over the Circuit Court. Congress created a new seat on the US Supreme Court to administer the Circuit Court, and President Jefferson appointed Thomas Todd to of Kentucky fill the vacancy.[269]

In its early days, there was little business before the court. At its first meeting, the officers took their oaths, five attorneys were admitted to practice, and the court issued rules. The next day, the court admitted two more attorneys, and the grand jury convened. There were no criminal indictments from 1803 to 1807, and the United States did not file its first civil suit until 1805. Most of the actions before the court were for the collection of money, based on diversity jurisdiction.[270]

Two major cases were before the court during the Byrd's tenure. The first involved former Vice President Aaron Burr, and the second was *Osborn v. Bank of the United States*, described previously.

A. Early Cases

In 1807, Burr and Harman Blennerhassett, purchased an island in the Ohio River near Marietta. The duo intended to use the island as a staging point for their plan to carve an empire out of the Spanish territories along the Mississippi River.

---

[267] Judiciary Act of 1789, 1 Stat. 73 (1789). Under this system, the Supreme Court justices were required to ride circuit for several months each year.

[268] *See,* 2 Stat. 201.

[269] An act establishing Circuit Courts, and abridging the jurisdiction of the district courts in the districts of Kentucky, Tennessee, and Ohio. 2 Stat. 420 (1807).

[270] The History of Ohio Law, *supra* note 16, 271 (quoting Roberta Sue Alexander, *The Changing Role of the Federal District Court*).

Blennerhassett ordered the construction of several riverboats near Marietta, and he published several articles to gain support for their plan.[271] After Burr's acquittal of treason charges in Virginia, the grand jury indicted both Burr and Blennerhassett, but neither of them ever appeared before the court. The case was eventually dismissed after several continuances spanning several years.[272]

In his book *The History of the United States District Court for the Southern District of Ohio*, Irwin Rhodes calculated that between 1807 and 1820, the District Court handled a total of 267 cases, averaging about 20 per year.[273] Most of the cases were default judgments.[274] Judge Byrd heard major civil and criminal cases as a circuit judge, and minor criminal and civil cases, and maritime cases, as a district judge.

B. The Docket Increases

Next, President Andrew Jackson appointed Humphrey H. Leavitt as judge of the District Court in 1834; Leavitt served in this capacity until his retirement in 1871. As Ohio's economy grew and its population increased, so did the District Court's docket. Congress enlarged the court's docket again in 1842, when it conferred concurrent jurisdiction with the Circuit Court for all criminal cases except for capital crimes.[275] The Bankruptcy Act of 1841[276] and the Fugitive Slave Act of 1850[277] added even more cases to the court's docket. By the 1850s, the court's docket had increased to the point where Congress divided Ohio into a northern and a southern district.[278]

The Fugitive Slave Act of 1850, while acting as a compromise between northern and southern states, strengthened abolitionist movements in the north, including

---

[271]   Knepper, *supra* note 3, 100–101.

[272]   The History of Ohio Law, *supra* note 16, 272–273 (quoting Roberta Sue Alexander).

[273]   Irwin S Rhodes, *The History of the United States District Court for the Southern District of Ohio*. U. Cin. L. Rev. 24 (Summer 1955), 341.

[274]   *Ibid.*

[275]   Judiciary Act of 1842. Stat. 516, 517 (1842).

[276]   Bankruptcy Act, 5 Stat. 440 (1841).

[277]   Fugitive Slave Act, 9 Stat. 462 (1850).

[278]   An Act to Divide the State Ohio into two Judicial Districts. 10 Stat. 605, 1855.

the Underground Railroad. These issues influenced Ohio's Constitution, even though an act to enfranchise African American men was defeated.[279]

III. Ohio's 1851 Constitution

As early as the 1810s, there were calls for reforming the judiciary, created by Article III of the 1802 constitution. The Supreme Court, which at that time had both original and appellate jurisdiction, had fallen behind on its docket. The requirement that the court sit in each county at least once per year made the problem even worse.

By the late 1840s, Ohio's population had increased from fewer than sixty thousand to more than two million. Eight counties became eighty-four, and as a result, the judges spent most of their time traveling from county to county.[280] In addition, the judges were chosen by the legislature rather than the voters, which made the court a subservient branch of government.

Another major problem involved the disproportionate power of the legislature, compared to the executive and judicial branches. In 1810, the legislature, incensed that the judiciary declared one of its acts unconstitutional, passed a bill that declared that all judicial offices in the state would become vacant effective March 1, 1810. This was the so-called Sweeping Resolution because it swept all judges in the state from office.[281]

The legislature later came to be seen as corrupt, conducting business through private bills, subsidizing private companies to construct canals, railroads, and other capital improvements, and granting special privileges in corporate charters. Democrats argued for some limitation in the General Assembly's ability to incur debt, since the state debt had increased to $20 million by 1849.[282] A new constitution, adjusting the checks and balances of power between the three branches of government, was crucial.

---

[279] All the supporters of the amendment represented the counties of the Western Reserve.

[280] The History of Ohio Law, *supra* note 16, 51 (quoting Barbara A. Terzian. *Ohio's Constitutional Conventions and Constitutions*).

[281] Fred Milligan, *Ohio's Founding Fathers* (Bloomington, IN: iUniverse.com, 2003), 148.

[282] *The History of Ohio Law, supra* note 16, 51.

A. Convention

Whether to hold a convention had been an issue for several years. By law, Ohio voters are asked whether a new constitutional convention should be called every twenty years. The voters overwhelmingly rejected a proposal to hold a convention in 1819, and Whig legislators blocked later efforts. However, by 1849 a Democratic-Free Soil coalition managed to pass an act providing for a referendum to be placed before Ohio voters at the next general election. In the October 1849 general election, voters approved the proposal by a three to one margin.[283]

The convention began in Columbus in May 1850. The voters chose 108 delegates; 68 were Democrats, 41 were Whigs, and 3 were members of the Free-Soil Party. The Democrats were split into two factions: the liberal wing favored working-class issues, while the conservative wing supported issues favoring the wealthy. Forty-three of the delegates were lawyers, and thirty were farmers. William Medill from Fairfield County, soon to be elected as governor, was chosen as president of the convention by the delegates. An outbreak of cholera that occurred in Columbus just after the convention started forced an adjournment until December, when the delegates reassembled in Cincinnati.[284] The delegates completed their work and adjourned the convention on March 10, 1851. A special ratification election was held on June 17, 1851, and by a margin of 113,237 to 104,255. Ohio's white male electorate approved the new constitution.[285]

In addition to judicial reform and adjusting the checks and balances of power between the branches, several of the delegates wanted to address social reform, including African American rights, women's rights, and temperance. The creation of

---

[283] Thomas Jefferson, for one, was very suspicious of unchanging constitutions. He proposed that each constitution expire after twenty years. This would ensure that every generation had a say in the document. See, John R. Vile. *Rewriting the United States Constitution—An Examination of Proposals from Reconstruction to the Present.* (New York: Prager Publishers, 1991). The 1802 constitution provided that "all white male inhabitants above the age of twenty-one years, having resided in the State one year next preceding the election, and who have paid or are charged with a State or county tax," are entitled to vote. Ohio Const. of 1802, Art. IV., § 1.

[284] Knepper, *supra* note 3.

[285] *The History of Ohio Law, supra* note 16, 59–60.

new counties was also of great interest to the delegates.[286] Although in the minority, Whigs and Free-Soilers teamed up with the two Democratic factions to mandate state-supported schools and other reforms.[287]

As was the case with Ohio's 1802 constitution, the delegates could rely on several recently written or rewritten constitutions from other states. The remaining states comprising the Northwest Territory, which had based their state constitutions in large part on Ohio's, were either writing or rewriting their state constitutions at around this time. Indiana, admitted in 1816, adopted a new constitution in 1851. Illinois, admitted in 1818, adopted a new constitution in 1848. Michigan, admitted in 1837, adopted a new state constitution in 1850. Wisconsin, whose 1846 constitution was rejected by the electorate, adopted their first constitution in 1848. Iowa, admitted in 1846, but not part of the Northwest Territory, adopted a new state constitution in 1857. Most of these states based all or part of their original constitutions on Ohio's 1802 constitution and experienced similar problems.

B. Changes to the Constitution

Compared to the 1802 constitution, the preamble is an exercise in brevity and reads as follows:

> We, the people of the State of Ohio, grateful to Almighty God for our freedom, to secure its blessings and promote our common welfare, do establish this Constitution.

C. Bill of Rights

Ohio's 1851 constitution contained a Bill of Rights, and like its predecessor, the new document contained provisions like the federal Bill of Rights. The new Ohio Bill of Rights contained twenty sections, but unlike its predecessor, these rights are spelled out at the beginning of the document, in Article 1.[288] "Indeed, unlike

---

[286]   Knepper, *supra* note 3, 204–205.

[287]   Kern & Wilson. *supra* note 193, 211.

[288]   The Bill of Rights in Ohio's 1802 constitution is set forth in Article VIII and consists of twenty-eight sections.

the federal Bill of Rights, the Ohio Constitution begins with its own Bill of Rights, thereby emphasizing the prominence our Constitution affords to the protection of individual rights."[289]

Like its 1802 counterpart, Ohio's 1851 Constitution recognized that:

> All political power is inherent in the people. Government is instituted for their equal protection and benefit, and may have the right to alter, reform, or abolish the same ...[290]

Ohio's 1851 Bill of Rights similarly granted to "all men" the right to peaceably assemble,[291] to bear arms,[292] to trial by jury,[293] to worship according to the dictates of their own conscience,[294] to speak, write, and publish his sentiments on all subjects,[295] to be free from unreasonable searches and seizures,[296] and have his property rights held inviolate.[297]

The delegates added a prohibition of slavery and involuntary servitude,[298] that the privilege of the writ of habeas corpus would not be suspended "unless, in cases of rebellion or invasion, the public safety require it,"[299] a prohibition on imprisonment for debt,[300] as well as other unremunerated rights.[301]

---

[289]   See, *Preterm Cleveland v. Voinovich* (1993), 89 Ohio App.3d 684, 627 N.E. 2d 570 (Young, concurring and dissenting).

[290]   Ohio Const. 1851, Art. I, §. 2.

[291]   Ohio Const. 1851, Art. I, § 3.

[292]   Ohio Const. 1851, Art. I, § 4.

[293]   Ohio Const. 1851, Art. I, § 5.

[294]   Ohio Const. 1851, Art. I, § 7.

[295]   Ohio Const. 1851, Art. I, § 11.

[296]   Ohio Const. 1851, Art. I, § 14.

[297]   Ohio Const. 1851, Art. I, § 19.

[298]   Ohio Const. 1851, Art. I, § 6.

[299]   Ohio Const. 1851, Art. I, § 8.

[300]   Ohio Const. 1851, Art. I, § 15.

[301]   Ohio Const. 1851, Art. I, § 20.

D. Balancing the Power

Next the delegates were tasked with the need to balance the three branches of government. While many changes were necessary to bring equality among the branches, the delegates wanted the General Assembly to maintain its preeminent standing within the government structure.

E. The General Assembly

Under Article II of Ohio's new constitution, the General Assembly was still the preeminent branch of government. The General Assembly would still consist of a Senate and a House of Representatives, with each chamber to be the judges of the election, returns, qualifications[302] and discipline[303] of its own members.

To address the state's debt crisis, the General Assembly was prohibited from drawing funds from the treasury except for specific appropriations, and no appropriation would be made for a period of more than two years.[304] A debt ceiling of $750,0000 was also established.[305]

The House of Representatives would have the sole power of impeachment, with the trials of any impeached officials to be conducted in the Senate.[306] The General Assembly was prohibited from enacting retroactive laws, or laws impairing the obligation of contracts.[307] Finally, the General Assembly was prohibited from establishing any new county containing fewer than four hundred square miles,[308] and from changing county lines or removing county seats without the express approval of the voters of the involved counties.[309]

Intending that the legislature convene just once every two years, the delegates passed a proposal for biennial elections and sessions of the General Assembly. This

---

[302] Ohio Const. 1851, Art. II, § 6.

[303] Ohio Const. 1851, Art. II, § 8.

[304] Ohio Const. 1851, Art. II, § 22.

[305] Ohio Const. 1851, Art. VIII, § 1.

[306] Ohio Const. 1851, Art. II, § 24.

[307] Ohio Const. 1851, Art. II, § 28.

[308] Ohio Const. 1851, Art. II, § 30.

[309] Since the ratification of Ohio's 1851 constitution, no additional counties have been established.

proposal was opposed by delegates, who felt that biennial sessions would disrupt the balance of power between the government's branches, because the executive and judicial branches were in session all year. Some delegates also believed that annual sessions would keep the business of the lawmakers closer to the people.[310]

While the new constitution took some powers away from the General Assembly, the voters, rather than the other branches of the government, were the primary beneficiaries of this power shift. Now, the electorate had the power to choose officers of the executive and judicial branches. Further, the ability of the General Assembly to create and divide counties was curbed, and stricter guidelines for apportionment, special acts of incorporation, retroactive laws, and legislatively granted divorces were enacted.[311]

The delegates did manage to curb the authority of the General Assembly to some extent, but the executive and judicial branches were still subordinate branches.

F. The Governor

Ohio's 1802 constitution eliminated nearly all the power that the territorial governor possessed. The governor could only appoint one state official, the adjutant general, and he could only fill vacancies in the other civil offices by recess appointment, subject to the approval of the General Assembly. The governor's term was set at two years; term limits were imposed, and he was chosen by popular vote, except for "[c] ontested elections," wherein the General Assembly had the power to select.[312]

One goal of the delegates was to restore some power to the governor.[313] The primary debates concerning the powers and duties of governor revolved around the veto power. One proposal suggested that the governor could hold an offending bill for a time certain, which would then be returned to the General Assembly for reconsideration. A simple majority could override this "pocket veto."[314] Debates

---

[310]   *The History of Ohio Law, supra* note 16, 102–103 (quoting David M. Gold. *The General Assembly and Ohio's Constitutional Culture*).

[311]   *The History of Ohio Law, supra* note 16, 102.

[312]   *The History of Ohio Law, supra* note 16, 140–141 (quoting John J. Kulewicz. *Reinventing the Governor: A History of Executive Power under Ohio Law*).

[313]   *The History of Ohio Law, supra* note 16, 147–148.

[314]   *The History of Ohio Law, supra* note 16, 147.

then began regarding the override margin, with some delegates favoring a simple majority while others demanded a two-thirds majority. Both proposals were eventually shelved.

Ohio's 1851 constitution established the new offices of lieutenant governor and attorney general and set a two-year term for these offices.[315] In addition, the offices of governor, lieutenant governor, secretary of state, auditor, treasurer, and attorney general would now be elected by popular vote.[316] The auditor was given a term of four years, while the remaining officers held two-year terms.[317]

While denied the veto power until 1903, the governor held the power to convene the General Assembly[318] on "extraordinary occasions," and, in the event of a disagreement between the two houses, he could adjourn the General Assembly as well.[319]

Other changes included eliminating term limits, changing the eligibility requirements to "the qualifications of the elector," expanding his appointment power of military officers to include the "Adjutant General, Quartermaster General, and other staff officers, as may be provided for by law," and to commission "all officers of the line and staff, ranking as such."[320] The governor was also included in the legislative reapportionment process, along with the auditor and secretary of state.[321]

Finally, the delegates would tackle the judiciary's much-needed independence from the General Assembly to complete the balance of power between the three branches of government.

---

[315]   Ohio Const. 1851, Article III, §§ 1, 2.

[316]   Ohio Const. 1851, Art. III, § 1. Several states have adopted this concept, called a plural executive, where the executive powers are distributed among several elected officials. The United States, by contrast, has a unitary executive, as established in Article II, Section 1 of the US Constitution.

[317]   Ohio Const. 1851, Art. III, § 2.

[318]   Ohio Const. 1851, Art. III, § 8.

[319]   Ohio Const. 1851, Art. III, § 9.

[320]   Ohio Const. 1851, Art. IX, § 3.

[321]   Ohio Const. 1851, Art. XI, § 11.

G. The Judiciary

The proposed constitution also called for major changes to Ohio's judiciary. One of the biggest problems of the 1802 constitution was the requirement that the court hold session in each county every year. This requirement was merely an inconvenience in 1802 when Ohio had nine counties, but by 1850 the state had grown to eighty-four counties. Complying with this provision proved an impossible burden for the justices, and the court's docket dragged. Further, allowing popular election of judges would help curb some of the power of the General Assembly and grant some independence to the judicial branch.

The final document completely restructured Ohio's judicial system. Article IV of the new constitution called for a Supreme Court, District Courts with appellate jurisdiction, Courts of Common Pleas, Probate Courts, Justice of the Peace Courts, and other inferior courts "and the General Assembly, may, from time to time, establish."[322]

The Supreme Court was increased to five members, and the requirement that the court meet in each county every year was dropped. Justices were elected to five-year terms in statewide elections.[323] The court had original jurisdiction in *quo warranto*, mandamus, habeas corpus, and *procedendo* "and such appellate jurisdiction as may be provided by law."[324] However, the General Assembly could increase or decrease the number of justices, and the number of Common Pleas districts; they could change the districts, and establish other courts upon vote of two-thirds of the members.[325]

District Courts, consisting of Common Pleas judges and one Supreme Court justice, were established at a level between the Supreme Court and the Common Pleas Courts. The District Courts had the same original jurisdiction as the Supreme Court and "such appellate jurisdiction as may be provided by law."[326] At the trial court level, nine Common Pleas districts were created, bounded by county lines, and as nearly equal in population as practicable.

---

[322]   Ohio Const. 1851, Art. IV, § 1.

[323]   Ohio Const. 1851, Art. IV, § 1.

[324]   Ohio Const. 1851, Art. IV, § 2.

[325]   Ohio Const. 1851, Art. IV, § 15.

[326]   Ohio Const. 1851, Art. IV, § 6.

The new constitution also created a Probate Court with one judge per county, elected to a three-year term by the voters of the county.[327] The Probate Court had existed previously under the territorial government but was eliminated by the constitution of 1802.[328] Justice of the Peace Courts were continued in each township in the several counties, elected by the voters to three-year terms. Their powers and duties "shall be regulated by law."[329]

Although Ohio's new constitution relaxed somewhat the chokehold that the General Assembly held on the judiciary, it was clear that the legislature remained as the dominant branch of government. Although members of the executive branch and the judiciary were now directly elected by the voters and term limits were eliminated, the governor still had no veto power. The General Assembly also retained the authority to increase or decrease the number of justices of the Supreme Court, the number of Common Pleas districts, and the jurisdiction of the remaining courts, giving them some coercive power over the judiciary.

Having completed the necessary changes to the branches of government, the delegates moved to the topic of social reform. They would attempt to include acts that would speak to the social issues of the times, including African American rights, women's rights, and temperance.

H. African American/Suffrage Issues

The abolitionist movement had strong support in Ohio during the prewar years. Prominent abolitionists, many of whom were affiliated with Oberlin College,[330] founded the Ohio Anti-Slavery Society in Zanesville in April 1835. Other organizers

---

[327]   Ohio Const. 1851, Art. IV, § 8.

[328]   From 1803 to 1851, the probate courts of Ohio were incorporated into the courts of common pleas, which were granted special "probate jurisdiction." John F. Winkler. *The Probate Courts of Ohio*. 28 U. Tol. L. Rev. 563, 569–570.

[329]   Ohio Const. 1851, Art IV, § 9.

[330]   Oberlin College, founded in 1833, was the first college in the United States to admit African American students (1835) and women (1837).

of the society included Quakers from Mt. Pleasant. The society's media outlet, the
Anti-Slavery Bugle, began publication in Lisbon in 1845 and continued until 1861.[331]

The society established chapters in every area of the state and employed speakers
to convince others to join. James Birney's newspaper, *The Philanthropist,* published
articles supporting the movement. One historian referred to Oberlin as the "town
that started the Civil War"[332] because of its reputation as a center of the abolitionist
movement. Over forty thousand runaway slaves utilized the over seven hundred
Underground Railroad safe houses and "depots" in Ohio on their journey to
freedom in Canada. Cincinnati was the home of the Lane Theological Seminary as
well as the home of abolitionist author Harriet Beecher Stowe. Stowe's father, Lyman
Beecher, became the first president of the seminary in 1832.[333] Charles Grandison
Finney, who became known as "The Father of Modern Revivalism," moved to Ohio
from Connecticut to teach at Oberlin College. From that platform, Finney became
a vocal advocate of abolitionism.[334] By the late 1830s, Ohio was home to over two
hundred antislavery organizations.[335]

Despite this, abolitionist sentiment in Ohio in the prewar period was hardly
overwhelming. In the early part of the nineteenth century, Ohio, reflecting its
southern roots,[336] was more hostile to blacks than other free states. While the
delegates to the 1802 constitutional convention overwhelmingly opposed slavery,
they did not necessarily support African-American rights. The convention proposed
limiting suffrage to white men only. Black laws, passed in 1804 and 1807, required

---

[331]   *About Anti-Slavery Bugle* (New Lisbon, Ohio). 1845–1861. Library of Congress. Available
        at http://www.chroniclingamerica.loc.gov/lccn/sn83035487 last visited July 27, 2013.

[332]   Nat Brandt, *The Town that Started the Civil War* (Syracuse, NY: Syracuse University Press, 1990).

[333]   Kern & Wilson, *supra* note 193, 142–143.

[334]   Kern & Wilson, *supra* note 193, 142–143.

[335]   Knepper, *supra* note 3, 201.

[336]   Ohio's earliest settlers hailed from the Piedmont, the Blue Ridge Mountains, the Shenandoah
        Valley and the Appalachian and Interior Low plateaus of the Upland South. Most arrived
        on flatboats via the Ohio River, except those who settled northern Ohio from New England.
        R. Hurt, *supra* note 23, 248–249.

African Americans entering Ohio to prove their freedom, register with local authorities, and find an Ohio resident to attest to their good behavior.[337]

In the 1830s, race riots in Cincinnati forced the students and faculty of the Lane Theological Seminary to relocate to Ohio's Western Reserve. The delegates to Ohio's constitutional convention of 1851 overwhelmingly defeated a proposal for black suffrage and a proposal to ban African Americans from moving to the state received serious consideration before being defeated.[338]

Although the final document created a more democratic government than the prior constitution, two suffrage provisions were soundly voted down. A proposal to enfranchise African American men was defeated seventy-five to thirteen, and an amendment dropping the word *male* from the voting requirements failed by a vote of seventy-two to seven.[339] Provisions to ban further African immigration and to deport all current African Americans residing in the state received more votes than the suffrage provisions, but these provisions were also defeated.[340] However, a temperance provision barring the state from licensing the sale of alcohol was placed on the ballot as a separate amendment and passed by a vote of 113,237 to 104,255.[341]

In 1852, Rutherford B. Hayes, then a young attorney practicing Cincinnati, summed up the general feelings behind the new constitution:

> Government no longer has its ancient importance. Its duties and powers no longer reach to the happiness of the people. The people's progress, progress of every sort, no longer depends on government.[342]

---

[337] An Act to regulate black and mulatto persons, 2 Laws of Ohio 63 (1804); An Act to amend the act, entitled 'An Act Regulating black mulatto persons, Laws of Ohio 53 (1807) (Act of 1807).

[338] Kern & Wilson, *supra* note 193, 212–213.

[339] All the supporters of both amendments represented the counties of the Western Reserve.

[340] Kern & Wilson, *supra* note 193, 204.

[341] The History of Ohio Law, *supra* note 16, 60.

[342] Rutherford B. Hayes, diary entry, September 24, 1852, in *Diary and Letters of Rutherford Birchard Hayes, 19th President of the United States* (Charles Richard Williams ed., Columbus: Ohio Archaeological and Historical Society, Iss. 422, 1922).

Although the 1851 constitution has been amended over 150 times since its ratification, it remains as the fundamental law of the state.

Summary

Congress created the US District Court for the District of Ohio upon Ohio's admission to the Union in 1803. This court served as both a District Court and a Circuit Court until Congress established the Seventh Circuit in 1807. In its early years, there were few cases before the court; most involved the collection of money based on diversity jurisdiction. Congress added to the Court's docket when they enacted the Bankruptcy Act of 1841 and the Fugitive Slave Act of 1850. By 1850 the Congress divided Ohio's federal courts into a northern and a southern district.

By 1850 Ohio had grown from fewer than sixty thousand residents to more than two million. The state courts had fallen behind on their dockets, and the General Assembly still controlled most of the governmental power. Several proposals to call a constitutional convention had been rejected by the voters, but in 1849 a Democratic-Free Soil coalition passed, and the voters approved, a referendum for a new constitution. The delegates met in Columbus in May 1850. A cholera outbreak forced the convention to recess until December, when the delegates reassembled in Cincinnati. The convention completed their work in March 1851, and that June Ohio's white male electorate approved the new document.

The new constitution addressed judicial reform and adjusted the power between the branches of government, but suffrage for African Americans and women was overwhelmingly defeated. A temperance provision was placed before the voters and approved as a separate issue. The delegates also placed a Bill of Rights, much more expansive than its federal counterpart, at the beginning of the document, as Article I.

The new constitution established the offices of lieutenant governor and attorney general and officials in the executive branch and the judiciary would now be elected. A debt ceiling was established, and some of the governor's power, except for the veto, was restored. The requirement that the Supreme Court meet annually in every county was also eliminated. District Courts with appellate jurisdiction, and Probate Courts were also established.

Ohio's 1851 constitution, with several amendments added in the intervening years, remains as the supreme law of the state.

Chapter 6

The Discordant Decade: 1850–1860

Disunion and civil war are at hand; and yet I fear disunion far less than compromise. We can recover from them. The free States alone, if we must go on alone, will make a glorious nation.

—Rutherford Birchard Hayes, January 4, 1861

I. Introduction

Once its new constitution was drafted and ratified, Ohioans could look to developments on the national scene, and how those developments would lead them into Civil War in the next decade. Events starting with 1) the Compromise of 1850, with its more stringent Fugitive Slave Act and the question of whether or not the new territories acquired as a result of the War with Mexico would be open to slavery, 2) the regional bloodshed that occurred as a result of the Kansas-Nebraska Act of 1854, later known as Bleeding Kansas, 3) the decision of the US Supreme Court in *Dred Scott v. Sandford,* 4) the publication of the antislavery novel *Uncle Tom's Cabin,* 5) the activities of the Underground Railroad, and 6) the election of Abraham Lincoln in 1860 all pointed the country down the path to war. The common thread among these rather disparate issues was the peculiar institution of slavery.

Ohioans have always been torn on the issue of slavery. While the Northwest Ordinance and the 1802 constitution banned slavery, the General Assembly enacted Black Codes designed to restrict African American liberties as well as their economic freedom. There was a strong abolitionist movement in the Western Reserve, but efforts to enfranchise African Americans had gone down to defeat in both of Ohio's constitutional conventions. Finally, Ohioans largely ignored the federal Fugitive

Slave Act of 1793, and some Ohioans had actively assisted runaways since the state's early years, but a movement in the 1851 constitutional debates to prohibit African American immigration to the state, and to deport those already residing here, was only defeated after much debate.[343]

II. The Compromise of 1850

The United States fought a war with Mexico from 1846 to 1848. As part of the treaty of Guadalupe Hidalgo, signed on February 2, 1848, and ending the war, the United States acquired a vast tract of land in the American Southwest, including the modern states of Arizona, New Mexico, California, and parts of Colorado, Utah, and Nevada.

The issue of the expansion of slavery into the territories had been percolating for several years. Previously this issue had been addressed by Congress in the Compromise of 1820. That bill admitted Maine as a free state and Missouri as a slave state, again equalizing the number of free and slave states in the Union. The bill further prohibited slavery in all parts of the Louisiana Territory north of 36°30' north latitude, except within the borders of Missouri.

Over the next three decades, Congress attempted to continue the balance between the slave and free states by admitting states from each category including Arkansas (1836) and Michigan (1837), Florida (1845) and Iowa (1846), and Texas (1845) and Wisconsin (1848). California, whose population exploded following the Gold Rush of 1849, threatened to disrupt this balance of power when it sought admission to the Union as a free state in 1850. The slaveholding states, already a minority in the House of Representatives because of their smaller populations, saw a threat to their "peculiar institution" of slavery if they became a minority in the Senate as well.[344]

In response to this "Crisis of 1850," Kentucky Senator Henry Clay joined forces

---

[343] Knepper, *supra* note 27, 206–216; *see, also*, David M. Potter, *The Impending Crisis: America Before The Civil War: 1848–1861*. (Harper Perennial: New York, 1976).

[344] Carl H. Moneyhon, *The Impact of the Civil War and Reconstruction on Arkansas* (Fayetteville, AR: The University of Arkansas Press, 2002), 90–91.

with Illinois Senator Stephen A. Douglas to propose the Compromise of 1850.[345] The final bill was a series of five bills, providing for, among other things:

- the admission of California as a free state;
- the organization of the remainder of the new territories without regard to the slave trade;[346]
- a prohibition of the slave trade (but not slavery itself) within the District of Columbia;
- transfer of Texas's state debt to the federal government in exchange for Texas ceding its claim to New Mexico; and
- enactment of a far more stringent Fugitive Slave Act.[347]

The compromise attempted to defuse sectional rivalry by granting concessions to both sides of the slavery issue. Instead, the compromise increased tensions between the sections, particularly about the new Fugitive Slave Act, adopted in large part to placate the slaveholding states. The new Fugitive Slave Act provoked hostility and resistance throughout the North. Mobs attacked slave catchers, and vigilance committees actively interfered with masters attempting to retrieve their property. Southern states became convinced that their comrades in the north had no intention of supporting, or complying with the new act.[348]

The new act's predecessor was the Fugitive Slave Act of 1793. That law guaranteed a slave holder the right to recover his escaped slaves.[349] The owner or his agent simply

---

[345] Kern & Wilson, *supra* note 161, 216–218.

[346] This provision would effectively repeal the 36° 30' provision of the Missouri Compromise.

[347] The Cambridge History of Law in America, supra note 6, 307–308 (quoting Ariella Gross, *Slavery, Anti-Slavery and the Coming of the Civil War*) (Grossberg & Tomlins, eds.).

[348] *The History of Ohio Law, supra* note 42, 769–770 (quoting Paul Finkleman, *Race, Slavery, and Law in Antebellum Ohio*).

[349] The original act gave effect to Article IV, Section 2 of the US Constitution, which provides that "No Person held to Service for Labour in one State, under the laws thereof, escaping into another, shall, in Consequence of any Law or Regulation therein, be discharged from such Service or Labour, but shall be delivered up on Claim of the Party to whom such Service or Labour, may be due."

had to appear before a federal judge and provide proof of ownership to obtain an order that allowed the removal of the slave from the state to which he or she fled.[350]

Despite Ohio's resistance to granting the franchise to African Americans, the state had a long-standing policy of protecting free blacks from kidnapping. In Ohio's early days, the ownership of fugitive slaves had to be proven to the satisfaction of an Ohio judge before the alleged slave could be returned.[351] The US Supreme Court addressed this issue in the case of *Prigg v. Pennsylvania*,[352] where the court held that the states were precluded from regulating the return of fugitive slaves. In response, the General Assembly repealed this "Fugitive Labor" law, but in 1831 they reinstated a statute that punished individuals who kidnapped free blacks.[353]

The new Fugitive Slave Act provided for stiff penalties against any federal marshal or other official who refused to aid in the capture of suspected runaways. The suspected slave was prohibited from requesting a jury trial or testifying in his or her own behalf, and fines of up to $1,000 and imprisonment awaited individuals convicted of aiding their escape. Abolitionists referred to this law as the "Bloodhound Law" after the dogs the slave owners used to track their runaway slaves.[354]

As with the earlier Fugitive Slave Act, northern states actively opposed the enforcement of the new act. In the case of *Ableman v. Booth*,[355] the defendant, Booth, was arrested by US Marshals for violating the Fugitive Slave Act. A Wisconsin state judge granted a writ of habeas corpus and released Booth from incarceration. The marshals appealed, and the Wisconsin Supreme Court found that the Fugitive Slave Act was unconstitutional and again ordered Booth's release. The case then went before the US Supreme Court. Chief Justice Roger Taney, writing for a unanimous

---

[350]   Earl M. Maltz, *Dred Scott and the Politics of Slavery (Landmark Law Cases & American Society)* (Lawrence, KS: University Press of Kansas, 2007), 26–27.

[351]   An Act relating to Fugitives from labor or service from other States, 37 Laws of Ohio 38 (1839).

[352]   *Prigg v. Pennsylvania*, 41 U.S. 539 (1842).

[353]   *The History of Ohio Law, supra* note 42, 764 (quoting Paul Finkleman. *Race, Slavery, and Law in Antebellum Ohio*).

[354]   The full text of the Fugitive Slave Act of 1850 is available at: http://www.nationalcenter.org/FugitiveSlaveAct.html

[355]   *Abelman v. Booth*, 62 U.S. 506 (1859).

majority, reversed the decision of the Wisconsin Court,[356] finding that the Wisconsin courts could not annul a judgment of conviction issued by a federal court.

State courts in Ohio were no less inclined to enforce the act than was the Wisconsin court. In March 1855, federal officers arrested a slave named Rosetta on a warrant from US Commissioner John L. Pendry. Attorney Salmon P. Chase sought and obtained a writ of habeas corpus, and Rosetta was brought before Judge Parker of the Hamilton County (Ohio) Common Pleas Court. Judge Parker determined that Rosetta was a free woman and ordered her release.[357] Federal Marshall H. H. Robinson then rearrested Rosetta under the federal warrant. State officers arrested Marshall Robinson and jailed him for contempt of court. Robinson applied for a writ of habeas corpus to US Supreme Court Justice John MacLean. Justice MacLean, invoking the supremacy clause of the US Constitution, held that state officials cannot interfere with federal officers performing duties on behalf of the federal government.[358]

The General Assembly also passed legislation making the Fugitive Slave Act more difficult to enforce in this state. In 1857, the Republican-dominated legislature enacted three new personal liberty laws. The first made holding a person as a slave in the state a criminal offense. The second declared that Ohio's jails were unavailable to slave catchers,[359] and the third punished individuals who kidnapped free blacks.[360] The next year, the General Assembly, now controlled by Democrats, repealed the

---

[356]   *Ableman v. Booth*, Encyclopedia Britannica: I: A-ak Bayes (15th ed.), 33–34 (Dale H. Hoiberg ed., Chicago, IL: Encyclopedia Britannica Inc., 2010).

[357]   As early as 1817, an Ohio justice held that slaves transported to Ohio by their masters were free. Ervin H. Pollack, Ohio Unreported Decisions 33, *State v. Carneal* (1817).

[358]   *Ex Parte Robinson*, 6 McLean 355, 20 F. Cas. 969 (S.D. Ohio, 1855).

[359]   An Act To prohibit the confinement of fugitives from slavery in the jails of Ohio, 54 Laws of Ohio 170 (1857).

[360]   An Act To prevent kidnapping, 54 Laws of Ohio 221 (1857).

latter two laws.[361] In 1858 another law, requiring jailers to accept fugitive slaves when they are in the company of federal officials, was enacted by the Democrats.[362]

In 1856, the Ohio Supreme Court issued another decision on the transient issue in the case of *Anderson v. Poindexter*.[363] Anderson was a slaveholder who resided in the state of Kentucky; Poindexter was Anderson's slave. For several years, Anderson allowed Poindexter to hire himself out as a laborer, sometimes performing work within the state of Ohio. Anderson agreed to allow Poindexter to purchase his freedom, and Poindexter signed several notes purchasing his freedom that were cosigned by his friends in Ohio. When Poindexter and his friends refused to pay on the notes, Anderson sued Poindexter for the value of the notes.

Justice Ozias Bowen held that Poindexter became free once he entered Ohio; his return to Kentucky did not make him a slave again. Therefore, Poindexter was free when he made the contract with Anderson, and since he was free when he signed the contract purchasing his freedom, the court found that the contract between Anderson and Poindexter was void for want of consideration.

Justice Bowen also noted that in Kentucky a contract between a free person and a slave was *void ab initio*. Had the court enforced the laws of Kentucky rather than the laws of Ohio, he wrote, Anderson still could not enforce payment of the notes.[364]

In *Commonwealth of Kentucky v. Dennison*,[365] the US Supreme Court declined to issue a writ of mandamus against the governor of Ohio. The commonwealth requested the writ, commanding the governor to deliver a fugitive slave to the agent of the commonwealth.

Chief Justice Taney, writing for the majority, held that it is the duty of the governor to cause the slave to be delivered to the agent of the governor of Kentucky.

---

[361]   An Act To repeal an act entitled 'An act to prohibit the confinement of fugitives from slavery in the jails of Ohio,' 55 Laws of Ohio 10 (1858); An Act To repeal an act therein named, 55 Laws of Ohio 19 (1858).

[362]   An Act To amend section one of an act for the confinement of persons under the authority of the United States in the jails of this state, passed December 20, 1806, and to repeal section two of said act, 56 Laws of Ohio 158 (1859).

[363]   *Anderson v. Poindexter*, 6 Ohio St. 622 (1856).

[364]   Paul Finkelman, *An Imperfect Union: Slavery, Federalism, and Comity* (The Lawbook Exchange, Ltd. Reprint of the first and only edition, June 12, 2000), 177.

[365]   Commonwealth of *Kentucky v. Dennison*, 65 U.S. 66 (1860).

The court further held that the governor's duty was ministerial, with no discretionary power. The word *duty* in the Fugitive Slave Act of 1793, he wrote, means the moral obligation of the state to perform a compact in the constitution. Congress cannot coerce a state officer to perform any duty by act of Congress. The state officer may perform if he thinks proper, and it may be a moral duty to perform it. But if he refuses, no law of Congress can compel him.[366]

Perhaps the most noteworthy of the fugitive cases from Ohio during this decade was the Oberlin–Wellington Rescue and trials of 1858–1859. John Price was a slave who escaped from his master in Kentucky. Price had recently been staying in the home of James Armstrong, who resided in Oberlin. On September 13, 1858, a group of slave catchers captured Price and rode to the nearby town of Wellington for the night.

When the news of this incident reached the community of Oberlin, a crowd of residents, including Oberlin College students, professors, townspeople, and free blacks rode to Wellington, recaptured Price from his captors and returned to Oberlin. Price was hidden in the home of Oberlin Professor James Fairchild, and he was taken across the border to Canada a few days later.

The Oberlin-Wellington Rescuers, 1858.
(Image courtesy of the Ohio History Connection).

---

[366] Ibid., at syllabus.

The US Marshalls arrested thirty-seven of the rescuers on federal warrants for violating the fugitive slave law. Two of the conspirators, Simeon Bushnell, a white clerk and printer, and Charles Langston, a black schoolteacher, were convicted and sentenced to sixty days and twenty days in jail respectively. Both defendants appealed their convictions to the Ohio Supreme Court. The court, citing the Supremacy Clause of the US Constitution, affirmed the convictions.

State authorities then arrested Price's kidnappers, including a federal marshal, and charged them with kidnapping. After negotiations, the federal charges against the remaining rescuers were dropped, and in exchange, Ohio officials dismissed the charges against the Kentucky kidnappers.[367] The continued tension between slave and free states reached the Kansas-Nebraska region in 1854.

III. Bleeding Kansas

In 1854, Senator Stephen A. Douglas of Illinois introduced the Kansas-Nebraska Act to Congress. This act would create the new territories of Kansas and Nebraska from the Louisiana Purchase. The prohibition of slavery above the line of 36° 30' from the Missouri Compromise was removed, and the voters of the territory would be allowed to determine whether slavery should exist there. Soon, pro-slavery "Border Ruffians" and anti-slavery "Free Staters" flooded into the territory to influence the election of the non-voting delegate to Congress.

On May 21, 1856, anti-slavery Missourians destroyed the town of Lawrence, Kansas. Three days later, abolitionists led by John Brown, a native of Summit County, Ohio, kidnapped five pro-slavery men and hacked them to death with broadswords. Brown and his men survived a retaliatory raid against their settlement soon afterward, but one of his sons was killed. Brown and his men escaped, and the party ended up in Harper's Ferry, Virginia, in 1859.[368] Brown's attempt to seize the Harpers Ferry arsenal and incite a full-blown slave revolt was quelled by US Marines under the command of Colonel Robert E Lee. Two more of Brown's sons were killed in the raid, while another son escaped. Brown, who was wounded in the raid, was tried and convicted of treason and hanged on December 2, 1859.

The sectional violence was not confined to the states of Kansas and Nebraska.

---

[367]   Kern & Wilson, *supra* note 161, 220–221.

[368]   *Ibid.*, 217–218.

On May 22, 1856, Congressman Preston Brooks, a Democrat from South Carolina, bludgeoned Free-Soil Senator Charles Sumner of Massachusetts on the floor of the Senate chamber with a heavy cane. The attack came in response to a speech Sumner had given two days earlier criticizing Brooks's uncle, Democratic Senator Andrew Butler from South Carolina. Sumner suffered serious injuries to his brain and spinal cord, and as a result he was unable to serve for three years. Brooks's actions were applauded throughout the southern states, but condemned in the North. The governor of South Carolina presented Brooks with a new walking stick in honor of his actions.[369]

The Kansas-Nebraska Act and bleeding Kansas sounded the final death knell of the Whig party. Begun in the 1830s to oppose the policies of President Andrew Jackson, the Whigs were a national force that elected two presidents (William Henry Harrison and Zachary Taylor) and several governors. Unable to deal with the slavery issue, the Whigs eventually split into Northern and Southern factions. Northern or "conscience" Whigs eventually joined forces with the new Republican Party, while Southern, or "Cotton" Whigs eventually joined the Democrats.[370]

A new political coalition came into being in 1854. Made up of former Free-Soilers, anti-Nebraska Democrats, "Conscience" Whigs, and other unaligned elements, the coalition soon adopted the name "Republican" to describe their new party.[371] Known as the Fusion party in Ohio, the coalition swept the statewide elections in 1854 and elected anti-slavery advocate Salmon P. Chase to the governor's office in 1855.[372] On a national level, the Supreme Court would hear a case that would make the conflict between slave and free states worse.

[369] Doris Kerns Goodwin, *Team of Rivals: The Political Genius of Abraham Lincoln* (New York: Simon & Schuster Paperbacks, 2005), 184–185.

[370] Ibid., 307–308.

[371] Ibid., 180–181.

[372] Knepper, *supra* note 27, 210–212.

Salmon P. Chase, 1808-1873.
(Image courtesy of the Ohio History Connection).

IV. Dred Scott Decision

In the case of *Dred Scott v. Sandford*,[373] the US Supreme Court issued a landmark decision on the slavery issue, addressing issues like, but not the same as those raised by *Prigg v. Pennsylvania*.[374] In *Scott*,[375] the issue revolved around the fate of a temporary resident of a free territory rather than that of a fugitive in a free state.

Dred Scott was a slave born in the slave state of Missouri. However, Scott's master, an army surgeon, relocated to the free state of Illinois with Scott and his family. Scott and his family later lived as slaves in the free territory of Minnesota. Upon the family's return to Missouri, Scott sued for his freedom.

The case was heard in various state and federal courts, including the Supreme Court

---

[373]   *Scott v. Sandford*, 60 U.S. 393 (1857).

[374]   *Prigg v. Pennsylvania*, 41 U.S. 539 (1842).

[375]   *Scott v. Sandford*, 60 U.S. 393 (1857) The full opinion is available at: http://supreme.justia.com/cases/federal/us/60/393/case.html

of Missouri, and finally came before the US Supreme Court for argument in 1856. The issue was whether Scott's living in a free state rendered him free when moved there by his master. The court first ruled that neither Scott nor any person of African descent could be a "citizen of a state," so the court lacked the jurisdiction to hear the case.[376]

Initially, the court was ready to issue an opinion that focused on the jurisdictional issue alone and did not analyze the constitutionality of the Missouri Compromise of 1820. However, the court later decided to address the broader slavery issue. Chief Justice Roger Taney, writing for the majority, held that a slave did not acquire freedom simply by being taken to a state where slavery is not permitted. The court also held that slaves could never become citizens and that the federal government did not have the authority to ban slavery in the territories.

Justice Benjamin R. Curtis dissented from the court's opinion because he felt that if the court lacked the jurisdiction to hear the case, the merits of the claims should not have been addressed.[377] Justice John MacLean of Ohio also dissented from the court's opinion. Justice MacLean cited the case of *Marie Louise v. Marot*,[378] (1836) wherein the Supreme Court of Louisiana held that a slave who is taken into a country where slavery is prohibited is immediately emancipated. Once the slave becomes free, he cannot be returned to slavery.[379]

Many legal scholars claim that the Dred Scott decision is the worst decision in the entire history of the US Supreme Court.[380] [381] Each of the nine justices issued their own opinion with intermingled concurrences and dissents. The result served only to inflame the tensions between the North and the South even more as Southerners celebrated the decision while Northerners condemned it.[382] Additionally, the decision represented only the second time that the Supreme Court overturned an act of Congress.

---

[376] *The Cambridge History of Law America, supra* note 6, 308–311.

[377] *Scott v. Sandford,* 60 U.S. 393, 564–565 (1857).

[378] *Louise v. Marot,* 9 Louisiana Rep. 476, 1836.

[379] *Scott v. Sandford,* 60 U.S. 393, 561 (1857).

[380] Paul Finkelman, *Scott v. Sandford: The Court's Most Dreadful Case and How It Changed History,* 82 Chi.-Kent L. Rev. 3, 3–48 (2007).

[381] Justice Felix Frankfurter referred to the *Dred Scott* case as "one of the Court's great self-inflicted wounds." Goodwin, *supra* note 369, 189.

[382] Daniel A. Farber, Lincoln's Constitution (Chicago: University of Chicago Press, 2004), 10.

Among those who criticized the decision were political rivals Abraham Lincoln and William Seward. Lincoln pointed out that in at least five states, free African Americans voted to ratify the Constitution and were thus a part of the *We the People* mentioned in the Preamble. William Seward, noting that the decision was announced a mere two days after the new President James Buchanan was inaugurated, accused the new president and the chief justice of engaging a conspiracy.[383] During this time, the horrors of southern slavery would be expressed by Stowe in her book *Uncle Tom's Cabin*.

V. Uncle Tom's Cabin

Harriet Beecher Stowe was born in Litchfield, Connecticut, on June 14, 1811. Harriet was one of thirteen children born to New England preacher Lyman Beecher. Seven of her brothers became ministers, including her younger brother Henry Ward Beecher.[384] Harriet received a classical education in a school run by her older sister.

Stowe moved to Cincinnati, Ohio, at the age of twenty-one, when her father became the head of the Lane Theological Seminary. While in Cincinnati, Stowe witnessed firsthand the proslavery Cincinnati Riots of 1836. Stowe then became involved in religion, feminism, and the abolition of slavery. She met and married Calvin Stowe, a Lane graduate, in 1836, and the pair moved to Brunswick, Maine, where her husband was teaching at Bowdoin College.[385]

Stowe wrote *Uncle Tom's Cabin* in part as a response to the Fugitive Slave Act of 1850.[386] Stowe's goal was to expose the horrors of Southern slavery to the northern population. Her book also served to lionize those slaves who escaped their captivity to flee to Canada and freedom. Cincinnati Attorney Salmon P. Chase contended that the character of John Van Trope, the abolitionist former slaveholder in *Uncle Tom's Cabin*, was based on his

---

[383]   Goodwin, *supra* note 369, 191.

[384]   Beecher's biographer called him "The Most Famous Man in America." Debby Applegate, *The Most Famous Man in America: The Biography of Henry Ward Beecher.* Image; Reprint edition (April 17, 2007)

[385]   One of Stowe's students at Bowdoin was Joshua Lawrence Chamberlain, who later won the congressional Medal of Honor defending Little Round Top, during the Second Day of the Battle of Gettysburg.

[386]   Harriet Beecher Stowe. *Uncle Tom's Cabin.* SparkNotes.com Available at: http://www.sparknotes.com/lit/uncletom/context.html

client John Van Zandt, whom he defended in a suit for monetary damages, brought by a slaveholder whose escaped slaves were aided by Van Zandt.[387] Chase lost the case, but the trial brought a great deal of attention to the abolitionist cause.[388]

The *National Era* published *Uncle Tom's Cabin* as a series of articles in 1851 and 1852. The book was published in its entirety the next year and immediately became a bestseller; over 300,000 copies were sold initially, and by the end of 1853 over 1.5 million copies had been sold. Except for the Bible, *Uncle Tom's Cabin* was the highest selling book of the nineteenth century.[389] Ironically, Stowe once remarked to her publisher: "I hope it will make enough so that I may have a silk dress."[390] The response to Stowe's book was so great, both pro and con, that ten years later, a smiling President Abraham Lincoln greeted her with: "So you're the little woman who wrote the book that made this great war."[391]

In addition, the Underground Railroad allowed many slaves to escape the horror of slavery described by Stowe.

VI. The Underground Railroad

One of the most active segments of the abolitionist movement was the organization known as the Underground Railroad. First, the Underground Railroad was neither underground nor a railroad. The Underground Railroad was a network of secret routes and safe houses established by Northerners committed to helping escaped slaves. Several of the primary escape routes ran across the Buckeye state, partly because Ohio bordered both the slave states and Canada and was the shortest distance between those two locations for many of the escaped slaves. Two of the most famous conductors of the Underground Railroad resided in Ohio, Levi Coffin from Cincinnati and John Rankin from Ripley. Coffin, sometimes referred to as "The President of the Underground

---

[387] *Jones v. Van Zandt*, 46 U.S. 215, How. 215 (1847).

[388] Kern & Wilson, *supra* note 161, 125–126.

[389] *The Civil War: A Visual History*, first edition. (London: DK Publishing, 2011), 26.

[390] *Ohio Authors and Their Books*, William Coyle ed. (Cleveland, OH: The World Publishing Company, 1962), 605.

[391] 2 Carl Sandburg, *Abraham Lincoln: The War Years* (New York: Harcourt, Brace and Company, 1939), 592.

Railroad," began assisting escaped slaves in 1847 and may have helped as many as three thousand slaves on their journey to freedom. Rankin, who built his home on a high bluff overlooking the Ohio River, would hang a lantern outside his home to help guide the escaped slaves to his safe house. Rankin may have aided as many as two thousand slaves that escaped from captivity in the South. Some of the conductors had religious motivations while others simply opposed the peculiar institution.[392]

Finally, the culmination of these events was met with the election of Abraham Lincoln and would bring the country towards the brink of war.

VII. The Election of 1860

At the Republican Convention in Chicago in May, the Ohio delegation stood behind its candidates Senator William Seward of New York, and two of her favorite sons, former Governor Salmon P. Chase and current Senator Benjamin F. Wade. By the fourth ballot, the delegates, including those from Ohio, had switched their votes to Abraham Lincoln, who became the Republican nominee. The party platform bitterly opposed the idea of extending slavery to the territories but did not threaten the institution where it already existed. Ohio Governor William Dennison returned to Ohio, pledging to work for Lincoln's election.[393]

The Democrats held their convention in Charleston, South Carolina, in April 1860. Ohio's delegates were solidly behind Illinois Senator Stephen A. Douglas. Delegates from the states in the Deep South bolted from the convention over a platform dispute. Six candidates were nominated, with Senator Douglas garnering most votes. By the fifty-seventh ballot, Douglas was still leading, but he fell short of the number of votes required for the nomination. On May 3, the delegates agreed to adjourn without nominating a presidential candidate.

The convention reconvened in Baltimore on June 18. The delegates from the Deep

---

[392] Kern and Wilson, supra note 161, 157–158. For an excellent account of the activities of the Underground Railroad during this era, see, Eric Foner. *Gateway to Freedom: The Hidden History of the Underground Railroad* (New York: W.W. Norton & Co., Inc., 2015). Foner's book concerns itself mostly with the routes along the eastern corridor and terminating in New York City. However, it is an excellent reference source.

[393] Walter Havinghurst, *Ohio: A Bicentennial History* (New York: W.W. Norton & Co., Inc., 1976), 94–95.

South again walked out of the convention when a resolution permitting slavery in the territories did not receive the required number of votes. Douglas eventually garnered the nomination, while Herschel Johnson Georgia received the nod for vice president.

The Constitutional Union Party, made up of former Southern Whigs and Know-Nothings, met in Baltimore and nominated former Tennessee Senator John Bell as their candidate. Bell formerly served as speaker of the House and as secretary of war. A slave owner, Bell opposed the extension of slavery and campaigned against secession. Bell and his followers believed that secession could be best avoided by ignoring the slavery question altogether.[394]

The Southern delegates, who walked out of the Democratic Convention in Baltimore, reconvened five days later and nominated former Vice President John C. Breckenridge as their candidate for president. Joseph Lane of Oregon was nominated for vice president.[395] Lincoln and Douglas were the main rivals in the Northern states, while Breckenridge and Bell were the primary candidates in the Southern states.

Although Lincoln only carried 40 percent (39 percent) of the popular vote nationwide, he carried almost all the states above Mason-Dixon Line as well as California and Oregon. Lincoln prevailed in the Electoral College with 180 electoral votes, even though he did not carry a single slaveholding state. He won 54 percent of the Northern popular vote, but nationwide, his opponents garnered nearly a million votes more than he did. Douglas carried only the states of Missouri and New Jersey, while Breckenridge and Bell failed to carry any states outside their section. Lincoln won Ohio, receiving 231,600 and votes, while Douglas received 187,232 votes. A mere 23,600 Buckeye votes were cast for Breckenridge and Bell combined.

Summary

Several occurrences during the 1850s set the stage for Civil War in the next decade. Ohio was at the center of these events; her political leaders helped to shape events on a national scale, and her resources contributed significantly to the country's wealth. The compromise of 1850, with its more stringent Fugitive Slave Act, the regional effect of the Kansas-Nebraska Act, the Dred Scott Decision, the publication of *Uncle Tom's Cabin*, the activities of the Underground Railroad, and the election of 1860

---

[394]   Goodwin, *supra* note 369, 259–260.

[395]   Kern & Wilson, *supra* note 161, 221–222.

contributed to the sectional tension during this decade. The common thread among these issues was the peculiar institution of slavery.

The California Gold Rush of 1849 swelled the population of that territory significantly, and by the next year, a petition for statehood was forwarded to Washington. Up to this time, the slave and the free states had been admitted mostly in tandem, but admitting California as a free state would tip the balance in the Senate to the free states. Senators Henry Clay and Stephen A. Douglas fashioned the Compromise of 1850 to mollify Southerners concerned about the "peculiar institution." Instead, the new Fugitive Slave Act provoked hostility and resistance throughout the northern states, including Ohio.

The Kansas-Nebraska Act provided that the voters of those respective territories would decide for themselves whether slavery should be allowed. This concept, called "popular sovereignty," was good in theory, but it caused free-soil advocates called Jayhawkers from the North as well as "Border-Ruffians" from Missouri to flood the territories to influence the local elections. Open warfare broke out between the two factions, and the federal army was dispatched to restore peace to the area.

In the case of *Dred Scott versus Sanford*, the US Supreme Court was called on to decide whether Scott, who was born as a slave but lived for several years in free territory, was still a slave. The court determined that neither Scott, nor any African American, could be a "citizen of a state," so the court lacked jurisdiction to hear the case. More importantly, the court held that the federal government did not have the authority to ban slavery in the territories. Ohio's Justice John MacLean was one of two dissenting justices in the case.

Harriet Beecher Stowe, a resident of Cincinnati, wrote *Uncle Tom's Cabin* in response to the Fugitive Slave Act. Her goal was to expose the horrors of slavery to the northern population. The book became a runaway bestseller, and, except for the Bible, it was the highest-selling book of the nineteenth century. Stowe's book helped to popularize the abolitionist movement known as the Underground Railroad, a series of secret routes and safe houses designed to assist escaped slaves.

The election of 1860 proved to be one of the most decisive in the country's early history. Republican Abraham Lincoln squared off against Democrat Stephen A. Douglas. Southern Democrats bolted the convention and nominated John C Breckenridge, while a coalition of former Whigs and Know-Nothings nominated John Bell. Lincoln prevailed in the Electoral College while garnering 40 percent of the popular vote nationwide. Lincoln won Ohio's vote, but he failed to carry any slaveholding state.

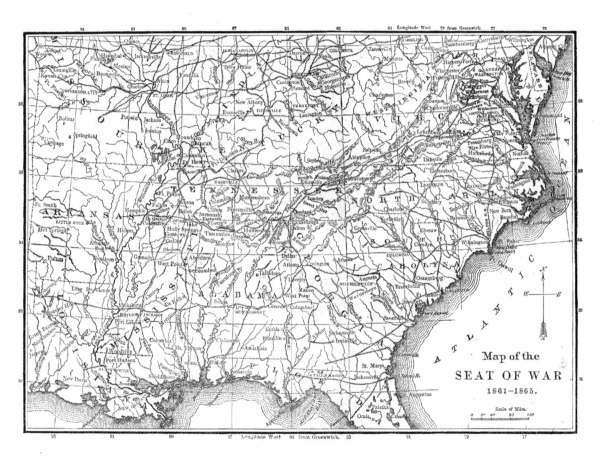

The Seat of War, 1861-1865.
(Image courtesy of the Ohio History Connection).

Chapter 7

Ohio Must Lead

Ohio must lead throughout the War!

—Ohio Governor William Dennison, 1861

I. Introduction.

The executive branch has frequently bent the Constitution and individual rights during times of war.[396] From 1789 to about 1846, the president largely respected congressional authority concerning declarations of war.[397] But from that point on, the president has stretched his executive power beyond the constitutional limits when it comes to war.[398] It is often argued, "'when national security is genuinely threatened, the president must be permitted to do whatever needs to be done to protect the United States.'"[399] This idea allows the president to burden individual rights in the name of security objectives while bypassing congressional approval.[400] The president's paramount responsibility is to protect the people of the United States and to keep the country secure even if it means bending the Constitution to

---

[396]   *See, generally,* Louis Fisher, *Presidential War Power,* second ed. (2004), 47 (discussing presidential war power through history).

[397]   Ibid., 17–39.

[398]   Ibid., 40–260. The majority of Fisher's book concerns itself with the ways in which the president has stretched his war power throughout the history of the country.

[399]   Scott M. Matheson, Jr., *Presidential Constitutionalism in Perilous Times* (2009), 17.

[400]   Ibid.

accomplish those purposes.[401] President Abraham Lincoln was no different when the Civil War broke out in 1861.[402]

Seven southern states passed Ordinances of Secession from the Union in the wake of Lincoln's election. These states formed the Confederate States of America in early 1861, with its capital in Montgomery, Alabama, and Jefferson Davis as its first president. Hostilities commenced when Confederate forces in Charleston, South Carolina, opened fire on Union forces occupying Fort Sumter in Charleston harbor. Four years later, more than 620,000 Union and Confederate soldiers were dead, the Southern infrastructure, including rail and riverboat service, was destroyed, the world's most advanced agrarian economy was in ruins, and slavery was abolished once and for all.

Lincoln responded to the attack on Fort Sumter by calling forth the state militias, suspending habeas corpus, and declaring a naval blockade of all southern ports.[403] Lincoln did this all while the Congress was in recess.[404] However, Lincoln did not claim that he had the authority to do these acts.[405] He acknowledged that he exceeded his executive powers when he asked Congress to validate his actions.[406] He explained why he did the things he did by stating, "whether strictly legal or not, were ventured upon under what appeared to be a popular demand and a public necessity, trusting then, as now, that Congress would readily ratify them."[407] Congress approved and legalized Lincoln's acts as if they had been done under the express authority of Congress.[408] Lincoln's actions caused another four states to

---

[401]   Ibid., 33.

[402]   Ibid., 33.

[403]   Fisher, *supra* note 396, 47.

[404]   Ibid., 47.

[405]   Ibid., 48.

[406]   Ibid.

[407]   Ibid.

[408]   Ibid.

secede,[409] and four additional border (slave) states with pro-Confederate sympathies seriously considered joining their comrades.[410]

President Lincoln resorted to other extraordinary measures to preserve the Union. During the four-year conflict, Lincoln assumed near-dictatorial powers that strained the Constitution in ways never seen before or since.

Lincoln gave his inaugural speech on March 4, 1861, before a crowd of approximately thirty thousand spectators. The speech itself was edited by Seward, and the tone was firm but conciliatory. Lincoln had "no purpose, directly or indirectly, to interfere with the institution of slavery in the States where it exists. I believe I have no lawful right to do so, and I have no inclination to do so."

However, Lincoln intended "to hold, occupy, and possess the property, and places belonging to the government, and to collect the duties and imposts; but beyond what may be necessary for these objects, there will be no invasion— no using of force against, or among the people anywhere …" Lincoln closed his speech with the words: "In your hands, my dissatisfied fellow countrymen, and not in mine, is the momentous issue of civil war. The government will not assail you. You can have no conflict, without being your selves the aggressors."[411]

Ohio's Republican governor, William Dennison, also stretched his more limited powers to the breaking point in dealing with the secession crisis. When Lincoln called for seventy-five thousand volunteers for the army, with thirteen thousand as Ohio's share, more than thirty thousand men appeared in Columbus to enlist. Ohio's First and Second Volunteer Infantry Regiments organized themselves so quickly that Dennison sent them to Washington to help protect the capital.[412] Dennison quickly appointed George B. McClellan, a railroad executive and West Point graduate, as major general and commander of the Ohio troops. Delaware County native and West Point graduate William S. Rosecrans was appointed as brigadier general and second in command.[413] In May 1861, Dennison telegraphed former Governor Salmon P. Chase, now serving as secretary of the treasury. Dennison was seeking a

---

[409]   Farber, *supra* note 382, 16. Arkansas, North Carolina, Virginia, and Tennessee seceded.

[410]   Farber, *supra* note 382, 16. Missouri, Kentucky, Maryland, and Delaware remained in the Union.

[411]   Goodwin, *supra* note 369, 326–328.

[412]   Kern & Wilson, *supra* note 161, 222–224.

[413]   Ibid., 222–224.

three-year commission as major general for McClellan, insisting that "Ohio must lead throughout the war."[414] President Lincoln soon appointed McClellan as major general in the regular army, to rank above all officers except commanding General Winfield Scott.

Dennison took additional steps that stretched his rather limited governing powers to the breaking point. Dennison took control over the railroads and telegraph lines to help with supply and communication problems. Dennison established several training camps for the troops, and he helped raise over one hundred thousand troops for the Union Army. Without waiting for Washington's approval, Dennison also convinced General McClellan to dispatch troops to western Virginia to aid the loyalists in that area and to control the line of the Baltimore & Ohio Railroad.[415] By July 1861, Union forces had driven the Confederates from the pro-Union region of western Virginia.[416] These pro-Union counties seceded from the state of Virginia and were admitted to the Union as the state of West Virginia in 1863.

Dennison's actions helped Ohio gain a war footing in record time, but he made powerful enemies in the process. Feeling that Dennison was a political liability, Republicans and War Democrats dumped Dennison in favor of Youngstown businessman David Tod for the gubernatorial nomination in 1861. Tod easily defeated Peace Democrat Hugh J. Jewett that November.[417] Dennison went on to chair the Republican National Convention in 1864, and he served as postmaster general in the Lincoln administration.[418]

Most historians describe the month of July 1863 as the turning point in the war. In that month Union forces captured the Confederate strongholds at Vicksburg and Port Hudson, thus opening the Mississippi River to the Union Navy. General George Meade defeated Lee's Army of Northern Virginia at Gettysburg; Lee attempted no further strategic offensives for the remainder of war. At the same time, William Rosecrans maneuvered Confederate General Braxton Bragg out of his strong

---

[414]   Ibid., 224.

[415]   Knepper, *supra* note 27, 223–224.

[416]   I Shelby Foote, *The Civil War: A Narrative, Fort Sumter to Perryville* (First Vintage Books Edition, 1986), 69–71.

[417]   Knepper, *supra* note 27, 224–25.

[418]   Goodwin, *supra* note 369, 659.

defensive positions at Tullahoma, Tennessee, in an almost bloodless campaign. The siege of the port of Charleston, South Carolina, continued, and the African American Fifty-Fourth Massachusetts Regiment unsuccessfully attacked Battery Wagner in Charleston harbor.

A thumbnail sketch of July 1863 also demonstrates the contribution of Ohio and its citizens to the war effort. Union General Ulysses S. Grant (Point Pleasant) accepted the surrender of Confederate forces at Vicksburg, Mississippi. Two of his corps commanders were William Tecumseh Sherman (Lancaster) and James B. McPherson (Clyde).

William Starke Rosecrans (Delaware County), commanding the Army of the Cumberland, drove General Bragg's army from Tullahoma in middle Tennessee to northern Georgia. Brigadier general and future President James A. Garfield (Orange Township) served as Rosecrans's chief of staff. Troops commanded by Generals Alexander McCook (Columbiana County) as well as the Ninth Ohio Infantry regiment held critical mountain passes that allowed Rosecrans to advance relatively unimpeded by Confederate forces. Major General Phillip Henry Sheridan (Somerset) commanded the Union division that first entered Tullahoma. Colonel and future President Benjamin Harrison (North Bend) commanded a regiment that guarded Rosecrans's supply lines in Kentucky and Tennessee.

July 1863 also saw the capture of Port Hudson, Louisiana, by forces under General Nathaniel Banks. Banks's division commanders included Godfrey Weitzel (born in Germany but living in Cincinnati) and Halbert Paine (Chardon). At Gettysburg, Brigadier General George Armstrong Custer (New Rumley) defeated a Confederate cavalry force attempting to attack the rear of the Union lines, while the Eighth Ohio Infantry helped blunt the left-flank attack during Pickett's charge on the third day of the battle. In Charleston Harbor, Union troops attacked the harbor defenses commanded by Confederate General Roswell Ripley (Worthington).

Back in Ohio, Confederate cavalry under General John Hunt Morgan invaded Ohio and were defeated by Union troops, including the Twenty-Third Ohio Infantry Regiment, with future Presidents Rutherford B. Hayes (Delaware) and William McKinley (Niles), at the Battle of Buffington Island. Copperhead Congressman Clement Vallandigham (Lisbon), recently convicted of making disloyal statements by a military commission and banished to the South by President Lincoln, accepted his party's nomination to run for governor, *in absentia*.

In his book entitled *Lincoln's Constitution*,[419] Professor Daniel Farber[420] examines the constitutional crisis that was the American Civil War. Farber gives emphasis to the secession crisis itself, the debate over state sovereignty versus federal supremacy, the legality of secession, the uses (and abuses) of presidential power, and the curtailment of individual rights.

Some curtailment of individual rights should have been expected in the theatre of war. The imposition of martial law, the seizure and destruction of personal property without compensation, and the liberation of millions of slaves[421] are natural consequences of warfare. Such intrusions were more difficult to justify in the states remaining loyal to the Union.

The intrusions on individual rights in the northern states, while of a more limited nature, still existed. Farber writes that at least thirteen thousand civilians were held under military arrest during the Civil War. Some of the arrestees, particularly draft dodgers, deserters, and blockade runners, were arguably under military jurisdiction. Others, most notably citizens of the Confederacy, those northern citizens caught trading with the Confederacy, and individuals accused of disloyal speech, were often denied their constitutional right to jury trial and other protections.[422]

Farber wrote in detail concerning four infringements on individual rights during this era, notably the suspension of *habeas corpus*, arrests without trials, trials of civilians by military commissions, and infringements on free speech.[423] This chapter will analyze the history of the Writ of Habeas Corpus; Lincoln's first suspension of Habeas Corpus; suspension and arbitrary arrests in Ohio; and other suspensions during Lincoln's presidency.

---

[419]   Farber, *supra* note 382, 14.

[420]   Farber serves as Sho Sato Professor of Law at the University of California, Berkeley.

[421]   Farber, *supra* note 369, 144. This article discusses Lincoln's actual reluctance in freeing the slaves because of its constitutional problems. http://quod.lib.umich.edu/j/jala/2629860.0005.104?rgn=main;view=fulltext

[422]   Farber, *supra* note 369, 145.

[423]   *See, generally,* Farber, *supra* note 369, chapter 7.

II. The Origin of the Great Writ

A. Habeas at English Common Law

Habeas corpus is a "judicial mandate directing a government official to present an individual held in custody to the court so that it can determine whether his detention is lawful."[424] A writ of habeas corpus "directs an agent of the crown detaining a citizen 'to produce the body of the prisoner, or person detained' to 'test the legality of the detention or imprisonment,' rather than to establish the guilt or innocence of the party." It is regarded as the "Great Writ" because it is the "sacred right of the people against sovereign authority."[425] When the founders drafted the Constitution, they understood it in the context of the English Habeas Corpus Act and with the belief that "national security interests should [not] be balanced against the right to individual liberty enjoyed by persons within protection, save one exception: in the event of a 'Rebellion or Invasion' where the political branches have taken the dramatic step of suspending the privilege."[426] The Suspension Clause was intended "to bestow on the new government a particular lever, drawn from English and colonial practice, by which it could—in a formal, transparent, and dramatic way—balance the needs of national security against the individual rights enshrined in the Constitution."[427]

The writ of habeas corpus came about in England and has since been recognized as the "'bulwark of our liberties' and the embodiment of the 'natural inherent right' of the 'personal liberty of the subject.'"[428] The writ is connected to "English conceptions of due process rooted in Magna Carta."[429] At the time the Constitution

---

[424] Geoffrey R. Stone, *Perilous Times: Free Speech in Wartime,* first ed. (New York: W. W. Norton & Co., 2004), 120.

[425] Robert G. Bracknell, Book Review, 47 Naval L. Rev. 208, 209–10 (2000) (Reviewing William H. Rehnquist, *All the Laws but One: Civil Liberties in Wartime* (1998)); *Black's Law Dictionary* (ninth ed. 2009).

[426] Amanda L. Tyler, *The Forgotten Core Meaning of the Suspension Clause,* 125 Harv. L. Rev. 901, 921 (2012).

[427] Ibid., 922.

[428] Ibid., 924.

[429] Ibid., 924.

was ratified, the writ of habeas existed in England as the specific right "not to be jailed on mere suspicion of criminal activity or of posing a danger to the state, but instead only upon formal criminal charges and timely trials commensurate with well-established procedural safeguards."[430] The writ was essentially "'a powerful guarantee that individuals would not be detained on executive fiat instead of legally recognized grounds.'"[431]

In 1627, the court in "Darnel's Case" simply stated that the prisoners were held "by the special command of the King."[432] The prisoners argued that due process must be afforded them, "'either by presentment or by indictment.'"[433] The prisoners' argument failed, but it laid the important groundwork for the parliamentary created Petition of Right.[434] The Petition of Right "essentially repudiated the holding in Darnel's Case" when Parliament cited the due process laid out in the Magna Carta and demanded that the king give cause before imprisoning and detaining his subjects.[435] The king signed the petition, giving the formerly declaratory statement the teeth to limit the power of the executive to arrest and detain "except upon a criminal charge or conviction, or for a civil debt."[436] Thus, while the writ was not codified until 1679, the "common law writ of habeas corpus, which continued to serve as the vehicle for redress available in 'all ... cases of unjust imprisonment' that were not covered by the [Habeas Corpus Act.]"[437]

B. The Habeas Corpus Act

The Habeas Corpus Act, promulgated in 1679, promised speedy trial, and release when a speedy trial was not held.[438] The writ under the act was described as "'the

---

[430]   Ibid., 924.

[431]   Ibid., 925

[432]   Ibid., 925.

[433]   Ibid., 925–26.

[434]   Ibid., 926.

[435]   Ibid., 926.

[436]   Ibid., 925–26.

[437]   Ibid., 927.

[438]   Ibid., 928–29.

first security of civil liberty' that 'protect[ed] the subject from unfounded suspicions, from the aggressions of power, and from abuses in the administration of justice.'"[439] The act also included specific provisions to protect individuals accused of treason that "would have been largely superfluous if the Crown could simply ignore them in the ordinary course by detaining persons thought to pose a danger to the state without charges in the first instance."[440] The act did not have any exceptions for times of war.[441] The Trial of Treasons Act of 1696 added more protections for those specifically accused of treason.[442] All of these developments together made it clear to the drafters of our Constitution that "'[t]he right to be either tried according to law or released is really the right that habeas corpus is supposed to secure.'"[443]

C. Parliamentary Suspensions of the Habeas Corpus Act

The British Parliament first suspended the writ ten years after the Habeas Corpus Act was promulgated, "in response to the events of the Glorious Revolution of 1688, which spurred James II to flight and installed William and Mary on the throne."[444] The Crown began to arrest those suspected of treason, all the while fearing "that persons detained without formal charges would be 'deliver[ed]' by habeas corpus" under the act.[445] Charles Boscawen asked the House of Commons for "'a short Bill, for two or three months, to enable the King to commit such persons as he shall have cause to suspect, without the benefit of Habeas Corpus.'"[446] After some debate, both houses of Parliament passed the first suspension of the Habeas Corpus Act.[447] Parliament later expanded the scope of the suspension of the act and

---

[439]   Ibid., 929.

[440]   Ibid., 929–30.

[441]   Ibid., 930.

[442]   Ibid., 931.

[443]   Ibid., 932.

[444]   Ibid., 934.

[445]   Ibid., 936.

[446]   Ibid., 935.

[447]   Ibid., 936.

lengthened its duration.[448] The suspension was later extended again for five more months.[449] A third attempt to extend the suspension was unsuccessful.[450]

In February of 1696, Parliament suspended the act again for six months after an assassination attempt on King William's life.[451] The act was again suspended in 1708, 1715, 1722, and 1744.[452] Notably, in 1777, "Parliament responded to the outbreak of rebellion in the colonies by enacting new suspension legislation. It provided:

> 'Whereas a Rebellion and War have been openly and traitorously levied and carried on in certain of His Majesty's Colonies and Plantations in America, and Acts of Treason and Piracy have been committed on the High Seas, and upon the Ships and Goods of his Majesty's Subjects, and many Persons have been seised and taken, who are expressly charged or strongly suspected of such Treasons and Felonies, and many more such Persons may be hereafter so seised and taken: And whereas such Persons have been, or may be brought into this Kingdom, and into other Parts of his Majesty's Dominions, and it may be inconvenient in many such Cases to proceed forthwith to the Trial of such Criminals, and at the same Time of evil Example to suffer them to go at large; be it therefore enacted … That all and every Person or Persons who have been, or shall hereafter be seised or taken in the Act of High Treason … or in the Act of Piracy, or who are or shall be charged with or suspected of the Crime of High Treason … and who have been, or shall be committed, in any Part of his Majesty's Dominions, for such Crimes … or for Suspicion of such Crimes … shall and may be thereupon secured and detained in safe Custody, without Bail or Mainprize … any Law, Statute, or Usage, to the contrary in anywise notwithstanding.'"[453]

---

[448]   Ibid., 938.

[449]   Ibid., 940.

[450]   Ibid., 941.

[451]   Ibid., 942.

[452]   Ibid., 942–43.

[453]   Ibid., 944–45.

D. Habeas Corpus in the Colonies

Arrestees were not afforded the protections of the Habeas Corpus Act in the colonies.[454] However, if they were captured and taken on English soil, English subjects were protected and owed due process.[455] Therefore, during the American Revolution, Americans were detained on English ships, until their number become unmanageable.[456] Parliament then suspended the Habeas Corpus Act in 1777 for any prisoners.[457] Instead of renewing the suspension in 1782, Parliament recognized Americans as members of a "wholly separate nation" and passed a statute authorizing the King "'to hold and detain … as Prisoners of War, all Natives or other Inhabitants of the thirteen revolted Colonies not at His Majesty's Peace.'"[458]

Americans were outraged at the disparate treatment.[459] In 1774, the Continental Congress wrote to the British "decrying the denial to the colonists of 'trial by jury' and 'the benefit of the habeas corpus Act, that great bulwark and palladium of English liberty.'"[460] The Continental Congress later wrote about the importance of habeas corpus:

> If a subject is seized and imprisoned, tho' by order of Government, he may, by virtue of this right, immediately obtain a writ, termed a Habeas Corpus, from a Judge, whose sworn duty it is to grant it, and thereupon procure any illegal restraint to be quickly enquired into and redressed.[461]

Thus, the colonists, having been denied the writ, intrinsically understood its fundamental importance and "[i]n breaking away from England, the colonists would

---

[454]   Ibid., 947.

[455]   Ibid., 947–48.

[456]   Ibid., 949.

[457]   Ibid.

[458]   Ibid., 950–51.

[459]   Ibid., 955.

[460]   Ibid.

[461]   Ibid.

claim the privilege as their own and in time incorporate it into a new constitutional framework that entrenched its protections from suspension far more than English law had."[462]

> Before the federal right to habeas was enshrined in the Constitution, "every state in the Union secured the writ of habeas corpus either by common law or state constitutional law."[463] The federal privilege was intended to protect the States' remedies.[464] Thus, the debate surrounding the incorporation of the suspension clause related to the allocation of power.[465] The Founders agreed that the suspension may be necessary in some cases.[466] Therefore, the provision in the Constitution as enacted in 1787 still reads: "[t]he Privilege of the Writ of Habeas Corpus shall not be suspended, unless when in Cases of Rebellion or Invasion the public Safety may require it."[467]

E. Context of the First Suspension

Lincoln was faced with extremely difficult circumstances immediately after becoming president. Lincoln committed severe abuses of civil rights, including the suspension of the writ of habeas corpus, to preserve the Union. Craig Lerner argues that in saving the Constitution, Lincoln "often took actions that skirted the outermost boundaries, and possibly exceeded his constitutional authority."[468] However, Lerner asserts that damage to the integrity of the Constitution is an

---

[462] Ibid.

[463] Eli Palomares, *Illegal Confinement: Presidential Authority to Suspend the Privilege of the Writ of Habeas Corpus During Times of Emergency*, 12 S. Cal. Interdisc. L.J. 101, 105 (2002).

[464] Ibid.

[465] Ibid.

[466] Ibid.

[467] U.S. Const. art. I, § 9, cl. 2.

[468] Craig S. Lerner, *Saving the Constitution: Lincoln, Secession, and the Price of Union*, 102 Mich. L. Rev. 1263, 1285, 1285 (2004).

inevitable cost of war.[469] Indeed, "Lincoln could count, and he knew he had the votes of both the people and the Congress" in restricting the rights and privileges in the Constitution.[470] Despite these abuses, "[t]he verdict of history is that Lincoln's use of power did not constitute abuse. Every survey of historians ranks Lincoln as number one among the great presidents."[471]

Lincoln's first inauguration took place on March 4, 1861.[472] He "immediately confronted a country literally splitting apart" as he watched states of the "Lower South," including South Carolina, Georgia, Florida, Alabama, Mississippi, Louisiana, and Texas secede.[473] Lincoln tried to prevent the "Upper South" states including Virginia, North Carolina, Tennessee, and Arkansas, and the "Border States" that included Missouri, Kentucky, and Maryland.[474]

Geoffrey R. Stone described the "tangled knot of complications" leading up to Lincoln's suspension of the Writ well:

> sharply divided loyalties, fluid and often uncertain military and political boundaries, and easy opportunities for espionage and sabotage. He also faced a set of additional dilemmas because of his need to retain the loyalty of the border states, address divisive questions of race, slavery, and emancipation, and impose conscription for the first time in the nation's history. Bitter disagreement, even within the Union, was inevitable.[475]

On April 12, 1861, only a month after Lincoln became president, the South fired

---

[469]   Ibid., 1285.

[470]   Frank J. Williams, *Abraham Lincoln, Civil Liberties and the Croning Letter*, 5 Roger Williams U. L. Rev. 319, 321 (2000).

[471]   Ibid., 321.

[472]   Ibid., 322.

[473]   Margaret A. Garvin, *All the Laws but One: Civil Liberties in Wartime*, 16 Const. Comment 691, 693 (1999); William H. Rehnquist, *Civil Liberty and the Civil War: The Indianapolis Treason Trials*, 72 Ind. L.J. 927, 927 (1997).

[474]   Rehnquist, *supra* note 473, 927.

[475]   Stone, *supra* note 424, 84.

on Union troops at Fort Sumter.[476] The Union surrendered the fort on April 14.[477] Lincoln called up the seventy-five thousand members of the militia.[478] The "Upper South" states immediately seceded, and Maryland threatened to secede, leaving "the Capital nearly surrounded by secessionists and their sympathizers."[479]

Former Chief Justice William H. Rehnquist explained how these events affected the dynamics between the South and the Union, putting Lincoln in a tight position.

> Their secession dramatically changed the military status of the nation's capital in Washington. When only the states of the "Lower South" had seceded, the border between the Confederate states and the United States was the southern border of North Carolina. But after Fort Sumter, that border was the Potomac River which separates Maryland from Virginia. Washington went from being an interior capital to a capital on the very frontier of the Union, raising the definite possibility of raids and even investment and capture by the Confederate forces. Lincoln, fully aware of this danger, was most anxious that the 75,000 volunteers for whom he had called would arrive in Washington and defend the city against a possible Confederate attack. The North, as a whole, had rallied to Lincoln's call to arms, and new volunteer regiments and brigades were oversubscribed. But the only rail connections from the North into Washington ran through the city of Baltimore, forty miles to the northeast. Herein lay a problem: there were numerous Confederate sympathizers in Baltimore, and the city itself, at that time, had a reputation for unruliness—it was known as "Mob City." Three rail lines—one from Philadelphia and the northeast, another from Harrisburg and the northwest, and the B&O from the west, converged in the city or close to it.[480]

---

[476] Michael B. Brennan, Book Review, 83 Marq. L. Rev. 221, 222 (1999) (Reviewing William H. Rehnquist, *All the Laws but One: Civil Liberties in Wartime* (1998)); Garvin, *supra* note 473, 694.

[477] Garvin, *supra* note 473, 694.

[478] Rehnquist, *supra* note 473, 928.

[479] Garvin, *supra* note 473, 694; Rehnquist, *supra* note 473, 928.

[480] Rehnquist, *supra* note 473, 928.

Maryland was "seething with secessionist tendencies."[481] Lincoln already had to avoid Baltimore en route to the capital for his inauguration because of an assassination attempt.[482] No one was sure what Maryland's intentions were, but it was clear that "if Maryland joined the Confederacy, the US capital would sit inside Confederate lines."[483] On April 19, "a violent mob" attacked Union soldiers from the Sixth Massachusetts militia "with bricks, stones, and pistols, to which they responded by firing into the crowd," which resulted in the deaths of four soldiers and twelve civilians.[484] The governor of Maryland, Thomas Hicks, allowed Confederates to burn bridges and interfere with telegraph lines and postal delivery to frustrate the Union troops' efforts to enter the city of Baltimore.[485] Governor Hicks also "convened the Maryland legislature on April 26 to discuss secession, and urged the General Assembly to adopt "a resolution affirming the preservation of Maryland's neutral posture."[486]

F. Lincoln First Suspends the Writ

On April 27, 1861, because "Lincoln believed that a military threat against Washington could have ended the War in favor of the South, or at least severely weakened the Union and put it in a compromising position at any future treaty negotiations," and the dissolution of the Union would threaten "the very existence of republican government, at home and abroad,"[487] he authorized the first suspension of habeas corpus "at any point he deemed necessary along the rail line from Philadelphia to Washington."[488] Lincoln wrote to the commanding general of the Army of the United States, Winfield Scott:

---

[481] Williams, *supra* note 470, 322.

[482] Brennan, *supra* note 476, 222,

[483] Bracknell, *supra* note 425, 210–11.

[484] Palomares, *supra* note 463, 110–11; Williams, *supra* note 439, 322.

[485] Bracknell, *supra* note 425, 210–11.

[486] Bracknell, *supra* note 425, 210–11.

[487] Jason A. Adkins, *Lincoln's Constitution Revisited*, 36 N. Ky. L. Rev. 211, 238 (2009).

[488] Rehnquist, *supra* note 473, 928.

You are engaged in suppressing an insurrection against the laws of the United States. If at any point on or in the vicinity of any military line which is now or which shall be used between the city of Philadelphia and the city of Washington you find resistance which renders it necessary to suspend the writ of habeas corpus for the public safety, you personally, or through the officer in command at the point where resistance occurs, are authorized to suspend the writ.[489]

Frank J. Williams emphasizes that Lincoln did not suspend the great writ lightly.[490] "The right of habeas corpus was so important, that the president considered the bombardment of Maryland cities as preferable to its suspension." Lincoln authorized General Scott to suspend the writ only "in the extremest necessity."[491] Lincoln's secretary of state, William H. Seward, said that the only reason the writ had not been suspended up to this point was "'because of Mr. Lincoln's extreme reluctance at that period to assume such a responsibility.'"[492]

G. Precedent for the Suspension

Lincoln did not have strong precedent to back his decision.[493] Before the Civil War, no branch of the government had suspended the writ.[494] Thomas Jefferson had attempted to suspend the writ during *Ex parte Bollman*,[495] but Jefferson did not even consider unilateral executive action when the bill passed in the Senate but was

---

[489]   Bracknell, *supra* note 425, 211; Palomares, *supra* note 463, 112; Garvin, *supra* note 473, 694.

[490]   Williams, *supra* note 470, 322.

[491]   Williams, *supra* note 470, 322. *See, also,* Frank J. Williams, *Judging Lincoln*, first ed. (Carbondale, IL: Southern Illinois Press, 2002), 62.

[492]   Palomares, *supra* note 432, 111.

[493]   Palomares, *supra* note 432, 111.

[494]   Saikrishna Bangalore Prakash, *The Great Suspender's Unconstitutional Suspension of the Great Writ*, 3 Alb. Gov't L. Rev. 575, 578 (2010).

[495]   8 U.S. (Cranch 4) 75 (1807).

rejected in the House.[496] In fact, Jefferson "could not conceive of a situation where the president should suspend the writ even during insurrection or rebellion."[497]

Therefore, Lincoln asked his attorney general, Edward Bates, for advice.[498] Bates's assistant, Titian J. Coffey, prepared a memorandum citing Matthew Hales, William Blackstone, and Joseph Story's *Commentaries on the Constitution*.[499] Story wrote, "'[h]itherto no suspension of the writ has ever been authorized by congress ... [i]t would seem, as the power is given to congress to suspend the writ of habeas corpus in cases of rebellion or invasion, that the right to judge, whether exigency had arisen, must exclusively belong to that body.'"[500]

H. Ex Parte Merryman

Many did not appreciate Lincoln's internal struggle, and felt that "Lincoln's suspension of the writ for the sake of military expedience struck a merciless blow to civil liberties."[501] At this time there were several dissenters in Maryland. John Merryman was a state legislator and a member of a secessionist unit of the Calvary.[502] He was a "Lieutenant Drillmaster." Thus, he not only exercised his constitutional right to disagree with what the government was doing, but he engaged in raising an armed group to attack and to attempt to destroy the government."[503] Just about a month after Lincoln suspended the writ, on May 25, 1861,[504] Merryman was arrested for "speaking out against the Union, recruiting soldiers to serve in the Confederate Army, and participating in the destruction of rail lines."[505] Merryman immediately

---

[496]   Palomares, *supra* note 463, 111; Prakash, *supra* note 494, 578.

[497]   Palomares, *supra* note 463, 111.

[498]   Goodwin, *supra* note 369, 355; http://www.fjc.gov/history/home.nsf/page/tu_merryman_doc_6.html

[499]   Stone, *supra* note 424, 121.

[500]   2 Joseph Story, *Commentaries on the Constitution of the United States* § 1336 (1833).

[501]   Bracknell, *supra* note 425, 210–11.

[502]   Williams, *supra* note 424, 323; Palomares, *supra* note 463, 112.

[503]   Williams, *supra* note 470, 323.

[504]   Palomares, *supra* note 463, 112.

[505]   Garvin, *supra* note 473, 694.

petitioned for a writ of habeas corpus, claiming he was being held illegally at Fort McHenry in Maryland.[506] Chief Justice Taney of the Supreme Court, famous for his decision in *Dred Scott*,[507] acting in his capacity as a circuit judge, quickly granted the writ on May 26.[508] Geoffrey R. Stone notes that Taney "welcomed the opportunity to consider Merryman's petition." Taney then issued the following Order:

> Ordered, this 26th day of May, A. D. 1861, that the writ of habeas corpus issue in this case, as prayed, and that the same be directed to General George Cadwalader, and be issued in the usual form, by Thomas Spicer, clerk of the circuit court of the United States in and for the district of Maryland, and that the said writ of habeas corpus be returnable at eleven o'clock, on Monday, the 27th of May 1861, at the circuit court room, in the Masonic Hall, in the city of Baltimore, before me, chief justice of the supreme court of United States. R. B. Taney.[509]

Taney's clerk, Mr. Spicer, then issued the following writ to General Cadwalader:

> You are hereby commanded to be and appear before the Honorable Roger B. Taney, chief justice of the supreme court of the United States, at the United States court-room, in the Masonic Hall, in the city of Baltimore, on Monday, the 27th day of May 1861, at eleven o'clock in the morning, and that you have with you the body of John Merryman, of Baltimore county, and now in your custody, and that you certify and make known the day and cause of the caption and detention of the said John Merryman, and that you then and there, do, submit to, and receive whatsoever the said chief justice shall determine upon concerning you on this behalf, according to law, and have you then and there this writ.[510]

---

[506] Palomares, *supra* note 473, 112; Stone, *supra* note 424, 85.

[507] Stone, *supra* note 424, 85; Williams, *supra* note 470, 323.

[508] Garvin, *supra* note 473, 694; Stone, *supra* note 424, 87.

[509] *Ex parte Merryman*, 17 F. Cas. 144, 146 (C.C.D. Md. 1861).

[510] Ibid.

The marshal served the writ on General Cadwalader on May 26. General Cadwalader replied by letter on May 27. He refused to comply, arguing that Colonel Yohe was authorized under Lincoln's suspension on April 27 to arrest and hold Merryman:

> [H]e is duly authorized by the president of the United States, in such cases, to suspend the writ of habeas corpus, for the public safety. This is a high and delicate trust, and it has been enjoined upon him that it should be executed with judgment and discretion, but he is nevertheless also instructed that in times of civil strife, errors, if any, should be on the side of the safety of the country. He most respectfully submits for your consideration, that those who should co-operate in the present trying and painful position in which our country is placed, should not, by any unnecessary want of confidence in each other, increase our embarrassments. He, therefore, respectfully requests that you will postpone further action upon this case, until he can receive instructions from the president of the United States, when you shall hear further from him.[511]

Therefore, when George Cadwalader failed to comply, Taney wrote the famous opinion in *Ex Parte Merryman*, and issued an attachment for Cadwalader for contempt.[512] Taney held that "only Congress was authorized to suspend the writ of habeas corpus," making Lincoln's executive order suspending the writ unconstitutional.[513] Taney believed the right belonged to Congress "because permissible suspension was in Article I § 9 of the Constitution, the section describing congressional duties," despite "the fact that it was placed there by the Committee on Drafting at the Constitutional Convention in 1787 as a matter of

---

[511]   Ibid.

[512]   Garvin, *supra* note 473, 694; Williams, *supra* note 470.

[513]   Stone, *supra* note 424, 87.

form, not substance."[514] Taney did not "acknowledge that a rebellion was in progress," threatening the fate of the Union.[515]

"Moreover, because Merryman was not a member of the military forces of the United States, and because the civil courts in Maryland were open and functioning, Taney held that ordinary judicial process, rather than military authority, had jurisdiction over the matter."[516] Taney wrote:

> I ordered this attachment yesterday, because, upon the face of the return, the detention of the prisoner was unlawful, upon the grounds: 1. That the president, under the constitution of the United States, cannot suspend the privilege of the writ of habeas corpus, nor authorize a military officer to do it. 2. A military officer has no right to arrest and detain a person not subject to the rules and articles of war, for an offence against the laws of the United States, except in aid of the judicial authority, and subject to its control; and if the party be arrested by the military, it is the duty of the officer to deliver him over immediately to the civil authority, to be dealt with according to law. It is, therefore, very clear that John Merryman, the petitioner, is entitled to be set at liberty and discharged immediately from imprisonment. I forbore yesterday to state orally the provisions of the constitution of the United States, which make those principles the fundamental law of the Union, because an oral statement might be misunderstood in some portions of it, and I shall therefore put my opinion in writing, and file it in the office of the clerk of the circuit court, in the course of this week.[517]

According to Eli Palomares, Taney's decision was based on four independent grounds:

---

[514] Ibid., 87.

[515] Ibid., 87.

[516] Ibid., 87.

[517] *Ex parte Merryman, supra* note 509.

First, President Jefferson believed that the President possessed no power to suspend the writ. Second, Taney reasoned that the location of the suspension clause in Article I, which deals with congressional powers, meant that Congress should have the sole power to suspend the writ. Third, Taney relied on Blackstone's Commentaries, which indicated that in England only Parliament could suspend the writ, and on Justice Story's Commentaries on the Constitution of the United States, which asserted that Congress had the sole power to suspend the writ. Finally, he relied on Chief Justice Marshall's statement in *Ex parte Bollman*, that "[i]f at any time the public safety should require the suspension of the powers vested by [the Judiciary Act of 1789] in the courts of the United States, it is for the legislature to say so."[518]

Taney's opinion reveals his Jacksonian constitutional philosophy, the belief that "power and liberty were at odds with each other and that concentrated power—whether political or economic—posed a grave threat to individual liberty."[519] Accordingly, Taney believed that "the courts possessed the authority to define the president's duty to faithfully execute the laws, and to command that the execution of laws conform to the interpretation of the law by the courts."[520] As Eli Palomares explains, this "assertion of judicial supremacy" went beyond Chief Justice Marshall's definition of judicial review in *Marbury v. Madison*.[521] While this was a stretch in actual judicial authority, a president is required to faithfully execute the laws, as interpreted by the judiciary. For this reason, Taney concluded the opinion with a reminder to the president: "[i]t will then remain for that high officer, in fulfillment of his constitutional obligation to 'take care that the laws be faithfully executed,' to determine what measures he will take to cause the civil process of the United States to be respected and enforced."[522]

---

[518]   Palomares, *supra* note 463, 115.

[519]   Timothy S. Huebner, *Lincoln's Legacy: Enduring Lessons of Executive Power*, 3 Alb. Gov't L. Rev. 615, 621 (2010).

[520]   Palomares, *supra* note 463, 115.

[521]   Ibid., 115.

[522]   *Ex parte Merryman*, *supra* note 509.

However, it was easy for Lincoln to ignore Taney's opinion because

> Taney's response to Lincoln's suspension of the writ [wa]s problematic. He ignored the general's request for postponement and made his ruling without the benefit of hearing the government's argument ... Taney's quick ruling without the benefit of oral argument foreclosed the opportunity for a more democratic resolution of the important issue of presidential authority to suspend the writ of habeas corpus under the Constitution. Although in the end Taney might not have changed his mind, a resolution after hearing the government's position would have legitimized his ruling.[523]

I. Lincoln Responds to Taney's Opinion

Lincoln had no difficulty disregarding Taney's ruling, in fact, Lincoln's administration did not even directly respond to Taney's opinion or order.[524] After the *Merryman* decision was handed down, Lincoln continued to delegate the suspension of the writ.[525] The suspension soon "became an effective tool to silence those interfering with the Administration's policies. Lincoln demonstrated that he was willing to sacrifice an individual's privilege of the writ of habeas corpus to fulfill what he believed to be his duty as Commander in Chief."[526] Soon after *Merryman*, on June 20, 1861,[527] Lincoln allowed the suspension of the writ in Florida, "and along the 'military line' from New York to Washington."[528]

---

[523] Palomares, *supra* note 463, 116.

[524] Brennan, *supra* note 476, 224; Stone, *supra* note 424, 87.

[525] Prakash, *supra* note 494, 579.

[526] Palomares, *supra* note 463, 113.

[527] 4 James D. Richardson, *A Compilation of the Messages and Papers of the Presidents, 1789–1897* (Published by Authority of Congress, 1900), 19. Lincoln wrote to Winfield Scott: "You or any officer you may designate will, in your discretion, suspend the writ of habeas corpus so far as may relate to Major Chase, lately of the Engineer Corps of the Army of the United States, now alleged to be guilty of treasonable practices against this government."

[528] Prakash, *supra* note 494, 579.

J. Lincoln's Constitutional Philosophy

Lincoln was a Republican, but he held many beliefs of the lifeless Whig Party, including "a deep respect for order and the rule of law."[529] In one of his most famous speeches, the "Lyceum Address," Lincoln said:

> Let reverence for the laws, be breathed by every American mother, to the lisping babe, that prattles on her lap—let it be taught in schools, in seminaries, and in colleges; let it be written in Primers, spelling books, and in Almanacs;—let it be preached from the pulpit, proclaimed in legislative halls, and enforced in courts of justice. And, in short, let it become the political religion of the nation; and let the old and the young, the rich and the poor, the grave and the gay, of all sexes and tongues, and colors and conditions, sacrifice unceasingly upon its altars.[530]

This idea seems to contradict Lincoln's treatment of civil liberties during the Civil War. Lincoln was committed to applying the Constitution in all circumstances, but "embrace[d] the view that the Constitution may be different in 'application' in these different circumstances. He derive[d] this largely from the habeas corpus provision of the Constitution, which allows the writ to be suspended in time of 'Rebellion or Invasion.'"[531] In a famous letter to Erastus Corning, in which Lincoln defended later suspensions, he stated:

> If I be wrong on this question of constitutional power, my error lies in believing that certain proceedings are constitutional when, in cases of rebellion or Invasion, the public Safety requires them, which would not be constitutional when, in absence of rebellion or invasion, the public Safety does not require them.[532]

---

[529]   Huebner, *supra* note 519, 627.

[530]   Huebner, *supra* note 519, 627.

[531]   Geoffrey R. Stone, *Abraham Lincoln's First Amendment*, 78 N.Y.U. L. Rev. 1, 22 (2003).

[532]   Palomares, *supra* note 463, 127.

In Lincoln's constitutional "religion," "[t]he Declaration of Independence is the sacred text … and represents the interpretive key to why he acted the way he did in particular circumstances … [a]bove all, Lincoln subordinated the particular provisions of the Constitution to its overall purpose of securing liberty and the true aims of republican government."[533] Lincoln also believed the preservation of the Union was his duty under the presidential oath in the "take care" clause in the Constitution since "[a]ny attempt at secession would be a breach of the fundamental law of the land. For this reason, he treated the Confederacy as a rebellion rather than a foreign state."[534] Lincoln's understanding of the clause was that "the existence of such a constitutional duty of the president very strongly implies the existence of legitimate constitutional power on the part of the president to carry out that duty."[535] A letter Lincoln wrote to Albert Hodges, the editor of a Kentucky newspaper, on April 4, 1864, evinces his construction of constitutional necessity:[536]

> It was in the oath I took that I would, to the best of my ability, preserve, protect, and defend the Constitution of the United States. I could not take the office without taking the oath. Nor was it my view that I might take an oath to get power, and break the oath in using the power … I did understand however, that my oath to preserve the constitution to the best of my ability, imposed upon me the duty of preserving, by every indispensable means, that government— that nation—of which that constitution was the organic law. Was it possible to lose the nation, and yet preserve the constitution?"

Lincoln analogized this duty to medicine, "noting that a limb must be sometimes be amputated to save a life, but that life must never be given to save a limb." [537] This

---

[533] Adkins, *supra* note 487, 213.

[534] U.S. Const. art. II, § 3, cl. 8; Jason A. Adkins, *supra* note 487, 243.

[535] Michael Stokes Paulsen, *The Constitution of Necessity*, 79 Notre Dame L. Rev. 1257, 1263 (2004).

[536] *Abraham Lincoln to Albert G. Hodges*, The Abraham Lincoln Papers at the Library of Congress, Series 1. General Correspondence. 1833–1916, April 4, 1864, *available* at: http://memory.loc. gov/cgi-bin/ampage?collId=mal&fileName=mal1/320/3207700/malpage.db&recNum=0

[537] Stone, *supra* note 424, 88.

belief justified ignoring Taney's opinion because "[o]therwise, there are few real checks on judicial power-an absurd result for a body considered by the Founders to be the 'least dangerous [branch].'"[538]

K. Lincoln's Defense Before Congress

Lincoln defended his actions in an address to a Special Session of Congress on July 4, 1861.[539] "By addressing Congress, Lincoln ignored Taney."[540] Jason A. Adkins posits that "the question in Lincoln's mind when he ignored Taney's opinion was: "How can we let the great experiment in republican government falter because of a slavish adherence to a legal doctrine in which the Constitution was unclear in proper application?'"[541] Lincoln's famous words to Congress were:

> [T]he attention of the country has been called to the proposition that one who is sworn to 'take care that the laws be faithfully executed,' should not himself violate them. Of course some consideration was given to the questions of power, and propriety, before this matter was acted upon. The whole of the laws which were required to be faithfully executed, were being resisted, and failing of execution, in nearly one-third of the States. Must they be allowed to finally fail of execution, even had it been perfectly clear, that by the use of the means necessary to their execution, some single law, made in such extreme tenderness of the citizen's liberty, that practically, it relieves more of the guilty, than of the innocent, should, to very limited extent, be violated? To state the question more directly, are all the laws, but one, to go unexecuted, and the government itself go to pieces, lest that one be violated? Even in such a case, would not the official oath be broken, if the government should be overthrown,

---

[538]   Adkins, *supra* note 487, 239–40.

[539]   Paulsen, *supra* note 535, 1265; Williams, *supra* note 470, 324; Rehnquist, *supra* note 473, 929; Stone, *supra* note 424.

[540]   Williams, *supra* note 470, 324.

[541]   Adkins, *supra* note 487, 241.

when it was believed that disregarding the single law, would tend to preserve it?[542]

In other words, Lincoln was willing to do whatever "was necessary to prevent the government from being overthrown, even if it meant 'disregarding' a 'single law,' because the alternative was the failure to execute all the laws, but that one."[543]

L. Attorney General Bates's Defense

Lincoln asked his attorney general, Edward Bates, to address "the issue of whether the president was justified in refusing to obey a writ of habeas corpus issued by a judge."[544] On July 5, 1861,[545] Bates wrote, "'[o]ur fathers, having divided the government into co-ordinate departments ... left [them] by design ... each independent and free, to act out its own granted powers, without any ordained or legal superior possessing the power to revise and reverse its action.'"[546] Bates supported Lincoln's decisions with "the sort of arguments made first in Federalist No. 49, and thereafter by Jefferson (pardoning those convicted under the Alien and Sedition Acts) and Jackson (vetoing the Bank), that the three co-ordinate federal branches each reserve the right to interpret the Constitution."[547] Bates believed the president's power was limited; however, and his suspension of the privilege was "'temporary and exceptional.' It was temporary, however, in the sense that it applied only when there was a rebellion or invasion. It was exceptional in that it sprung into existence only when the 'ordinary course of judicial proceeding' was too weak and ineffectual."[548]

Bates concluded his argument by claiming that he "discussed habeas corpus

---

[542] Paulsen, *supra* note 535, 1265; Williams, *supra* note 470, 324; Rehnquist, *supra* note 473, 929; Stone, *supra* note 424, 121.

[543] Paulsen, *supra* note 535, 1265.

[544] Palomares, *supra* note 463, 118.

[545] Garvin, *supra* note 473, 695.

[546] Palomares, *supra* note 463, 118.

[547] Lerner, *supra* note 468, 1285 and 1289.

[548] Prakash, *supra* note 494, 582.

only because others had raised the matter," comparing it to suspending the writ of replevin in order to seize arms from enemy troops."[549] Saikrishna Bangalore Prakash explains that this claim was remarkable for two reasons:

> First, Lincoln had hinted that an Attorney General opinion would defend his assertion of suspension authority. The actual opinion, however, suggested that a defense was wholly gratuitous. Second, Lincoln's orders had authorized the suspension of the writ of habeas corpus. If Bates was right, however, these authorizations were superfluous because suspensions of habeas corpus were unnecessary. Indefinite detention of the rebels was legal even without any suspension of habeas corpus. In other words, Bates' opinion argued that all the hand-wringing (by the President, Taney, and others) about the writ of habeas corpus and any orders Lincoln had issued were much ado about nothing.[550]

M. John Merryman's Fate

John Merryman was never tried because Taney refused to participate in a trial in his capacity as a circuit judge and would not allow Merryman to be tried while he was serving as a Supreme Court justice.[551] It is very possible that Taney's obstinacy saved Merryman's life because rather than being executed under Lincoln's order, he was eventually freed on bail.[552]

II. Suspension and Arbitrary Arrests in Ohio: *Ex Parte Vallandigham*

A. General Burnside Issues General Order No. 38

Lincoln appointed General Ambrose Burnside as the commanding general of the Department of Ohio in March of 1863, assuming it was a safe position for a "'man

---

[549] Ibid., 582–83.

[550] Ibid., 583.

[551] Brennan, *supra* note 476, 224.

[552] Bracknell, *supra* note 425, 213; Brennan, *supra* note 476, 224.

of zealous and impulsive character.'"[553] When Burnside arrived in Ohio, "[h]e was appalled to discover that newspapers in Ohio were full of 'reasonable expressions' and the 'large public meetings were held, at which our Government authorities and our gallant soldiers in the field were openly and loudly denounced for their efforts to suppress the rebellion.'"[554] Burnside "assumed that it was for the military to define the boundaries of legitimate dissent that any criticism of the administration was treasonable, and that civil officials and civil courts had failed in their duty to suppress such expression."[555]

Therefore, on April 19, 1863, Burnside issued General Order No. 38, without informing Lincoln or receiving his approval.[556] The order warned that "'[t]he habit of declaring sympathy for the enemy will no longer be tolerated in this Department. Persons committing such offenses will be at once arrested' and subject to military procedures."[557] The order further stated that "'all persons found within our lines who commit acts for the benefit of the enemies of our country, will be tried as spies or traitors, and, if convicted, will suffer death.'"[558]

B. "Mr. V" Criticizes "King Lincoln"

Clement Laird Vallandigham was a prominent Ohio "Copperhead," known for his criticism of Lincoln and abolitionists, who he blamed for the war.[559] Vallandigham's philosophy was Jeffersonian, and he advocated for a limited government and popular sovereignty.[560]

Vallandigham "opposed the war, the draft, the military arrest of civilians, the

---

[553]   Stone, *supra* note 424, 95.

[554]   Ibid., 96.

[555]   Ibid., 98.

[556]   Garvin, *supra* note 473, 697; Stone, *supra* note 424, 96.

[557]   Garvin, *supra* note 473, 697; Stone, *supra* note 424, 98; Brennan, *supra* note 476, 225–26.

[558]   Williams, *supra* note 470, 329.

[559]   Adkins, *supra* note 487, 241; Stone, *supra* note 424, 98.

[560]   Stone, *supra* note 424, 98.

suspension of habeas corpus, and the Emancipation Proclamation."[561] On July 10, 1861, Vallandigham criticized Lincoln before Congress for his

> "[W]icked and hazardous experiment" of calling the people to arms without counsel and authority of Congress; with violating the Constitution in declaring a blockade of Southern ports; with "contemptuously" setting at defiance the Constitution in suspending the writ of habeas corpus; and with "coolly" coming before the Congress and pleading that he was only "preserving and protecting" the Constitution and demanding and expecting the thanks of Congress and the country for his "usurpations of power."[562]

In efforts to secure the Democratic nomination for governor of Ohio, on May 1, 1863, Vallandigham challenged Burnside's general order, and called the war "'wicked, cruel, and unnecessary."[563] Vallandigham "defended the constitutional right of people to debate the policies of the national administration."[564] Vallandigham's speech "brought cheers from the largely antiwar, anti-Lincoln crowd" of fifteen to twenty thousand.[565] Vallandigham ended his speech with the plea to the public to "'hurl King Lincoln from his throne.'"[566]

[561] Ibid.

[562] Williams, *supra* note 470, 328–29.

[563] Williams, *supra* note 470, 329; Stone, *supra* note 424, 101; Garvin, *supra* note 473, 697; Stone, *supra* note 424, 100.

[564] Ibid., 101.

[565] Ibid.

[566] Brennan, *supra* note 476, 226.

Clement L. Vallandigham, 1820-1871.
(Image courtesy of the Ohio History Connection).

C. Vallandigham's Arrest and Detention

General Burnside arrested Vallandigham without consulting the president or his superiors after two of his captains, disguised as civilians, witnessed the speech.[567] On May 5, over one hundred soldiers arrived at Vallandigham's home, arrested him, and then took him to a military prison in Cincinnati.[568] Despite Vallandigham's arguments that "he was being persecuted for mere 'word of criticisms of the public policy, of the public servants of the people,'" since no one could claim that he "'counseled disobedience to the Constitution or resistance to law or lawful authority,

---

[567]   Ibid.; Williams, *supra* note 470, 330.

[568]   Ibid.

Vallandigham was found guilty by a military tribunal."[569] After a two-day trial, he was convicted of "'publicly expressing, in violation of general Orders No. 38, ... sympathy for those in arms against the government of the United States, and declaring disloyal sentiments and opinions with the object and purpose of weakening the power of the government in its efforts to suppress an unlawful rebellion.'"[570] Vallandigham was then incarcerated at Fort Warren in Boston Harbor.[571]

Vallandigham's lawyer immediately filed a petition for a writ of habeas corpus from the circuit court in Cincinnati, arguing that he was denied due process, access to a grand jury, and opportunity to summon and confront witnesses.[572] Judge Humphrey H. Leavitt denied the writ, although it was not suspended in the area at the time.[573] Judge Leavitt's decision was a balancing test between the suspension of fundamental rights enumerated in the Constitution and the preservation of the Constitution itself.[574] Judge Leavitt's justification was that "the president ... is invested with very high powers,' and 'in deciding what he may rightfully do' under these powers, 'the president is guided solely by his own judgment and discretion, and is only amenable for an abused of his authority by impeachment.'"[575] He held that General Burnside's actions

---

[569]   Stone, *supra* note 424, 101. Judge Leavitt's opinion can be found in *ORW*, Series II, Volume 5, pp. 573–584.

[570]   Stone, *supra* note 424, 101. The transcript of the Vallandigham trial can be found at *ORW*, Series II, Volume 5, pp. 633–646. It is interesting to note that the tribunal granted Vallandigham a half-hour continuance for him to secure counsel.

[571]   Stone, *supra* note 424, 101; Williams, *supra* note 470, 330.

[572]   Stone, *supra* note 424, 11; Stone, *supra* note 424, 103.

[573]   Stone, *supra* note 531, 11; Stone, *supra* note 424, 103.

[574]   Stone, *supra* note 531, 11 ("Judge Leavitt reasoned that '[t]he court cannot shut its eyes to the grave fact that war exists, involving the most imminent public danger, and threatening the subversion and destruction of the constitution itself.' 'Self-preservation,' he added 'is a paramount law,' and this is 'not a time when anyone connected with the judicial department' should in any way 'embarrass or thwart the executive in his efforts to deliver the country from the dangers which press so heavily upon it.' In the face of a rebellion, Leavitt argued, 'the president ... is invested with very high powers,' and 'in deciding what he may rightfully do' under these powers, 'the president is guided solely by his own judgment and discretion, and is only amenable for an abuse of his authority by impeachment.'")

[575]   Stone, *supra* note 424, 103.

were reasonable in view of the "'pestilential leaven of disloyalty in the community,'" that "'must learn that they cannot stab its vitals with impunity.'"[576]

Vallandigham petitioned the Supreme Court for a writ of certiorari to review Judge Leavitt's decision, but this was also denied for lack of jurisdiction.[577] The court said:

> Whatever may be the force of Vallandigham's protest, that he was not triable by a court of military commission, it is certain that his petition cannot be brought within the [Judiciary Act of 1789]; and further, that the court cannot, without disregarding its frequent decisions and interpretations of the Constitution in respect to its judicial power, originate a writ of certiorari to review or pronounce any opinion upon the proceedings of a military commission.[578]

During his incarceration, Vallandigham continued to speak out against the government. On his first day in prison, he wrote to "the Democracy of Ohio" and "urged his fellow Democrats to 'stand firm.'"[579] Vallandigham pledged that he would "'adhere to every principle'" and "'make good through imprisonment and life itself, every pledge and declaration which [he had] ever made, uttered or maintained from the beginning.'"[580] Vallandigham maintained that he was "'in a military bastille for no other offense than [his] political opinions.'"[581]

D. Lincoln Responds to Public Outcry

While many of Lincoln's abuses of civil liberties were ignored by the press and generally accepted by the public, "the Vallandigham case was important, and newspapers did pay attention to it."[582] In Vallandigham's hometown, Dayton, Ohio, a mob of "Peace

---

[576] Stone, *supra* note 531, 11–12.

[577] Garvin, *supra* note 473, 698; Williams, *supra* note 470, 330.

[578] Garvin, *supra* note 473, 697–98.

[579] Williams, *supra* note 470, 330.

[580] Ibid.

[581] Stone, *supra* note 424, 105–06.

[582] Michael Les Benedict, *Lincoln and Constitutional Politics*, 93 Marq. L. Rev. 1333, 1350 (2010).

Democrats" burned down the Republican newspaper building.[583] Almost every major Northern city experienced a similar public outcry, spurred on by local Democratic press.[584] Many Republicans also criticized Vallandigham's detention.[585]

General Burnside was not dismayed by the public outrage. In fact, he caused further public outcry when he closed the *Chicago Times* for criticizing Lincoln's handling of the Vallandigham situation. [586] However, Judge Thomas Drummond issued a restraining order preventing "General Burnside from taking action against The *Chicago Times* or its editor Wilbur Fiske Storey."[587] Lincoln himself was extremely embarrassed and surprised by Vallandigham's arrest.[588] Once again, he was in a difficult position: should he allow the incarceration to continue, fueling secessionist movements, or undermine his own appointed general?[589] Lincoln chose to defend General Burnside's actions, while ultimately commuting Vallandigham's sentence to banishment from the Union.[590]

A group of Democrats met in May of 1863 in Albany, New York, to draft a set of resolutions criticizing Lincoln for the Vallandigham debacle. Lincoln responded to the "Albany Resolves" with two defenses: "first, the entire country was a war zone and military arrests were justified anywhere the enemy used speech or the press to conduct war; and second, the arrest was not for Vallandigham's speaking in public but for his war on the military."[591] Lincoln responded to Erastus Corning on June 29, 1863:

> You claim ... that according to my own position in the Albany response, Mr. V. should be released; and this because, as you claim, he has not damaged the military service, by discouraging enlistments,

---

[583]   Stone, *supra* note 424, 105–06.

[584]   Ibid., 105–06.

[585]   Ibid., 82.

[586]   Ibid., 107.

[587]   Ibid., 107–08.

[588]   Ibid., 108.

[589]   Ibid., 109.

[590]   Williams, *supra* note 470, 330.

[591]   Garvin, *supra* note 473, 698.

encouraging desertions, or otherwise … I certainly do not know
that Mr. V. has specifically, and by direct language, advised against
enlistments, and in favor of desertion, and resistance to drafting.
We all know that combinations, armed in some instances, to resist
the arrest of deserters, began several months ago … These had
to be met by military force, and this … has led to bloodshed and
death. And now, under a sense of responsibility more weighty and
enduring than any which is merely official, I solemnly declare my
belief that this hindrance, of the military, including maiming and
murder, is due to the course in which Mr. V. has been engaged, in
a greater degree than … to any other one man. These things have
been … known to all, and of course known to Mr. V … When it is
known that the whole burthen of his speeches has been to stir up
men against the prosecution [sic] of the war, and that in the midst of
resistance to it, he has not been known, in any instance, to counsel
against such resistance, it is next to impossible to repel the inference
that he has counseled directly in favor of it.[592]

That same month, the Ohio Democratic Convention met in Columbus to
nominate a candidate for governor.[593] They chose the still-exiled Vallandigham and
approved resolutions that challenged the suspension of the writ of habeas corpus and
demanded Vallandigham's release.[594] On June 25, Judge Mathias Birchard personally
delivered the resolutions to Lincoln at the White House.[595] Lincoln's response was
prompt, and almost identical to his response to Erastus Corning:

> "You claim that men may, if they choose, embarrass those whose
> duty it is to combat a giant rebellion, and then be dealt with in turn,
> only as if there was no rebellion. The constitution itself rejects this
> view. The military arrests and detentions, which have been made,

---

[592]   Stone, *supra* note 531, 20–21; Benedict, *supra* note 582, 1364.

[593]   Stone, *supra* note 531, 20.

[594]   Stone, *supra* note 531, 20.

[595]   Stone, *supra* note 531, 20.

including those of Mr. V. which are not different in principle from the others, have been for prevention and not for punishment—as injunctions to stay injury, as proceedings to keep the peace."[596]

Lincoln agreed to release Vallandigham if a majority of members of the committee would agree:

"1) That there is now a rebellion in the United States, the object and tendency of which is to destroy the national Union; and that in your opinion, an army and navy are constitutional means for suppressing the rebellion. 2) That no one of you will do anything which in his own judgment, will tend to hinder the increase, or favor the decrease, or lessen the efficiency of the army or navy, while engaged in the effort to suppress that rebellion; and, 3) That each of you will, in his own sphere, do all he can to have the officers, soldiers and seamen of the army and navy, while engaged in the effort to suppress the rebellion, paid, fed, clad, and otherwise well provided and supported."[597]

The *Cleveland Herald* thought the president's letter was "a perfect response" and begged everyone to read it, saying, "'[t]he temper and the abnegation of self are charming traits in the president's reply, while the sound, invulnerable logic will command the respect of every man who has sense enough to appreciate correct deductions.'"[598] Of course the Democratic press thought differently: "'[t]he president's constitutional justification for suspending habeas corpus meant that '[t]he people … have no liberties, but hold them and their lives simply at the pleasure of Mr. Lincoln. The Constitution is utterly swept away and annihilated.'"[599] The Ohio committee quickly replied, and "spurned Lincoln's concluding proposals and asked

---

[596]   Williams, *supra* note 470, 335.

[597]   Williams, *supra* note 470, 335.

[598]   Benedict, *supra* note 582, 1364–65.

[599]   Ibid., 1364–65.

for the revocation of the order of banishment, not as a favor, but as a right, without sacrifice of their dignity and self-respect."[600] Lincoln did not answer.[601]

III. Other Suspensions During Lincoln's Presidency

A. Habeas Corpus Act of 1863

The question of who could suspend the writ became moot when Congress authorized it in the 1863 Habeas Corpus Act. The Act "permitted the president the right to suspend the writ while the rebellion continued."[602] The language of the act implies that Congress "did not believe that the president had such authority under the Constitution itself," but nonetheless wanted to support the president's emergency measures."[603] The act was silent on whether Lincoln's suspensions over the past two years were authorized.[604] It also placed limits on the president's power to suspend habeas corpus.[605] It required the secretary of state and the secretary of war to provide a list of all the persons arrested by the military to the local judge.[606] It also required a judge to order prisoners who had not been indicted by a grand jury to be discharged. If either of these conditions was not met within twenty days, "any person or prisoner could petition for release."[607] While Lincoln cited the act as authorization for future suspensions,[608] he did not comply with these act's limitations.[609]

---

[600]   Williams, *supra* note 470, 335.

[601]   Ibid.

[602]   Williams, *supra* note 470, 324.

[603]   Prakash, *supra* note 494, 584.

[604]   Palomares, *supra* note 463, 122.

[605]   Palomares, *supra* note 463, 123.

[606]   Palomares, *supra* note 463, 123.

[607]   Palomares, *supra* note 463, 123.

[608]   Prakash, *supra* note 494, 585.

[609]   Palomares, *supra* note 463, 123.

B. Extent of the Suspensions under Lincoln

Not only did Lincoln exercise what he believed was his authority under the Constitution, to suspend the privilege of habeas corpus in times of "Rebellion or Invasion," but he also delegated that authority to his generals and cabinet members.[610] Lincoln's secretary of state, William H. Seward, had over eight hundred civilians arrested by the military. Lincoln granted him "authority to arrest all persons suspected of disloyalty in those areas where habeas corpus has been suspended."[611] Seward is rumored to have told the British prime minister, "'I can touch a bell on my right hand and order the arrest of a citizen in Ohio. I can touch the bell again and order the imprisonment of a citizen in New York, and no power on earth but that of the president can release them. Can the Queen of England, in her dominions, say as much?'"[612]

Despite Seward's bragging, it was Lincoln's secretary of war, Edwin M. Stanton, who truly took advantage of this power.[613] Under Stanton, the "suspension of the writ was used to arrest draft resisters and 'persons arrested for disloyal practices,'"[614] resulting the arrest of over thirteen thousand people.[615] All in all, scholars estimate that there were from thirteen thousand to thirty-eight thousand military arrests and detentions of civilians during the Civil War.[616]

C. Other Suspensions of the Writ under Lincoln

The writ of habeas corpus was suspended eight times during Lincoln's presidency.[617] Lincoln first suspended the writ around Baltimore on April 27, 1861.[618] Soon after,

---

[610]   Robert H. Jackson, *Wartime Security and Liberty Under Law*, 55 Buff. L. Rev. 1089, 1096 (2008).

[611]   Stone, *supra* note 424, 88.

[612]   Ibid., 124.

[613]   Francis P. Sempa, *The Wartime Constitution: The Charging Balance of Power Among the Three Branches of Government in Wartime*, 26 T.M. Cooley L. Rev. 25, 39 (2009).

[614]   Bracknell, *supra* note 425, 213.

[615]   Sempa, *supra* note 613, 39.

[616]   Stone, *supra* note 424, 124.

[617]   Ibid., 120.

[618]   *See supra* Section II.b.

he suspended the writ in all of Florida on May 10, 1861.[619] On June 20, Lincoln suspended the writ with regard to "Major Chase" of the Army Engineer Corps.[620] Just two days before Lincoln's speech before Congress, "he authorized General Scott to suspend the writ 'at any point, on or in the vicinity of any military line which is now, or which shall be used between the City of New York and the city of Washington.'"[621] Unlike the preceding two suspensions, which were "narrowly tailored to protect the capital from imminent attack," the suspension on July 2, 1861, "aimed to stop any resistance to the Union forces over a broad area. Furthermore, this suspension was neither directed at an imminent harm nor aimed at protecting the public safety."[622]

The next suspension order occurred on October 14, 1861. It similarly "extended the military line to Bangor, Maine, even though no record of disturbances in New England existed to justify this action".[623] The Militia Act authorized conscription in 1862.[624] Riots broke out in Pennsylvania, Wisconsin, Ohio, and Indiana.[625] Nicholas Kemp, one of the leaders of the resistance in Wisconsin, was arrested and obtained a writ of habeas corpus from the Supreme Court of Wisconsin.[626] On September 24, 1862, Lincoln issued a nationwide proclamation "'discouraging volunteer enlistments, resisting militia drafts, or guilty of any disloyal practice, affording aid and comfort to Rebels' should 'be subject to martial law and liable to trial and punishment by Courts Martial or Military Commission.'"[627] The jailer at the military prison refused because Lincoln had suspended the writ nationwide on September 24, 1862.[628] The Supreme

---

[619]   *See supra* Section II.e.

[620]   *See supra* Section II.e.; Palomares, *supra* note 432, 120.

[621]   Palomares, *supra* note 463, 120.

[622]   Ibid., 120–21.

[623]   Ibid.

[624]   Ibid., 122.

[625]   Bethany Keenan & Colby Blanchete, Northern Draft Riots. Wentworth Institute of Technology: Civil War, available at: http://blogs.wit.edu/hist-415/northern-draft-riots/

[626]   Brennan, *supra* note 476; Stone, *supra* note 424, 91–92.

[627]   Garvin, *supra* note 473, 697.

[628]   Stone, *supra* note 424, 91–92.

Court of Wisconsin held "that the president did not have the authority by himself to suspend the writ of habeas corpus, and that martial law could not control in areas of the country where there was no insurrection or combat."[629] However, the court refused to have the jailer arrested "out of respect for federal authorities."[630]

On August 8, 1862, the president empowered the secretary of war to suspend the writ.[631] On that same day Lincoln issued an order authorizing "all U.S. marshals and police chiefs to 'arrest and imprison any person or persons who may be engaged, by act, speech, or writing, in discouraging volunteer enlistments, or in any way giving aid and comfort to the enemy, or in any other disloyal practice against the United States.'"[632] Lincoln suspended the writ in Kentucky on July 5, 1864, citing his authority from the Habeas Corpus Act and the Constitution.[633]

D. Events in Ohio

Union Army records show that no fewer than three facilities held civilian prisoners under military arrest during the war. As early as July 1862, when the recordkeeping began,[634] Camp Chase held 550 civilian prisoners and 1,726 military prisoners. The number of civilian prisoners soon swelled, reaching a high of 738 in October 1862. These numbers dropped off quickly, but for the remainder of the war, Camp Chase usually held between one hundred and two hundred civilians under military arrest.[635]

MacLean Barracks held as many as many as sixty citizens in November 1863 and as few as fourteen in September 1864. No returns are recorded for Camp Chase after December 1864. Records also show that the Ohio Penitentiary housed one civilian

---

[629]   Brennan, *supra* note 476, 225.

[630]   Brennan, *supra* note 476, 225; Stone, *supra* note 29, 91–92.

[631]   Palomares, *supra* note 463, 121–22.

[632]   Ibid.

[633]   Prakash, *supra* note 463, 582.

[634]   A War Department Circular dated 7 July 1862 required returns on prisoners. Those individuals, both civilian and military, detained in civilian prisons and hospitals are not counted in the returns. Other returns do not distinguish between civilian and military prisoners.

[635]   *ORW*, Series II, Volume 8, pp. 986–1004.

under military arrest in February and March 1864.[636] Other records indicate that Johnson's Island housed civilians "who were deemed disloyal to the Union."[637]

IV. The Final Word: *Ex Parte Milligan*

A. Background

The final member of our triumvirate of Civil War individual rights cases is *Ex Parte Milligan*.[638] Milligan is significant because it was the first such case decided after the war was over, and the issue of civil liberties was easier to discuss. A Latin maxim provides that: *silent leges inter arma*, which means that during times of war the laws are silent and the guns speak. With *Milligan,* the court could calmly reflect on issues in a more rational way than when the war was raging. The principal defendant, Lambdin Purdy Milligan, like Vallandigham, was a vocal opponent of President Lincoln and the war. Like Vallandigham, Milligan was arrested, tried by a military commission, and sentenced to death. Unlike Vallandigham, when Milligan's death sentence was forwarded to Lincoln for approval, Lincoln returned the commission's record for correction of certain errors. Lincoln was assassinated before the record was returned to him, and Milligan's conviction was quickly approved by Lincoln's successor, President Andrew Johnson.

Born in Belmont County, Ohio, Milligan studied law with Edwin M. Stanton, Lincoln's future secretary of war. When he completed his law studies, Milligan married, moved to Fort Wayne, Indiana, and opened a law practice. Dissatisfied with Lincoln's conduct of the war, particularly the Emancipation Proclamation, Milligan joined the Knights of the Golden Circle, a secret political society hostile to the government. Founded in the 1850s, the Knights' purpose was to colonize a Mexico that permitted slavery and to align this new country with the American South. After

---

[636] Ibid.

[637] Docnews.com-the magazine. *Rebel Soldiers Lived and Died in Johnson's Island Prison on Lake Erie.* Available at: http://www.docsnews.com/johnsons.html

[638] *Ex Parte Milligan*, 71 U.S. (4 Wall.) 2 (1866).

some public disclosure of its activities, the members changed the society's name to the Order of the Sons of Liberty (OSL), and Milligan became a prominent member.[639]

B. Unrest in the Heartland

By 1863, many citizens of the states in the Old Northwest Territory were becoming disillusioned by the war. A series of Union defeats on the battlefield coupled with an unpopular draft law cooled the ardor of some of these individuals. States like Ohio, which had opposed slavery from the beginning of its history, still opposed granting full citizenship to African Americans. By issuing the Emancipation Proclamation, Lincoln changed the nature of the war from preserving the Union to abolishing slavery. In the election of 1862, the Democrats gained control of the state legislatures in Indiana, Illinois, and Ohio. Battlefield successes for the Union were for few and far between during this period, and the farmers in these states felt they were being gouged by railroads who charged excessively high prices to ship their goods to market.

Indiana, like Ohio and Illinois, was initially settled by transplanted Southerners who migrated down the Ohio River or through the Cumberland Gap. Starting in the 1820s, these settlers were joined by immigrants from New York and New England, traveling across New York State via the newly completed Erie Canal. By 1860, all three states had a significant portion of their population with close ties, both familial and economic, to the Southern states. In the political culture of the day, the Democratic Party stood for states' rights and generally favored the institution of slavery. Conversely, the new Republican Party desired a strong federal government and the abolition of slavery. Milligan, a staunch Democrat, spoke out loudly and often about his opposition to Lincoln's policies, which quickly became known to Indiana Republicans.

---

[639] At about the same time, Union supporters formed "Union Clubs" or "Loyalty Leagues." One of the goals of these organizations was to spy on the Democratic societies and individual suspected of disloyalty. Gilbert Treadway, *Democratic Opposition to the Lincoln Administration in Indiana* (Indianapolis, IN: Indiana Historical Bureau, 1973), 122–23; James M. McPherson, *Battle Cry of Freedom* (New York, Oxford University Press), 599.

Milligan was not alone in his sentiments. The *Fort Wayne Sentinel* expressed the following opinion and editorial dated September 27, 1862:

> The Constitution has been set aside, freedom of speech and the press destroyed, are citizens subjected to arbitrary arrests, and the right of habeas corpus suspended. If the overthrow of the Constitution … Is to be excused on the plea of military necessity, it must be obvious that the sooner the war is brought to an end the better.[640]

C. Governor Morton Responds

Two events served to galvanize the Republican response to the secret societies in Indiana. The first event was a Democratic triumph in the elections of November 1862. Although Governor Oliver Morton, a Republican and staunch Lincoln ally, was not up for election, the Democrats took over the Indiana legislature. The second event was the raid of Confederate General John Hunt Morgan into Indiana during the summer of 1863. General Henry Carrington, the commander of the Military District of Indiana, predicted that Morgan's forces could be potentially joined by as many as twenty thousand Indiana citizens, and that the secret societies had persuaded Morgan to invade the state.[641]

A failed assassination attempt against Governor Morton strengthened the governor's resolve to wipe out the secret societies.[642] Morton continued his attacks against the societies from the lectern while Carrington increased the surveillance against the societies. Once Morgan's troops were forced from the state, the panic

---

[640] Treadway, *supra* note 639, 24.

[641] William Dudley Foulke, *Life of Oliver P. Morton* (Indianapolis, IN: The Bowen-Merrill Company, 1899), 374.

[642] Treadway, *supra* note 639, 383–84.

subsided somewhat, but by the summer of 1864, another election, and still another threat of invasion, increased the scrutiny again.[643]

D. The Plot

The Democratic National Convention was to convene in Chicago in late August 1864. Confederate agents and sympathizers were scheduled to be in Chicago at the same time, and some plans were made to secure a cache of arms, free the Confederate prisoners held at Camp Douglas, near Chicago, and start an uprising.[644] Acting on a tip, Carrington's soldiers raided the office of Harrison H. Dodd, the "Grand Commander" of the order in Indiana. The soldiers seized hundreds of firearms and thousands of rounds of ammunition, and perhaps more importantly, correspondence that linked several prominent Democratic politicians, including Milligan, to the Order of the Sons of Liberty.[645]

Carrington, using the information he had discovered in the raid, ordered the arrest of Dodd, Milligan, William Bowles, Stephen Horsey, Andrew Humphries, Horace Heffren, and J.J. Bingham.[646] Carrington wanted to try the prisoners in federal court; however, he bowed to the wishes of Governor Morton and War Secretary Edwin M. Stanton to try the defendants before a military commission.

---

[643] Morgan was captured by Union forces in late July 1863. He was imprisoned in the Ohio State Penitentiary but escaped his confinement in November and returned to active service. In June 1864, Morgan led his troops into Kentucky and threatened to cross the Ohio River a second time. Morgan was killed in September 1864 during a raid near Greenville, Tennessee. Lester V. Horwitz, *The Longest Raid of the Civil War* (Cincinnati: Farmcourt Publishing, Inc., 2001), 356–78.

[644] The plan was remarkably similar in scope and intent to John Brown's Harper's Ferry Raid in 1859.

[645] A similar plot was unfolding in Ohio at about the same time. Confederate agents and sympathizers planned to steal a steamboat on Lake Erie, capture a federal gunboat, and use the gunboat to free the Confederate prisoners held at Johnson's Island. The newly freed prisoners would then travel to Camp Chase in Columbus, free the prisoners held there, and conduct raids throughout Ohio. The perpetrators were captured soon after they stole the steamboat, and the plot came to nothing. Kern & Wilson. *supra* note 161, 232–33.

[646] Major Henry Burnett, the judge advocate, estimated that some three to four hundred prisoners were being held at the Soldiers' Home after the OSL arrests. Treadway, *supra* note 639, 219.

Dodd's trial began on September 17, 1864, but before the trial concluded, he escaped from confinement and fled to Canada. The commission convicted him *in absentia* and sentenced him to death.[647]

E. Trial by a Military Commission

Bingham, who was the editor of the *Indianapolis Sentinel*, was released, but the remaining five defendants faced the commission in October in what was called the Indianapolis Treason Trials, even though none of the defendants were charged with treason.[648]

Milligan and his cohorts were charged with "conspiracy against the government of the United States," "affording aid and comfort to rebels," "inciting insurrection," "disloyal practices," and "violations of the laws of war," none of which were part of the US Criminal Code. Further, the defendants were not accorded many of the rights of defendants facing trial in federal court. Under the Sixth Amendment, defendants are entitled to:

> … A speedy and public trial, by an impartial jury of the State and
> District wherein the crime shall have been committed …[649]

In contrast, when tried before a military commission, a defendant has no guarantee that members of the commission be residents of Indiana, and a unanimous verdict was not required for conviction. In addition, the defendant tried before a military commission has no protection against *ex post facto* laws, as guaranteed to civil defendants in Article I of the Constitution. The deck was clearly stacked against the defendants from the beginning.

The trial began on October 21, 1864, and the testimony ended on December 1. A review of the testimony showed damning evidence against Dodd, but little against the other defendants other than attending a few meetings, accepting offices in the organization, and making some vague plans. The charges against Heffren were dropped midtrial, and Humphreys' sentence of hard labor for the duration of the

---

[647] Rehnquist, *supra* note 473, 82–4.

[648] Ibid.

[649] U.S. Const. amend. VI.

war was commuted to parole by General Hovey, who had succeeded Carrington. Milligan, Bowles, and Horsey were found guilty and sentenced to be hanged. The commission then forwarded a record of the trial to President Lincoln for approval, but by that time Lincoln had been handily reelected, the war was winding down, and punishment was no longer the order of the day.

F. Temporary Reprieve

Once the record was returned, President Andrew Johnson, who had succeeded Lincoln, quickly approved the sentences, and General Hovey set the execution date for May 9, 1865.

Just prior to the scheduled execution date, lawyers for the Milligan, Bowles, and Horsey filed a petition for a writ of habeas corpus with the circuit court. Johnson, perhaps bowing to popular opinion, commuted the sentence of Horsey to life imprisonment and granted a stay of execution until June 1 for the two remaining defendants.[650] By the end of May, Johnson had commuted the sentences of Milligan and Horsey and Bowles to life imprisonment. Despite the commutation, the petition for habeas corpus went forward. The petitioners continued to argue that the military court could not sentence them.

The case was heard by Supreme Court Justice David Davis,[651] sitting in his capacity as circuit judge, and David McDonald, a recently appointed district judge. The judges were in a difficult position. If they issued the writ, the military was likely to disregard it, as they had disregarded Chief Justice Taney's writ in *Merryman*. Instead, after hearing testimony, the judges issued a split decision and certified the issue to the U.S. Supreme Court for resolution.

G. US Supreme Court

Oral arguments before the Supreme Court began on March 6, 1866, and continued for six days. Ohio was well represented among the appellate counsel, with Henry

---

650   Rehnquist, *supra* note 473, 104.

651   Davis and Lincoln had ridden the Eighth Judicial Circuit in Illinois together. Davis served as Lincoln's campaign manager in 1860 and helped him to secure the Republican presidential nomination that year. Lincoln appointed Davis as associate justice of the Supreme Court in 1862.

Stanbery, future US attorney general, and Johnson's lead counsel during his impeachment proceedings, as well as current Attorney General James Speed, and Benjamin Butler, current Massachusetts congressman and former Union major general representing the government. Congressman and former Union Major General James Garfield,[652] former attorney general and Secretary of State Jeremiah Black, Ohio native and future Indiana Senator Joseph E. McDonald, and David Dudley Field, brother of Justice Stephen J. Field, represented the petitioners.[653]

Oral arguments ended on March 13, 1866, and on April 3, the court issued an order directing that the writ should issue. The opinion itself was not released until December. Justice Davis wrote the majority opinion, joined by Justices Field, Nelson, Clifford, and Grier. Chief Justice Chase wrote a concurring opinion, joined by Justices Swayne, Miller, and Wayne.

Both court factions agreed that the defendants' trials by military commission were contrary to law and that they should be released from confinement. Both factions also agreed that the Bill of Rights could be suspended during times of war or rebellion. Davis opined that civilians could not be tried in a military court so long as the civilian courts were open and operating. Davis also opined that neither Congress nor the president could authorize military trials under these circumstances. Chase, conversely, wrote that under the Habeas Corpus Act of 1863, Congress could authorize such trials, even though Congress never tried to do so.[654]

This split decision occurred because the court attempted to address an issue that was not before it; whether Congress could authorize military commissions to try civilian defendants when the federal courts were open and operating. All the justices agreed that the *Milligan* commission was contrary to law and that the guarantees contained in the Bill of Rights were not suspended during wartime. The inclusion of *obiter dicta* by the justices resulted in a far lesser impact than a unanimous opinion on the issue before it would have had.

---

[652] Garfield made his first oral argument in any courtroom here. Allen Peskin, *Garfield: A Biography* (Kent, OH: Kent State University Press, 1978), 270.

[653] Rehnquist, *supra* note 473, 118–26.

[654] Ibid., 128–29.

The *Milligan* decision could have caused a severe blow to Congress's attempts at reconstructing the governments in the southern states. Although the court did not address the issue, Radical Reconstruction included the installation of military governments in the former Confederate states. The court could have easily applied the doctrine to determine the insurrection was over and that martial law could not be used indefinitely in these conquered regions.

Although Davis's opinion was a stunning reversal of his policies, Governor Morton suffered little or no political backlash for his actions. His actions seeking clemency for the condemned men greatly gained him more publicity than his role in their arrests and trials, which were largely orchestrated by General Hovey. Morton continued as governor, and in 1867 he was elected to the US Senate. He remained in that post until his death ten years later.[655]

Summary

Seven southern states enacted Ordinances of Secession in the weeks after Lincoln's election. These states formed the Confederate States of America with its capital in Montgomery, Alabama, and Jefferson Davis as its first president. Hostilities began when Confederate forces in Charleston, South Carolina, opened fire on the federal garrison at Fort Sumter, located in Charleston Harbor.

In response, Lincoln called forth the state militias, suspended habeas corpus, and declared a naval blockade of all southern ports; he also assumed near-dictatorial powers to preserve the Union. During this period, Ohioans were subjected to infringements on their rights of speech and press, suspension of habeas corpus, arrests without trials, and trials of civilians by military commission, among others. These infringements certainly violated the rights of Ohioans under both the federal and the state Bill of Rights. Most of the infringements were the result of federal, not state action, and most of these infringements ceased after the conflict.

Ohio was quick to respond to Lincoln's call. Ohio Governor William Dennison quickly dispatched two Ohio regiments to Washington to protect the capital. He also sent troops to Western Virginia to guard the line of the Baltimore & Ohio Railroad and to drive Confederate troops from the area.

---

[655] Treadway, *supra* note 639, 254–255.

Ohio's military and political leaders had a prominent role in the conflict. Ohio's generals, including Ulysses Grant, William Sherman, and Philip Sheridan, led the armies while over three hundred fifty thousand of their fellow Ohioans served in the ranks. Future presidents Grant, Rutherford B. Hayes, James A. Garfield, Benjamin Harrison, and William McKinley held commissions in the Union Army. Although only one military campaign occurred within the state boundaries, that being Morgan's Raid in July 1863, over thirty-five thousand Ohioans lost their lives during the war.

Chapter 8

Preserving the Fruits of Victory

> I repeat again, the people of the United States have the right to say when those rebels may again exercise the rights and powers of States in the Union, and, in my judgment, should see that they are not so restored except upon conditions of security for the future, if not also indemnity for the past.
>
> —John A. Bingham, 1865

I. Introduction

The surrender of General Robert E. Lee and the ratification of the Thirteenth Amendment to the Constitution in 1865 created a whole new set of problems for the now-reunited country. The Union had incurred a huge war debt that needed to be paid, and the fate of some 4 million former African slaves, emancipated by the Thirteenth Amendment, had to be resolved. Meanwhile, several Southern states passed "Black Codes" meant to restrict the freedom of the former slaves. Vigilante groups such as the Ku Klux Klan terrorized freedmen who attempted to vote, run for political office, or purchase land.

Furthermore, the issue of whether former Confederates should be allowed to vote and hold office needed resolution. Throughout the South, former Confederate military officers and government officials were elected to local and national offices while the former slaves were denied the right to vote. President Johnson, who supported a moderate approach to Reconstruction and reunification, was issuing wholesale pardons to former Confederates and was attempting to reconstruct the governments of the Southern states without congressional input.

Nearly three hundred twenty thousand Ohioans served during the four-year conflict, over thirty-five thousand of these were killed, and many times that number were wounded or permanently disabled by illness. After such catastrophic losses, it is not surprising that Ohioans would think that to merely win the war was not enough. Instead, they needed to take measures to ensure that the issues that led to the war were fully resolved.[656]

The feelings of many Ohioans were expressed by first-term Congressman Martin Welker, who in a speech before Congress on reconstruction policy, declared:

> Let these men so lately engaged in the rebellion have time to satisfy us that they are thoroughly cured of many of the heresies they have heretofore entertained. They can afford to wait after what they have done against their Government, after the great injury they have inflicted upon the country-the deluge of blood, the ravages of war they have caused all over our broad land, the widows and orphans may have made, the crippled and maimed soldiers they have scattered everywhere among us. There is much for them to do in the way of improvements and reforms in their localities before they are ready to assume all responsibilities of Government. As a matter of law most of them have forfeited their lives, and if the laws were enforced strictly against them, many of them would be hung for treason, as they ought to be. They should remember that during these bloody four years they have caused the sacrifice of millions of precious lives and thousands of millions of treasure in this mad attempt to disconnect themselves from the Government, and establish forever the infernal institution of slavery.[657]

The Thirty-Ninth Congress left its own mark on the Reconstruction Era.

---

[656] William E. Nelson, *The 14th Amendment from Political Principle to Judicial Doctrine* (Cambridge, MA: Harvard University Press, 1988), 61; Robert D. Sawrey, *Dubious Victory: The Reconstruction Debate in Ohio* (Lexington, KY: University of Kentucky Press, 1992).

[657] Congressional Globe, Thirty-Ninth Cong., First Sess., 727 (1866).

II. The Thirty-Ninth Congress

William Horatio Barnes chronicled, and Richard L. Aynes summarized,[658] the history of the Thirty-Ninth Congress. Aynes's work was published as part of the University of Akron Constitutional Law Center Thirty-Ninth Congress Project. The project[659] is an excellent source of research material and biographical summaries of members of the Thirty-Ninth Congress.[660] Magliocca referred to this Congress as "the most important Congress since the first one in 1789."[661]

The Thirty-Ninth Congress held session from March 4, 1865, to March 3, 1867.[662] When the session began, Abraham Lincoln was still president and the Civil War was still in progress. Robert E. Lee surrendered his army to Ulysses S. Grant on April 9, 1865, but Confederate troops were in the field and fighting until almost the end of 1865. President Johnson did not declare the insurrection to be officially at an end until August 20, 1866.[663] [664]

Because of the election of 1864, the Republican majority in the House of Representatives increased from 56 percent to 77 percent, and the Republican percentage in the US Senate increased from 64 percent to 79 percent. This majority gained for the Republicans not only a veto-proof Congress, but also the supermajority

---

[658] Richard L. Aynes, *The Thirty-Ninth Congress (1865–1867) and the 14th Amendment: Some Preliminary Perspectives.* 42 Akron Law Rev. 1019 (2009).

[659] More information about the Thirty-Ninth Congress Project is available online at: http://www.uakron.edu/law/constitutionallaw/39th-congress-project/

[660] William Horatio Barnes, *History of the Thirty-Ninth Congress of the United States* (New York: Harper and Brothers Publishers, 1868).

[661] Gerard N. Magliocca, *American Founding Son: John Bingham and the Invention of the Fourteenth Amendment* (New York: NYU Press, 2013), 110.

[662] Ohio's Delegation to the Thirty-Ninth Congress is listed in Appendix C.

[663] Aynes, *supra* note 658, 5–6.

[664] It was assumed that peace would restore the constitutional checks and balances that were in place before the war. Some scholars have suggested that it was up to the national government to decide exactly when peace had arrived. This gave the national government the ability to extract concessions from the former Confederate states in exchange for a declaration that peace had been restored. Michael Les Benedict, *A Compromise of Principle Congressional Republicans and Reconstruction, 1863–1869*, first ed. (Norton, 1974).

necessary to propose constitutional amendments. This majority not only allowed the Congress to ignore veto threats from the president, but it also gave them very little incentive to negotiate with the Democratic minority.[665] In addition to their overwhelming congressional majority, the prestige and authority of the US. Supreme Court had been in decline since the *Dred Scott* decision, so the actions of Congress could go virtually unchallenged.

Three great challenges faced the Thirty-Ninth Congress: 1) the losses of life and property in the war; 2) the uncertainty about whether the war was really over; and 3) the enormity of the task of economic and political reconstruction.[666]

During its term, the Thirty-Ninth Congress passed 714 pieces of legislation, more than any Congress had passed up to that time.[667] Included in the legislation enacted by this Congress was: 1) the Civil Rights Act of 1866; 2) the extension of the Freedman's Bureau for another two years; and 3) the Fourteenth Amendment.[668] Congress also established the Joint Committee of Fifteen on Reconstruction, made up of leading members of the House and Senate, and tasked this committee with addressing the issues involved in securing a final peace.[669] This Congress also enacted the Judicial Circuits Act,[670] which reduced the number of federal circuits from ten to nine and the number of Supreme Court Justices from nine to seven.

Ohio's contribution to the Thirty-Ninth Congress came from John Armor Bingham.

---

[665]   Barnes, *supra* note 660, 577–624.

[666]   Aynes *supra* note 658, 4.

[667]   In contrast, the 113th Congress enacted fewer than sixty bills from the beginning of 2013 through December 26, 2013. CNN Political Unit. *Poll: This is a 'do-nothing' Congress.* Available at: http://politicalticker.blogs.cnn.com/2013/12/26/poll-this-is-a-do-nothing-congress/

[668]   14 Stat.1–809 (1865–1867).

[669]   Benjamin B. Kendrick, *The Journal of the Joint Committee of Fifteen on Reconstruction*, 155–69 (1914).

[670]   Sess. 1, ch. 210, 14 Stat. 209.

III. John Armor Bingham

John Armor Bingham (1815–1900), then serving as congressman from Ohio's Sixteenth House District, was the principal author of section 1 of the Fourteenth Amendment. Born in Pennsylvania, Bingham moved to Ohio, studied law at Franklin College,[671] and began a law practice in 1840. Bingham served as district attorney for Tuscarawas County from 1846 to 1849.

Elected to Congress in 1855, he served until defeated for reelection in 1863. After his defeat, President Lincoln appointed Bingham as judge advocate; he served in this capacity during the trial of the Lincoln assassination conspirators and as chairman of the seven House managers in the impeachment trial of President Andrew Johnson.[672]

As early as 1859, Bingham had argued that "whenever the Constitution guarantees to its citizens a right, either natural or conventional, such a guarantee is in itself a limitation upon the States."[673] Bingham's view was contrary to the precedent established by the US Supreme Court in its holdings in *Barron v. Baltimore*[674] and *Livingston v. Moore*.[675] In those cases the court found that the Fifth Amendment's guarantee that government takings of private property for public use required just compensation and are restrictions on the federal government alone. By 1866, Bingham was advocating a constitutional amendment binding the states to the Bill

---

[671]   Magliocca describes Franklin College as "a haven for abolitionists led by a member of the Underground Railroad," and suggests that Bingham's relationship with Titus Basfield, an ex-slave and one of the first African-Americans to receive a college degree in Ohio, influenced his opposition to slavery and his belief in racial equality. Gerard N. Magliocca, *The Father of the 14th Amendment*, The New York Times Opinionator, September 17, 2013. available at: http://opinionator.blogs.nytimes.com/2013/09/17/the-father-of-the-14th-amendment/?_r=0

[672]   Magliocca, *supra* note 661, 111.

[673]   Cong. Globe, Thirty-Fifth Cong., Second Sess. 982 (1859).

[674]   *Barron v. Baltimore,* 32 U.S. (7 Pet.) 243 (1833).

[675]   *Lessee of Livingston v. Moore,* 32 U.S. (7 Pet.) 469 (1833).

of Rights.[676] Bingham was not the first person to refer to the first ten amendments as the "Bill of Rights," but his use of that term was innovative for that time.[677]

John Armor Bingham, 1815-1900.
(Image courtesy of the Ohio History Connection).

Despite being a freshman congressman, Bingham had a formidable reputation in Washington due to his previous congressional service, the fame he gained from the Lincoln Conspirators Trial, and because he represented Ohio, a large and

---

[676]   Cong. Globe, Thirty-Ninth Cong., First Sess. 1088–94 (1866).

[677]   For example, both Article VIII of Ohio's 1802 Constitution and Article I of Ohio's 1851 Constitution were entitled "Bill of Rights."

influential state. Bingham needed to craft the proposed amendment in such terms as to satisfy the competing interests of President Johnson and his followers, who thought that no amendment was necessary at all, with those of Thaddeus Stevens and the Radical Republicans, who believed that a much harsher Reconstruction policy was required.[678] Bingham wasted no time in introducing a proposed amendment seeking to "empower Congress to pass all necessary and proper laws to secure to all persons in every State of the Union equal protection in their rights, life, liberty and property."[679]

Rather than act on Bingham's proposed amendment, Congress established the Joint Committee on Reconstruction, consisting of six members from the Senate and nine members from the House, including Bingham. The Committee became known as the Committee of Fifteen, with twelve members from the Republican Party and the remaining three from the Democrats,[680] leading to the enactment of the Fourteenth Amendment.

IV. The Fourteenth Amendment

Before the Civil War, few individual rights merited protection from the national government. The founding fathers saw state officials as the most likely threat to human rights, since human affairs were mostly governed by the states. Most states, including Ohio, wrote specific guarantees protecting individual rights into their state constitutions, and they looked to state courts as guarantors of individual rights.[681] To protect the civil rights of the newly freed slaves, particularly in the former Confederate states, Congress passed the Civil Rights Act of 1866 over President Johnson's veto. However, many politicians, including the Radical Republicans,

---

[678]   Magliocca, *supra* note 661, 114–115.

[679]   Ibid., 110–111, quoting Cong. Globe, Thirty-Ninth Cong., First Sess.14 (1865).

[680]   *Civil Rights Debate,* Harpweek: Explore History. Text, Illustrations and Cartoons from the Pages of Harper Weekly., Winter 1865–1866: Congressional Joint Committee on Reconstruction. Available at: http://14thamendment.harpweek.com/HubPages/CommentaryPage.asp?Commentary=02Committee

[681]   Archibald Cox, *The Court and the Constitution* (Boston: Houghton Mifflin Company, 1987), 111–113.

supported a constitutional amendment guaranteeing African American rights rather than relying on temporary political majorities.[682]

A. The Debates

The state of Ohio played a leading role in the drafting and ratification of the Fourteenth Amendment, thought by some scholars to be the most important amendment to the Constitution.[683] The purpose of the Fourteenth Amendment was to finally settle the issues that led to the US Civil War. This amendment created a constitutional definition of US and state citizenship, and prohibited the abridgment of privileges and immunities of US citizens. The amendment secured the rights of equal protection and due process of law, determined the basis of representation in Congress, disqualified individuals from holding office if they had previously taken an oath to support the Constitution and later joined the rebellion, guaranteed the (US) public debt while repudiating the Confederate debt, and granted Congress the authority to enforce the amendment by enacting the appropriate legislation.

James Madison, future president and principal author of the Virginia Plan at the Federal (Constitutional) Convention of 1787, kept an unofficial record of the daily proceedings in the convention that drafted the US Constitution. Madison's notes are the only comprehensive record of what occurred during the convention and have served as a valuable historical tool in discerning the intent of the drafters.

Like the Constitutional Convention, the debates surrounding the framing of the Fourteenth Amendment are veiled in secrecy. Unfortunately, the Joint Committee of Fifteen had no Madison present to transcribe the daily debates and other activities that led to the enactment of the Fourteenth Amendment. In his essay *Debating the Fourteenth Amendment, The Promise and Perils of Using Congressional*

---

[682] Lawrence Goldstone, *Inherently Unequal: The Betrayal of Equal Rights by The Supreme Court, 1865–1903* (Walker & Company, 2011).

[683] Bernard Hibbitts. *Law Professor prompts Ohio to ratify 14ᵗʰ Amendment.* Jurist: Paper Chase Newsburst, March 17, 2003, available at: http://jurist.org/paperchase/2003/03/law-professor-prompts-ohio-to-ratify.php

Sources,[684] Professor Daniel Hamilton describes the limits and possibilities of using congressional sources to write the history of the Fourteenth Amendment.

Hamilton dissected Fourteenth Amendment originalism into its two component parts: that originalism practiced by lawyers and judges and that practiced by historians and constitutional scholars. The first group used originalism to answer constitutional questions, while the second group were seeking answers to questions such as: 1) Did the framers of the amendment intend to apply the Bill of Rights to the states? Did the framers intend to prohibit individual discrimination or just state action? Did they intend to prohibit racial discrimination? These questions remain unanswered, since the framers left no definitive record of their intent.[685]

B. The Joint Committee of Fifteen

The Joint Committee of Fifteen first met on January 6, 1866. The early meetings focused on the issue of apportionment, but on January 12, Bingham introduced his first draft of the proposed amendment, which read as follows:

> The Congress shall have power to make all laws necessary and proper to secure to all persons in every state within this Union equal protection in their rights of life, liberty and property.[686]

It is apparent that Bingham favored African American suffrage, but when asked about the subject, he replied, "I will answer with all of my heart that I am ready to go for that. But a majority of those with whom I am associated think that this is all that is needed at present."[687]

The Committee met again on April 21, 1866, and Congressmen Stevens introduced the second draft of the amendment, which was substantially similar to the final product. Bingham moved to delete Section 1 of the current draft, which

---

[684]   *Making Legal History: Essays in Honor of William E. Nelson* (quoting Daniel W. Hamilton. *Debating the Fourteenth Amendment: The Promise and Perils of Using Congressional Sources,* (Hulsebosch & Bernstein, eds., New York University Press, 2013).

[685]   Ibid., 76–77.

[686]   Kendrick, *supra* note 669, 46 (1914).

[687]   Cong. Globe, Thirty-Ninth Cong., First Sess. 431 (1866).

prohibited discrimination based on race, color, or previous condition of servitude, and substitute his language, which became the final version of Section 1.[688]

Section 1 of the proposed amendment contained four important clauses: the citizenship clause; the privileges and immunities clause; the due process clause; and the equal protection clause. The citizenship clause specifically repudiated the holding of the US Supreme Court in the *Dred Scott Decision*.[689] The privileges and immunities clause was crafted in broad terms to protect liberty, human dignity, or property from governmental action. The due process clause protects against any act of Congress or a state that is unduly restrictive to the enjoyment of personal liberty, the use of property, or fundamental rights. The equal protection clause was designed to protect the former slaves, but in practice it extended to women, minorities, and other victims of discrimination.[690] As with the recently ratified Thirteenth Amendment, the final section granted Congress the power to enforce the prohibitions by appropriate legislation.

Historians today spend most of their time discussing Section 1 of the amendment. However, politicians of the day considered other sections more important. Congressmen Stevens once declared that Section 2 and Section 3, addressing apportionment and enfranchisement of former Confederates to be far more critical as these would determine control of the country for the next several years.[691]

C. Enactment and Ratification

The Fourteenth Amendment passed the House by a vote of 128–37, with Bingham delivering the final speech in support. Ohio's delegation voted strictly on party lines, with the nineteen Republicans voting in favor of the amendment and the two Democrats voting against. The Senate approved the measure by a vote of 33–11, with both of Ohio's Senators voting in favor. The House approved the Senate's amendments to the bill on June 13, 1866.[692] The Radicals were happy with the

---

[688]   *History of Ohio Law*, supra note 42, 383.

[689]   *Dred Scott v. Sandford*, 60 U.S. 393 (1857), discussed *supra*.

[690]   Cox, *supra* note 681, 112–113.

[691]   Amar, supra note 14.

[692]   Aynes, *supra* note, 658, 384–385.

amendment but disappointed that it did not secure political rights, including the right to vote, for the former slaves.[693]

Connecticut was the first state to ratify the new amendment on June 30, 1866, and by the end of that year six states, including Tennessee, had ratified. Twenty-two states ratified by June 1867, and on July 9, 1868, South Carolina, the twenty-eighth state, ratified.[694] In the meantime, two states, Ohio and New Jersey, attempted to rescind their ratifications.[695] Congress refused to recognize the two states' attempt to rescind ratification, and on July 20, 1868, Secretary of State Seward certified that the amendment had become part of the Constitution.[696]

The Fourteenth Amendment became the foundation for sustaining the Union and readmitting the rebel states. The Fourteenth Amendment would later serve as the legal basis for the desegregating public schools, securing equality for women, and creating a right of privacy.[697] Today, the Fourteenth Amendment is the basis of more litigation than all other provisions of the Constitution.[698]

V. The Reconstruction Era 1863-1877

The rejection of the Fourteenth Amendment by ten of the Southern states posed a dilemma for Congress. Since there were thirty-six states at the time, including the states still "excluded" from Congress, some twenty-seven states needed to ratify the amendment for it to become law. Proponents of the amendment offered three proposals to ensure ratification: 1) Admit more states to the Union; 2) keep the ten holdout states in political limbo until they ratified the amendment; and, 3) declare

---

[693] Congress enacted the Fifteenth Amendment two years later to address those concerns.

[694] Joseph B. James, *The Ratification of the Fourteenth Amendment* (Macon, GA: Mercer University Press, 1984), 11–219.

[695] Ibid., 282–286. Both states subsequently re-ratified the amendment in 2003.

[696] Ibid., 294–298.

[697] Brown v. Board of Education of Topeka, 347 U.S 483 (1954); West Coast Hotel v. Parrish, 300 U.S. 379 (1937); and Griswold v. Connecticut, 381 U.S. 479 (1965) are probably the best-known examples.

[698] Felix Frankfurter, *John Marshall and the Judicial Function.* 69 Harv. L. Rev. 217, 229 (1955). ("[The 14th Amendment] is probably the largest source of the Court's business.").

that the ten holdouts to not be "states" to ratifying the amendment. None of these proposals was considered to be politically viable.

Instead, the Thirty-Ninth Congress enacted the Reconstruction Acts on March 2, 1867. This series of four acts established military rule for the former Confederate states and required that each seceding state draft a new state Constitution, ratify the Fourteenth Amendment, and grant voting rights to African American males before their congressional delegates would be seated.[699] The initial legislation was entitled "an act to provide for the more efficient government of the Rebel States" and was codified as March 2, 1867, 14 Stat. 428-430, c. 153. This act and the remaining three acts passed by Congress on March 23, 1867, July 19, 1867, and March 11, 1868, applied to all the former Confederate states except Tennessee, which had already ratified the Fourteenth Amendment and was readmitted to the Union. When the original Reconstruction Act was presented to President Johnson for approval, he promptly vetoed it, and Congress promptly overrode his veto.[700]

Soon, the term *Reconstruction* became synonymous with the era from 1863 to 1877. Most scholars agree that Reconstruction began with the Emancipation Proclamation, on January 1, 1863, and concluded with the informal Compromise of 1877. Historians typically divide Reconstruction into three separate eras: 1) Wartime Reconstruction, from January 1, 1863, until the termination of hostilities in 1865; 2) Presidential Reconstruction, from the end of the war until after the congressional elections of 1866; and 3) congressional (Radical) Reconstruction, from the 1866 elections until the end of the era in 1877.

A. Wartime Reconstruction

President Lincoln announced his first plan for Reconstruction on December 8, 1863. Entitled a "Proclamation of Amnesty and Reconstruction," Lincoln established a plan for full pardon and restoration of rights, except the right to own slaves, to individuals in the seceding states. Some individuals, most notably high Confederate civil and military officials, were excluded. When 10 percent of the electorate in 1860

---

[699] Eric Foner, *Reconstruction: America's Unfinished Revolution, 1863–1877* (New York: HarperCollins Publishers Inc., 1988), 276–277.

[700] Ibid., 276.

took a loyalty oath and repudiated slavery, a new government could be established.[701] Lincoln's plan was hardly comprehensive, but it was a start.

Andrew Johnson, who succeeded to the presidency on Lincoln's assassination, agreed with Lincoln's moderate approach to Reconstruction. Johnson, a Democrat, previously served as congressman, governor, and senator from his native Tennessee. A strong Unionist, Lincoln appointed Johnson as military governor of Tennessee in 1862, soon after Union forces had retaken control of the state. As military governor, Johnson helped implement Lincoln's Reconstruction policies in Tennessee. Partly because of Johnson's efforts, Tennessee ratified the Thirteenth and later the Fourteenth Amendment, and its congressional delegation was seated in the US Congress on July 24, 1866, the first of the seceding states to gain readmission.[702]

B. Presidential Reconstruction

Johnson was Lincoln's running mate in the 1864 presidential election, and six weeks after he was sworn in as vice president, he became president upon Lincoln's death.[703] Lincoln believed that since secession was contrary to the Constitution, the Confederate states were still part of the Union. Lincoln also felt that he should be in control of Reconstruction policies in his capacity as commander-in-chief. Congress, on the other hand, wanted to treat the former Confederate states as defeated territory, and that they should oversee Reconstruction.[704]

Johnson acted quickly to initiate his plan. While Congress was in recess, he moved to readmit the former Confederate states, if they accept the Thirteenth Amendment and rescind their ordinances of secession. Former high-ranking Confederate civil and military officers were not automatically pardoned, but Johnson would consider pardoning those former officials who applied personally.[705]

By the summer of 1865, most of the former Confederate states were reorganizing

---

[701]   Foner, *supra* note 699, 35–36.

[702]   Andrew Glass, *Tenn. is readmitted to the Union July 24, 1866.* Politico.com, available at: http://www.politico.com/news/stories/0708/11990.html

[703]   Foner, *supra* note 699, 42–43.

[704]   II The Cambridge History of Law in America,*supra* note 6, 328–329.

[705]   Ibid.

under Johnson's plan. While they complied by rescinding their secession ordinances and renouncing slavery, many of the reorganized states attempted to withhold civil rights from the former slaves, such as limiting their access and participation in the court system, requiring them to work and carry passes from their employers, to marry, and to enter into contracts. That fall, delegates from the defeated states, including many former Confederates, arrived in Washington to take their seats in Congress,[706] but Congress had other plans.

C. Congressional (Radical) Reconstruction

Early in the new congressional Session, Congressman Thaddeus Stevens introduced three new resolutions: 1) declaring that the task of Reconstruction was "the exclusive business of Congress;" 2) finding that President Johnson's policies were provisional and subject to oversight by Congress; and 3) denying seats to members elected from the former Confederate states.[707] Thus began the period of Congressional Reconstruction. Congressional Reconstruction was characterized by: 1) Congress repudiating Johnson's policies; 2) Johnson vetoing congressional legislation, and 3) Congress overriding Johnson's vetoes.

From the beginning of 1866 until the end of his term, a political struggle ensued between Johnson and Congress. The former Confederate states were divided into military districts, and Congress required major changes to the legal and social structure of these states for them to gain readmission, including ratifying the Fourteenth Amendment and enfranchising the former slaves.[708] The Radicals were in no great hurry to readmit the Southern states, because their admission could dilute the overwhelming Republican majority in Congress. Congress also passed the Tenure of Office Act, which restricted the ability of the president to remove officers of the executive branch without Senate approval.[709]

The elections of 1867 featured President Johnson, who opposed the Fourteenth Amendment and was attempting to block its ratification, and Congressman Stevens,

---

[706] Ibid., 329.

[707] Harpweek, available at: http://14thamendment.harpweek.com/HubPages/CommentaryPage. asp?Commentary=02Committee

[708] II The Cambridge History of Law, *supra* note 6, 329.

[709] Foner, *supra* note 699, 333–336.

who thought the Fourteenth Amendment did not go far enough and who urged a much stricter Reconstruction policy. In Ohio, Democrat Allen Thurman ran against war hero Rutherford B. Hayes for governor, and the Democratic platform stood for opposing African American suffrage and rescinding Ohio's ratification of the Fourteenth Amendment. Hayes won the governorship by 2,983 votes, but the Democrats gained control of the General Assembly and the suffrage measure lost by 50,000 votes.[710] Johnson stated that he was "gratified, but not surprised by the result of the recent elections,"[711] Bingham, on the other hand, interpreted the results as the voters' rejection of Stevens's more radical Reconstruction policies.[712] On the national level, Republicans triumphed in the Southern states, due to a large turnout among African American voters combined with white voter apathy and the continued disenfranchisement of former Confederates, but in the Northern states, Democrats cut steeply into the Republican majority and suffrage issues were defeated in Minnesota and Kansas, as well as Ohio.[713]

VI. Impeachment and McCardle

The battle between Congress and the president reached its zenith in 1868. Their defeat in the 1867 elections convinced the Radicals that the Fourteenth Amendment needed to be in place before another presidential election. When impeachment of the president seemed to be their only recourse, Johnson touched the match to the fuse by suspending War Secretary Edwin Stanton, an Ohio native, during the congressional recess. When Congress reconvened in December, Johnson reported Stanton's suspension to the Senate. The Senate promptly refused to sanction Johnson's actions, and Grant, who served as Interim Secretary, allowed Stanton to return to his office in the War Department. Stanton immediately began interfering with Johnson's orders to his military commanders, and in January 1868, Johnson fired Stanton and appointed General Lorenzo Thomas to serve as interim secretary.

---

[710]   Kern & Wilson, *supra* note 161, 242.

[711]   Hans L. Trefousse, *Andrew Johnson: A Biography* (New York: W.W. Norton, 1989), 299.

[712]   Magliocca, *supra* note 661, 141.

[713]   Foner, *supra* note 699, 314–315.

Meanwhile, Stanton refused to relinquish power, and for a brief period there were two war secretaries issuing conflicting orders to the army commanders in the field.[714]

On February 24, 1868, the House approved an impeachment resolution, accusing Johnson of "high crimes and misdemeanors" by violating the Tenure of Office Act, by a vote of 126 to 47. On February 25, Congressmen Bingham and Stevens formally notified the Senate of the impeachment vote.[715]

As was the case with the war, Ohioans played a pivotal role in the impeachment trial, which began in the Senate on March 30, 1868. Chase, in his role as chief justice, presided over the trial. Bingham, who refused to serve under Butler and threatened to resign, was selected as chairman of the seven impeachment managers, whose duty was to try the case before the Senate. Stanton was the victim of Johnson's illegal action, and Benjamin Wade, then serving as president pro tem of the Senate, would have become the eighteenth president had Johnson been convicted.[716]

Johnson's trial began on March 30, 1868. Bingham played only a small role in this part of the trial, mostly arguing procedural issues. The "jury" of senators was torn. Did Johnson really violate the law, or was he being tried for opposing the ratification of the Fourteenth Amendment? Bingham, who had been receiving death threats from the Ku Klux Klan, delivered the closing argument on May 4, 1868.[717]

Johnson had argued throughout the trial that as president, he had the right to either execute or disregard what he considered to be an unconstitutional law. Years before, Thomas Jefferson had voiced a similar opinion. Bingham rejected that theory outright. Congress, he argued, could pass an invalid law over presidential veto, and Johnson had no power to stop it. Congress's actions in that instance could only be overruled by the courts, or by the voters in the next election.[718]

On May 16, the Senate voted on Article 11 of the impeachment, the catch-all

---

[714] Harold M. Hyman, *A More Perfect Union: The Impact of The Civil War and Reconstruction on The Constitution* (New York: Alfred A. Knopf Inc., 1973), 504–506.

[715] Magliocca, *supra* note 661, 144.

[716] Ibid., 645, 146.

[717] Ibid., 147.

[718] Ibid., 148–149.

provision, and fell one vote short of the two-thirds majority necessary for conviction. The Senate then recessed briefly so the congressman and senators could attend the Republican National Convention. Upon reconvening on May 26, the Senate again fell one vote short of conviction on Articles 2 and 3.

Johnson may have helped secure his acquittal by actions he took in April and May. First, he appointed General John Schofield, a candidate perfectly acceptable to moderate Republicans, as Stanton's replacement. Next, he let it be known that he would stop actively opposing the ratification of the Fourteenth Amendment. Finally, Johnson provided patronage, and perhaps some outright bribes, to some of the undecided senators.[719]

In a way, the impeachment trial benefitted both sides. Johnson could continue to serve as president until the end of his term, and in exchange he stopped interfering with the ratification process. Bingham also got what he wanted, because in the next two months, six former Confederate states ratified the amendment, and on July 28, Secretary of State Seward declared that the proposed amendment had been adopted.[720] The Johnson era ended when General Grant, another Ohioan, took the oath as president on March 4, 1869.

Another issue came to a head when William McCardle, a newspaper editor from Mississippi, was arrested for advocating violent resistance to Radical Reconstruction policies. While awaiting trial before a military commission, McCardle applied for a writ of habeas corpus to the Circuit Court of the Southern District of Mississippi, alleging that his detention was contrary to law. The court promptly denied his petition and remanded him to the army for trial. Since the *Vallandigham* matter set the precedent that the US Supreme Court had no jurisdiction to hear appeals from military commissions, McCardle instead sought to invoke the Habeas Corpus Act of 1867,[721] a bill originally sponsored by Bingham.[722]

---

[719] Ibid., 152.

[720] Ibid., 152–53.

[721] Sess. 2, Chap 28, 14 Stat. 385.

[722] This law allowed nonresident plaintiffs, as well as defendants, to transfer or "remove" certain cases in state courts, involving questions of national importance, to federal courts if the petitioner can show that he would be unable to obtain justice in the state court system. Hyman, *supra* note 714, 473.

After the oral arguments were heard, but before a decision was announced, Congress suspended the jurisdiction of the Supreme Court to hear McCardle's petition. The court then unanimously upheld Congress's authority to strip the court of jurisdiction pursuant to Article III, Section 2 of the Constitution.[723]

VII. Grant and the Retreat from Reconstruction.

Ohio native Ulysses Grant assumed the presidency in March 1869. Born in Point Pleasant in 1822, Grant had an average upbringing. Using his political influence, Grant's father, Jesse, secured a coveted appointment at West Point for his son. Grant graduated in 1843, twenty-first in his class of thirty-nine cadets. Grant excelled at mathematics, drawing, and horsemanship while a student, and not much else.[724] Despite being disillusioned by the war with Mexico, Grant won brevet promotions to first lieutenant at the Battle of Molino Del Ray and to captain at the Battle of Chapultepec.[725] Upon his return from the war, Grant married Julia Dent, the sister of his West Point roommate.

Grant resigned from the army in 1854 because of allegations of drunkenness. Bouncing from job to job throughout the late 1850s, Grant was working in his father's dry goods store in Galena, Illinois, at the start of the Civil War. Dogged by the past allegations of drunkenness,[726] Grant was initially unable to secure a commission with the rapidly expanding army.[727]

With the help of his political supporter, Illinois Congressman Elihu B. Washburne, Grant was commissioned first as a colonel, then a brigadier general

---

[723] Ex Parte McCardle, 74 U.S. (7 Wall.) 506. The full text of Ex Parte McCardle is available at: https://supreme.justia.com/cases/federal/us/74/506/case.html

[724] *American President: A Reference Resource.* Ulysses S. Grant Front Page. Miller Center, University of Virginia. Available at: http://millercenter.org/president/grant/essays/biography/print

[725] George Washington Cullum, *Biographical Register of The Officers and graduates of The U.S. Military Academy, From 1802–1867.* Available at: http://penelope.uchicago.edu/Thayer/E/Gazetteer/Places/America/United_States/Army/USMA/Cullums_Register/1187*.html

[726] Historynet.com. *Ulysses S. Grant's Lifelong Struggle with Alcohol.* Available at: http://www.historynet.com/ulysses-s-grants-lifelong-struggle-with-alcohol.htm

[727] American President, *supra* note 724.

in the volunteer army.[728] After suffering a tactical defeat at Belmont Missouri in November 1861, Grant's forces captured the Confederate Forts Henry and Donaldson in early February 1862.[729]

On April 6, 1862, Grant's army was surprised by Confederate forces under Albert Sidney Johnston at Pittsburg Landing (Shiloh), Tennessee. Initially driven back toward the Tennessee River, Grant's army drove the Confederates from the field the next day.[730] In 1863, Grant won major victories at Vicksburg[731] and Chattanooga, and in March 1864, Lincoln promoted him to command all the Union Armies. Thirteen months later Grant accepted the surrender of Robert E. Lee and the Confederate Army of Northern Virginia, effectively ending the war.[732]

After the war, Grant remained in the army and took charge of the army's efforts at Reconstruction. Initially Grant agreed with Johnson's moderate approach to Reconstruction, but his compliance with the Reconstruction Acts put him at odds with the president.[733] In July, 1866 Congress established the rank of general of the Army of the United States, and promoted Grant into the position.[734] Grant also served briefly as interim secretary of war when Johnson suspended Edwin M. Stanton during a congressional recess, but when the Senate refused to sanction the suspension, Grant surrendered the office to Stanton.[735] Johnson subsequently fired Stanton, and the House drew up articles of impeachment against him for violating the Tenure of Office Act.[736]

The Radicals hoped for a Johnson conviction, which would place their fellow Radical, Ohio Senator Benjamin Wade, in the presidency, and help secure the 1868

---

[728]   Foote, *supra* note 416, 148.

[729]   Goodwin, *supra* note 369, 417.

[730]   Foote, *supra* note 416, 333–350.

[731]   McPherson, *supra* note 639, 636.

[732]   Ibid., 725–726.

[733]   Foner, *supra* note 699, 337. See, also, Hyman, *supra* note 714, 501–514.

[734]   Ulysses S. Grant. Available at: http://www.granthomepage.com/grantchronology.htm

[735]   William S. McFeeley, *Grant: A Biography* (New York: W.W. Norton & Company, 1981), 275.

[736]   Magliocca, *supra* note 661, 144. Discussed at page 215, *supra*.

Republican nomination for Wade. When Johnson was acquitted, the nomination went to Grant, who campaigned under the slogan "Let Us Have Peace."[737]

The most immediate effect of Grant's election was a truce in the war between the executive and the legislative branches. As commander of the army, Grant was charged with implementing Reconstruction policy in the conquered South. However, Grant played no role in the impeachment or Johnson's trial.

Several events that occurred during Grant's presidency led to the decline, and finally the end of Reconstruction. Among these events were the adoption and ratification of the Fifteenth Amendment, the need to use the army for frontier duty, several scandals that occurred among Grant's closest advisors, the economic Panic of 1873, the reemergence of the Democratic Party and the establishment of the Democratic "Solid South," and finally the election of 1876.

A. The Fifteenth Amendment

Although the Reconstruction Acts established African American suffrage in the former Confederate states, eleven of the twenty-one northern states, including Ohio, still refused to allow African-American citizens to vote. Between the time of Grant's election in November and his inauguration in March, Congress crafted the Fifteenth Amendment to address this issue. Three different versions were proposed:

- Prohibited the states from denying the vote to any citizen because of race, color, or previous condition of servitude;
- Prevented the states from denying the vote to any citizen because of issues relating to property, literacy, or the condition of their births; and
- Ensured that all male citizens over the age of twenty-one have the right to vote.[738]

Citing concerns about ratification in the Northern states, Congress finally settled on the first and most moderate version. This version passed Congress on February 26, 1869, just days before Grant assumed office.

---

[737] Foner, *supra* note 699, 338.

[738] PBS.org. Ulysses S. Grant: The Passage of the Fifteenth Amendment. Available at: http://www.pbs.org/wgbh/americanexperience/features/general-article/grant-fifteenth/

The proposed amendment faced a firestorm of opposition. The Radicals complained because the proposed amendment failed to establish nationwide voting standards. States could easily enact literacy or property standards to deny the vote. Further, the proposed amendment made no guarantees regarding the right to hold office. Democrats, on the other hand, considered the proposed amendment as an attempt by the Radicals to establish equality for the former slaves.[739]

Bingham sided with the Radicals in opposing the moderate verbiage. He feared that some states might establish religious, educational, and property requirements to vote.[740] Even some Northern states restricted the right to vote. California, for instance, denied Chinese residents the right to vote. Rhode Island required that non-native-born citizens own property, and Pennsylvania required the payment of state taxes. Massachusetts and Connecticut had a literacy test.[741] Bingham proposed adding the words *creed* and *property* to the proposed language, but the House-Senate conference committee removed Bingham's language.[742]

Women's rights groups also opposed the amendment. Suffragists complained that the amendment would allow barely educated African Americans to make laws while denying educated and refined women the right to vote.[743] The controversy caused a split in the abolitionist-feminist alliance that had existed for decades.[744]

Three-quarters of the states (twenty-nine of thirty-seven) needed to ratify the amendment for it to become part of the Constitution. Nevada was the first state to ratify the Fifteenth Amendment, on March 1, 1869. By the end of that month, eleven other states had ratified. In April, Senator Oliver Morton of Indiana proposed legislation requiring those Southern states not yet "readmitted" to the Union to ratify the amendment to gain readmission. Congress quickly enacted Morton's

[739]   Foner, *supra* note 699, 446.

[740]   Ibid.

[741]   Ibid., 447.

[742]   Magliocca, *supra* note 661, 156.

[743]   Foner, *supra* note 699, 447–448.

[744]   Ibid., 447.

proposals.[745] Ohio ratified the amendment by one vote in the Senate and two votes in the House, on January 27, 1870,[746] and on March 31, Secretary of State Hamilton Fish declared that the amendment had become part of the Constitution.[747]

B. The Army

By the summer of 1866, the Union Army, Lincoln's "Terrible Swift Sword," was a shadow of its' former self. Almost one million volunteers had been mustered out by that time, and the regular army now consisted of about thirty thousand troops, up from a prewar strength of about eighteen thousand.[748]

In July, Congress passed an act to increase and fix the military peace establishment of the United States, which established the organization of the postwar army. The army created by this act was a mixture of Regulars and Civil War veterans, and the officers were a mixture of West Point graduates and former volunteer officers. Four regiments of infantry and two regiments of cavalry were to consist entirely of African American soldiers, commanded by white officers.[749]

Congress enacted a series of cutbacks during the next several years that severely weakened the army. In 1869 Congress cut the number of infantry regiments from forty-five to twenty-five, and the authorized strength was set at 37,313. The next year Congress limited the number of enlisted men to 30,000. By 1874 the authorized strength was capped at 25,000, but because of desertions, discharges, and death, the rolls at the regimental level rarely exceeded 19,000 men.[750]

Once the war was over, migration westward began to increase dramatically. The population of the western states increased by one million between 1860 and 1870,

---

[745]   Fifteenth Amendment Ratification, Harpweek. Available at http://15thamendment. harpweek.com/HubPages/CommentaryPage.asp?Commentary=03Ratification

[746]   Kern & Wilson, *supra* note 161, 244.

[747]   Harpweek, *supra* note 745.

[748]   Robert M. Utley, *Frontier Regulars: The United States Army and The Indian 1866–1891* (Lincoln, NE: University of Nebraska Press, 1973), 11.

[749]   Ibid., 11.

[750]   Ibid., 16.

and by another 2.5 million between 1870 and 1880.[751] Some of the migrants sought to strike it rich in the gold and silver mines, and others wanted to take advantage of the free land offered by the government via the Homestead Act. The construction of the Transcontinental Railroad brought more settlers west.[752]

By 1866, there were about 270,000 Native Americans on the frontier. There were about ten times as many white settlers, and thousands more were on the way. Some of the tribes chose to coexist peacefully with the whites. Some of the tribes had clashed with whites before the war and were defeated. Some of the tribes had been so decimated by war and disease that they were incapable of resisting the whites. Only a few of the remaining tribes had the numbers to contest white settlement.[753]

During this era, the army served two masters—the president on the frontier and Congress in the Reconstruction South. Events in the West had increased the need for troops in that region, and Reconstruction duties required up to one-third of the army's strength.[754] Only in Texas, which at the time was part Old South and part frontier, did the army's duties come together.

The duties of the army in the South also evolved over time. From military occupation as a tactical concept, to military government for conquered territory, to Reconstruction, army commanders struggled to enforce civilian rules without much guidance.[755] Vengeful Southerners filed lawsuits in state courts against federal officials and soldiers throughout the South. Defendants did not receive much sympathy from Southern juries. In response, Grant issued orders allowing transfer of such cases to federal courts.[756]

As part of their Reconstruction duties, military commanders had to deal with rioting, moonshining, horse theft, as well as registering voters, supervising elections, establishing procedures for civil courts, and approving constitutions. The army also

---

[751]   Ibid., 2.

[752]   Ibid., 3.

[753]   Ibid., 5.

[754]   Ibid., 12.

[755]   Hyman, *supra* note 714, 157.

[756]   Allen R. Millett & Peter Maslowski, *For the Common Defense: A Military History of The United States of America* (New York: The Free Press, 1994), 258.

engaged in irregular warfare with former Confederates, who were determined to resist federal authority, preserve white supremacy, and maintain local rule.[757] As the Southern states were restored to full status, and with the public outcry for more troops in the West, the number of troops on occupation duty dwindled.[758] Once a state was readmitted to full status, the army could only intervene upon the request of the civil authorities.

In 1867, about 12,000 troops were on occupation duty in the South. Nine years later, fewer than 2,800 federal troops were garrisoning the eleven former Confederate states.[759] In 1866, 2,000 troops helped supervise elections in Louisiana, but just two years later the number dwindled to 598. As the number of troops decreased, the instances of violence against the freedmen spiked.[760] Despite the rise in violence, Congress gradually reduced the army's presence from one soldier to every 708 southern civilians to one solder to every 3,160 southern civilians.[761] By 1871, the principal duty of the army was to support federal marshals who were trying to suppress the activities of the Ku Klux Klan.[762]

---

[757]   Millet & Maslowski, *supra* note 756, 257.

[758]   I *American Military History*, Chapter 13. Darkness and Light the Interwar Years, 1865–1898. Available at: http://www.history.army.mil/books/AMH-V1/ch13.htm

[759]   Douglas R. Egerton, *The Wars of Reconstruction: The Brief, Violent History of America's Most Progressive Era* (New York: Bloomsbury Press, 2014), 313.

[760]   Ibid., 287.

[761]   Ibid., 313.

[762]   Ibid.

Rutherford B. Hayes, 1822-1893.
(Image courtesy of the Ohio History Connection).

In 1876 the Republicans nominated Ohio native Rutherford B. Hayes as president. Hayes, a Harvard graduate, served as a major general in the war, Ohio representative to the Thirty-Ninth Congress, and three-time governor.[763] In a contest against Democratic Governor Samuel Tilden of New York, Republican election boards in four Southern states had invalidated enough votes to give the election to Hayes. Democrats, naturally, disputed the results.[764]

Rival state governments were established in South Carolina and Louisiana, while in Florida the state supreme court determined that the Democratic candidate

---

[763] Foner, *supra* note 699, 569.

[764] Ibid., 575–576.

prevailed, but they let Hayes's margin of victory stand.[765] To solve the crisis, Congress appointed a fifteen-member commission to determine the victor. While the committee deliberated, Hayes's supporters secretly met with moderate Southern Democrats. The opposing sides reached a compromise: The Democrats withdrew their opposition to Hayes, and in exchange, the remaining occupation troops were withdrawn from the South and assigned to other duties.[766]

C. Scandals.

During Grant's administration, several scandals took place among Grant's closest friends and advisors that shifted the focus of the country away from Reconstruction issues. Among these scandals were the Black Friday Gold Panic, the Whiskey Ring, the Trading Post Scandal, the Credit Mobilier Scandal,[767] and several others. Allegations of nepotism also dogged the administration.

The first of these scandals was the Black Friday Gold Scandal. This scandal was the result of an attempt by Wall Street financiers Jay Gould and James "Diamond Jim" Fisk to corner the gold market. Gould and Fisk enlisted the aid of Grant's brother-in-law, Abel Rathbone Corwin. Corwin hoped to convince Grant to stop selling gold on the open market to increase the price of American agricultural products overseas. Concerned about the price of agricultural products, Grant initially agreed to stop government sales of gold.[768]

Starting in September 1869, Gould and Fisk began to buy gold. When the price quickly rose from $37 to $141 per ounce, Grant asked his treasury secretary, George Boutwell, to investigate.[769] Corbin wrote to Grant urging him to withhold gold sales. By this time Gould and Fisk jointly owned some $50 to $60 million in gold. Grant, at Boutwell's urging, began selling gold on the open market again. Grant did not

---

[765] Ibid., 575–576

[766] History.com, Compromise of 1877. Available at: http://www.history.com/topics/us-presidents/compromise-of-1877

[767] Since the Credit Mobilier was formed during Lincoln's administration, some historians credit Lincoln with this scandal.

[768] *Kenneth Ackerman, The Gold Ring: Jim Fisk, Jay Gould and Black Friday 1869* (New York: DeCampo Press, 2005), 91.

[769] Jean Edward Smith, Grant 481–490 (New York: Simon and Schuster, 2001).

reply directly to Corbin's letter, but Julia wrote a letter to Corbin's wife urging her to stop speculating in gold.[770]

Gould learned about Julia's letter and Grant's suspicions, so he began selling gold, while still purchasing small amounts to avoid suspicion. Gould never informed Fisk of Grant's suspicions, so Fisk kept buying gold.[771] By September 23, 1869, the price of gold peaked at $160 per ounce. To foil the scheme, Boutwell released $4 million in gold to the market and purchased $4 million in government bonds.[772] The market crashed, and investors, including Grant's private secretary, were ruined. The economy tanked, and the prices of stock and agricultural products dipped. Thousands of farmers were ruined.[773]

Another scandal involved an organized network of (mostly Republican) politicians, government revenue agents, and whiskey distillers and distributors intent on bilking the government of millions in tax revenues, known as the Whiskey Ring. The ring began in St. Louis but quickly spread to other cities.[774]

Treasury Secretary Benjamin Bristow broke the ring in 1875, and several high-ranking politicians, including Grant's personal secretary Orville Babcock and his personal friend General John McDonald, were implicated. Grant refused to believe the allegations against his friend, and he planned to travel to St. Louis to testify at Babcock's trial. More pressing duties kept Grant in Washington, but he signed an affidavit in support of Babcock, who was eventually acquitted of the charges.[775]

The Trading Post Scandal erupted soon after the Whiskey Ring trials concluded. Early in Grant's administration, War Secretary William W. Belknap convinced Congress to authorize his department to award trading post contracts for the posts around the country who traded with the Native Americans. Belknap was accused

---

[770]　Ulysses S. Grant 96–98 (Josiah Bunting III & A.M. Schlesinger Jr., eds., Times Books, Henry Holt and Company, LLC, 2001).

[771]　Ibid.

[772]　Smith, *supra* note 769, 481–490.

[773]　Ibid., 481–490.

[774]　Foner, *supra* note 699, 486.

[775]　Foner, *supra* note 699, 566. *See, also,* Ralph Kirschner, *The Class of 1861: Custer, Ames, and Their Classmates After West Point* (Carbondale, IL: Southern Illinois University Press, 1999), 132–135.

of accepting kickbacks from the government-appointed Indian trader at Ft. Sill, Oklahoma, Caleb P. Marsh, a friend of Belknap's wife.[776]

Marsh testified before a House committee that both Belknap and his wife accepted bribes in return for the trading post concession at Ft. Sill. Lt. Colonel George Custer later gave testimony before the same committee that supported Marsh's allegations,[777] incurring Grant's wrath in the process. Belknap resigned to avoid impeachment by the House.[778]

The Credit Mobilier Scandal had its origins in the Lincoln administration. In 1864 the government chartered the Union Pacific Railroad and tasked that agency with building the Transcontinental Railroad. Certain railroad officials, including Thomas C. Durant, created a sham corporation, the Credit Mobilier, to give the impression that the Railroad had hired an independent company to be the primary construction contractor. The actual purpose of establishing a separate company was to shield the railroad's officials from personal liability.

Because of wartime needs, construction on the railroad was nearly at a standstill. In 1865, Lincoln asked Congressman Oakes Ames of Massachusetts to take control of the Union Pacific.[779] Ames didn't want Congress to discover that the Credit Mobilier was a sham corporation, so he began selling shares to influential members of Congress, including Bingham, at a price below market value. When Bingham sold his shares back to Ames the next year, he realized a profit of $6,500.[780] A House investigating committee cleared Bingham of any wrongdoing but also recommended that Ames be expelled from that body.[781]

---

[776]   Ibid.

[777]   James Donovan, *A Terrible Glory* (New York: Back Bay Books, 2008), 106–107.

[778]   Foner, *supra* note 699, 566.

[779]   Logan Douglas Trent, *The Credit Mobilier* (New York: Arno Press, Inc., 1981), 6. Oaks Ames was a partner in his father's business Oliver Ames and Sons, a manufacturer of shovels and picks. The business prospered because of the gold discoveries in California and Australia. During the Civil War, the company obtained government contracts for the manufacture of shovels and swords, and Ames became quite wealthy. *Encyclopedia Americana* (1920)/Ames, Oaks, available at: http://en.wikisource.org/wiki/The_Encyclopedia_Americana_(1920)/Ames,_Oakes

[780]   Magliocca, *supra* note 661, 165. See, also, *New York Herald*, February 19, 1873, claiming that Bingham realized a profit more than $10,000 on the sale of his shares.

[781]   Magliocca, *supra* note 661, 166.

Other party leaders, including Vice President Schuyler Colfax and Ohio Congressman James Garfield, were also named in the scandal.[782] Garfield emerged from the scandal relatively unscathed and was elected president in 1880.[783] Colfax was not nominated for another term as vice president; he was replaced on the ticket by Henry Wilson, who was also implicated.[784]

Finally, on the last day of its session, the Forty-Second Congress enacted a bill that would double the salary of the president and Supreme Court justices, but also included was a provision to increase the salaries of members of Congress by 50 percent.[785] After a public outcry, the next Congress quickly repealed this "Salary Grab" law.[786]

D. The Panic of 1873

The Panic of 1873 was the largest economic downturn in America's history, lasting from October 1873 to March 1879. The seeds of this panic were sown during the Civil War, when the United States released paper greenbacks into circulation to fuel the Union war machine. A greenback is basically a promissory note, redeemable in gold or silver. Adding fuel to the fire was a decision by several European countries to end the use of silver as currency.

When Germany put the deutschmark on the gold standard in 1871, a worldwide glut of silver was the result, meaning less value per ounce. For countries like the United States, which backed its currency with gold and silver, it was possible to exchange devalued silver for precious gold, and devaluing the relative value of the

---

[782]   Kern & Wilson, *supra* note 161, 244.

[783]   History.com, James A. Garfield-U.S. Presidents-. Available at: http://www.history.com/topics/us-presidents/james-a-garfield

[784]   The Expulsion Case of James W. Patterson of New Hampshire (1873) Credit Mobilier Scandal. U.S. Senate Historical Office. Available at: http://www.senate.gov/artandhistory/history/common/expulsion_cases/064JamesPatterson_expulsion.htm

[785]   John W. Dean (September 27, 2002). *The Telling Tale of The Twenty-Seventh Amendment: A Sleeping Amendment Concerning Congressional Compensation is Later revived.* Available at: http://writ.corporate.findlaw.com/dean/20020927.html

[786]   Magliocca, *supra* note 661, 166.

US dollar. This deflation caused a ripple effect throughout countries that still used silver and gold to back their currency.[787]

Pressured to follow Germany's lead, Congress passed the Coinage Act of 1873, which set the country on the road to the gold standard. This act ended the government's purchase of silver at market value and ended the minting of the silver dollar. Western silver-producing states were outraged by the act. Senator William Stewart of Nevada wrote the following:

> I am persuaded history will write (the Act of 1873) down as the greatest legislative crime in the most stupendous conspiracy against the welfare of the people of the United States and of Europe which this or any other age has witnessed.[788]

The immediate effect of this act was to decrease the supply of money available, which was limited by the amount of gold held by the treasury. Investors' access to currency and credit shrank, and interest rates skyrocketed.

The banking industry was one of the first to notice the change. The investment bank owned by Jay Gould & Co. was one of the biggest investors in the Northern Pacific Railroad. The railroad would receive huge land grants from the federal government for every mile of track they built. The railroad would then use the land grants as collateral for new loans. Less available currency made it difficult for private investors to buy up the railroad lands, making less money available to the railroads to pay its debts.

Unable to pay its debts, the Cooke Company filed for bankruptcy protection in September 1873. The stock markets, investment houses and banks, and railroads and other industries felt the pinch. Thousands of American companies defaulted on their loans, nine of every ten railroad companies folded, and wages fell by up

---

[787] Teaching History.org: Panic of 1873. Available at: http://teachinghistory.org/history-content/beyond-the-textbook/24579

[788] Milton Friedman, *The Crime of 1873*. Available at: file:///C:/Users/tminahan/Downloads/E-89-12.pdf

to 25 percent.[789] Jobs disappeared, the price of agricultural products dropped, and Grant had no solution.[790]

The panic, combined with the Grant administration scandals discussed *supra*, cooled the ardor of most northerners toward Reconstruction. Grant and the Republicans were blamed for the crisis, but the root causes went well beyond the Grant administration.[791]

E. Revival of the Democrats

During the Civil War, the Democratic Party split into two factions, the War Democrats, who supported the Union and Lincoln's policies, and the Peace Democrats or Copperheads, who opposed the war. After the nominal head of the party, Senator Stephen A. Douglas, died in June 1861, the War Democrats were without a national leader.[792] In the meantime, the Copperheads gained strength. The story of one of their national leaders, Congressman Clement Vallandigham, is discussed *supra*.

Nationally, the Democrats made gains in the 1862 elections, an increase of thirty-four members in the House, the legislatures of Indiana and Illinois, the New York governor, and the governor and legislature of New Jersey.[793] Historian James McPherson considered it fortuitous that the elections in Pennsylvania and Ohio were held in odd-numbered years, and that the Republican governors in Indiana and Illinois were elected to four-year terms in 1860, or these offices may have gone to the Democrats that year as well.[794]

Conversely, most of the Democratic gains were in the six lower-North states from New York to Illinois, and the margins in these states was very small, including just six thousand votes in Ohio.[795] The absence of soldiers at the front could have

---

[789]   Teaching History, *supra* note 787.

[790]   Kern & Wilson, *supra* note 161, 245.

[791]   Teaching History, *supra* note 787.

[792]   McPherson, *supra* note 639, 274–275.

[793]   Ibid., 561.

[794]   Ibid., 561.

[795]   Ibid., 561–562.

easily explained away the Democratic gains. In addition, the Republicans retained the governor's mansion in seventeen of the nineteen northern states, as well as sixteen of the state legislatures. Republicans gained five seats in the US Senate and had a twenty-five-vote majority in the House.[796]

By 1864 the Republicans were in trouble. Two of the main reasons were the lack of success on the battlefield and the impression that the War was being fought for abolition, not reunification. To satisfy both the Peace Democrats and the War Democrats, the party nominated disgraced General George McClellan for president and Congressman George Pendleton, an Ohio Copperhead and Vallandigham supporter, for vice president on a peace platform.[797]

Lincoln expected to be beaten by McClellan. If Lincoln was defeated, he planned to cooperate with the president-elect, and to try to save the Union in the months between the election in November and the inauguration the following March.[798]

As it turned out, Lincoln and his supporters were worried needlessly. Admiral Farragut's capture of Mobile Bay in August and General Sherman's capture of Atlanta in September reenergized the Republicans.[799] Later that month the Union forces were buoyed by General Phil Sheridan's victory over Confederate General Jubal Early at Winchester, Virginia.[800] Additionally, General McClellan had to run a gauntlet between the Peace Democrats and the War Democrats, and in the end, he succeeded in pleasing neither faction.[801]

When the votes were counted, Lincoln had prevailed by half a million votes and by an electoral count of 212–21. As in 1860, Lincoln won big majorities in the states of the upper North, including New England. Democrats were strongest in the southern Midwest. Republicans won all the states except Kentucky, Delaware (both slaveholding states), and New Jersey (McClellan's home state). As discussed *supra*, Republicans won a "supermajority" (a large enough majority to propose

---

[796]   Ibid., 561.

[797]   Ibid., 771–772. This information is discussed in more detail in chapter 6, *supra*.

[798]   Ibid., 561.

[799]   Goodwin, *supra* note 369, 652–657.

[800]   McPherson, *supra* note 639, 776–777.

[801]   Goodwin, *supra* note 369, 652–657.

Constitutional Amendments and override presidential vetoes) in Congress that year.[802]

By 1866, the election had become a referendum on Reconstruction. Johnson campaigned against the Radical Republicans over whether the policy should be lenient or harsh. Bingham used his reelection campaign to stump for ratification of the Fourteenth Amendment.[803] Grant, believing that hostilities were about to resume, removed the arms from southern arsenals and had them quietly relocated in northern warehouses.[804]

Republicans won in another landslide, winning every state but Delaware, Kentucky, and Maryland. Republicans also retained their "supermajority" in Congress for another two years. Republicans interpreted this landslide as an endorsement of Reconstruction and the Fourteenth Amendment, while Democrats saw the defeat of several African-American suffrage issues as a repudiation of Radical Reconstruction policies.[805]

By 1868, things had changed. Radicals hoped that Grant's nomination would help them keep their congressional majority, but the failed impeachment bid cast them in a bad light. The party platform endorsed Radical Reconstruction but left the issue of African American suffrage to the Northern states, while demanding suffrage in the former Confederate states.[806]

The Radicals retained control of Congress by a wide margin, but Grant won by only three hundred thousand votes nationwide, and Bingham won his seat by only 416 votes.[807] By 1870, Republicans still retained control of Congress, but their "supermajority" was gone. By this time, however, actions of the Ku Klux Klan and other paramilitary groups threatened to destroy the Republican Party

---

[802]   McPherson, *supra* note 639, 804–805.

[803]   Magliocca, *supra* note 661, 124–127.

[804]   Joseph Wheelan, *Terrible Swift Sword: The Life of General Phillip H. Sheridan* (Boston: DeCappo Press, 2012), 221–222.

[805]   William Gillette, *Retreat from Reconstruction 1869–1879* (Baton Rouge, LA: Louisiana State University Press, 1979), 9–10.

[806]   Ibid., 12–13.

[807]   Magliocca, *supra* note 61, 154–155.

in the Southern states.[808] Historians coined the term "Redemption" to describe the process where white Southern Democrats regained control of the Southern state governments. Redemption ushered in an era where the interests of the planter aristocracy and the business interests were supported over the interests of small farmers and laborers, and where the government did little or nothing to promote the interests of the freedmen.[809]

By 1872, the scandals discussed previously began to haunt the Grant administration. The liberal wing of the Republican Party, opposed to corruption, nominated Horace Greely to oppose the president, and the Democrats soon nominated Greeley as well.[810] Grant jettisoned the scandal-plagued Schuyler Colfax as vice president, and the party added Senator Henry Wilson of Massachusetts to the ticket. Southern freedmen only remembered Grant's enthusiastic endorsement of the Fifteenth Amendment, and that was enough for them.[811] Perhaps by riding Grant's coattails, the Republicans gained over sixty seats in the House, but Bingham, a victim of congressional redistricting, lost his seat in the primary.[812]

As a practical matter, the election of 1874 spelled the end of Reconstruction. Democrats, who opposed Radical Reconstruction and the regular army that carried out its policies, gained control of the House. Sixty-two incumbent Republicans were not re-elected, and the large Republican majority in the House gave way to a seventy-nine-member Democratic majority.[813] Except for a short period (1881–83, 1889–91), the Democrats maintained control of the House for the next twenty

---

[808]   Egerton, *supra* note 759, 295.

[809]   New Georgia Encyclopedia. Civil War and Reconstruction: Available at: http://www. georgiaencyclopedia.org/articles/history-archaeology/redemption

[810]   Earl Dudley Ross, The Liberal Republican Movement (1910). Available at: http:// books.google.com/books?id=ZX2q-h-xYFcC&pg=PA202&dq=%22liberal+republica ns%22+%22consent%22&lr=&num=100&as_brr=0&ei=su24SKSzAY32sgPo8pDFD g#v=onepage&q=%22liberal%20republicans%22%20%22consent%22&f=false

[811]   Egerton, *supra* note 759, 280.

[812]   Magliocca, *supra* note 661, 164–165.

[813]   Civil Rights Bill of 1875, Legislative Interests, The Fifteenth Amendment in Flesh and Blood, Black Americans in Congress Series. Available at: http://history.house. gov/Exhibitions-and-Publications/BAIC/Historical-Essays/Fifteenth-Amendment/ Legislative-Interests/

years. Starting with intimidation and fraud, Southern Democrats and paramilitary groups like the Ku Klux Klan resorted to targeting leading African-Americans and Republicans in order to prevail at the ballot box.[814] Fatigue and indifference toward Reconstruction in the Northern states helped this shift in control.[815]

Perhaps the death knell of Reconstruction was sounded when the lame-duck Forty-Third Congress passed the Civil Rights Act of 1875.[816] First proposed by Senator Charles Sumner (1811–1874) of Massachusetts in 1870, the bill was passed by Congress in February 1875 and signed by President Grant on March 1, 1875.[817] Sumner had long argued that since equality was now the law of the land, racial segregation was contrary to law. He intended to sweep away the last vestiges of segregation with one "all-encompassing" bill.[818]

The bill as written provided for equal access to "public accommodations" such as railroads, stagecoaches, steamboats, streetcars, hotels, and theatres.[819] The bill also provided for equal entry into schools and land-grant colleges as well as the right to serve on juries.[820] After much delay and debate, three versions of the bill were introduced: the Senate bill, with its provisions to desegregate and federally fund common schools, the amended House version, which called for "separate but equal" public schools, and a last-minute version which deleted all references to education.[821] The third version was eventually passed by both the House and Senate.[822] This "watered-down" version accomplished very little and was struck down by the US Supreme Court in 1883.[823]

---

[814]   II The Cambridge History of Law, *supra* note 6, 334.

[815]   Hyman, *supra* note 714, 538.

[816]   18 Stat. 335–337.

[817]   Civil Rights Bill of 1875, *supra* note 797.

[818]   Gillette, *supra* note 805, 196–197.

[819]   Ibid., 196–197.

[820]   Ibid.

[821]   Civil Rights Bill of 1875, *supra* note 797.

[822]   Civil Rights Bill of 1875, *supra* note 797.

[823]   Foner, *supra* note 699, 587.

F. The Election of 1876

The election of 1876 served to drive the final nail into the casket of Reconstruction. Democrats, sensing their first victory in a presidential election since 1856, nominated the reform governor of New York, Samuel J. Tilden. Although primarily responsible for the overthrow of the "Boss Tweed" corruption ring in New York City, Tilden was wealthy himself and had the backing of the country's leading industrialists, including Jay Gould and Jim Fisk, lately of the Gold Scandal.[824]

Former House Speaker James G. Blaine was the Republicans' first choice as nominee, but a series of scandals and accusations of influence peddling marred his candidacy. When Blaine failed to gain a majority of the delegates in the early convention balloting, the party again turned toward the moderate Midwest and nominated Ohio governor and Union Major General Rutherford B. Hayes. Hayes, a Harvard law graduate, was the first choice of very few of the delegates; however, in the end he was the one candidate who was acceptable to all.[825] Hayes was a former congressman and had voted for the Fourteenth Amendment, but he spent most of the Reconstruction years in Ohio, and thus he escaped most of the taint of Radical Reconstruction and the accompanying corruption.[826]

The election was held on November 7, 1876. The early election returns foretold a Tilden victory.[827] Tilden led in popular votes by some 250,000 and garnered 184 electoral votes, one short of a majority, to Hayes's 165. Tilden carried New York and most of the Southern states while Hayes prevailed in New England, the Midwest, and the West. Twenty electoral votes, from the still-Republican controlled states of Louisiana, Florida, and South Carolina, plus one from Oregon, were disputed.[828]

Republican election boards in the three Southern states, citing fraud and voter intimidation, invalidated enough Democratic votes to allow Hayes to prevail in all three states. Hayes also ended up with all three of Oregon's electoral votes. By contrast, South Carolina and Louisiana established rival administrations, one

---

[824]   Foner, *supra* note 699, 568. William H. Rehnquist, Centennial Crisis: The Disputed Election Of 1876, 76–78 (New York: Vintage Books, 2004).

[825]   Foner, *supra* note 699, 567. Rehnquist, *supra* note 824, 54–55.

[826]   Gillette, *supra* note 805, 303–304.

[827]   Rehnquist, *supra* note 824, 95–96.

[828]   Foner, *supra* note 699, 575–576.

Democratic and one Republican, while Florida awarded the gubernatorial contest to the Democratic candidate while certifying Hayes' victory.[829]

Article II, Section 1 of the U.S. Constitution provides as follows:

> The President of the Senate shall, in the presence of the Senate and the House of Representatives, open all the Certificates, and the Votes shall then be counted. The Person having the greatest Number of Votes shall be the President … [830]

Republican leaders determined that this clause meant the president pro tempore of the Senate, Republican Senator Thomas W. Ferry of Michigan,[831] would determine which electors were legitimate, and thus which electoral votes to count, while the Democrats, who controlled the House, determined that Congress should have a role in the process. Unfortunately, the Constitution did not address this dilemma. Grant, claiming to be neutral, stationed troops around the three Southern capitals to prop up their Republican legislatures, and he moved more troops to Washington, DC, to prevent unrest in the capital.[832]

In response to the crisis, Congress created the Electoral Commission. A panel of fifteen members, five each from the Senate and the House, as well as five Supreme Court justices, would make up the commission. The commission was initially intended to consist of seven Republicans and seven Democrats, with Justice David Davis, a Republican with close ties to the Democrats and liberals, to be the deciding vote. Before the commission met, the Illinois legislature selected Davis as their next senator, and he promptly resigned from the commission.[833] Three members of the commission (20 percent of the total members) hailed from the Ohio, Senator Allen G. Thurman (D), Congressmen James A. Garfield (R), and Henry B. Payne (R).[834]

Davis was quickly replaced by Justice Joseph P. Bradley, a Republican, and in a

---

[829]   Ibid., 575–576.

[830]   U.S. Const., art. II, § 1.

[831]   Foner, *supra* note 699, 576. Rehnquist, *supra* note 808, 113.

[832]   Gillette, *supra* note 805, 325.

[833]   Foner, *supra* note 699, 580.

[834]   Rehnquist, *supra* note 824, 163.

series of 8–7 party line votes, the commission awarded all twenty of the disputed electors, and the election, to Hayes. Tilden's supporters, unhappy with the outcome, threatened to obstruct the electoral vote count in the House and prevent a March 4 inauguration.[835] Opponents were already referring to Hayes as "Rutherfraud" and "His Fraudulency."[836]

As part of the informal Compromise of 1877, Southern Democrats agreed to support Hayes for president, and Hayes agreed to withdraw the remaining federal troops from the South. Hayes also agreed to appoint a Southerner to his cabinet; David M. Key from Tennessee was soon appointed as postmaster general. Hayes also promised to support a Pacific Railroad, with its eastern terminus in Texas.[837] In this way, the era of the Solid South, where "the base of the Democratic Party was the white, voting South," began and continued until after Lyndon Johnson signed the Voting Rights Act of 1965 into law.[838]

G. The Reconstruction Era in Ohio

In his book *The Impact of the Civil War and Reconstruction on Arkansas*,[839] author Carl Moneyhon describes the level of devastation in that state at the end of the war. While some property was either stolen or seized by federal authorities, other property was put to the torch or otherwise wasted. The armies had confiscated all of the horses and other animals, and the government was controlled by a completely different set of people.

County tax records showed that the number of horses and mares decreased by 50 percent from 1860 levels, while the number of cattle decreased by 43 percent and the number of mules, essential to an agrarian economy, decreased by 39 percent.

---

[835]   Foner, *supra* note 699, 580.

[836]   Kern & Wilson, *supra* note 161, 264–265.

[837]   Foner, *supra* note 699, 580. Knepper, *supra* note 27, 254–255.

[838]   PBS, The American Experience: Freedom Riders. Available at: http://www.pbs.org/wgbh/americanexperience/freedomriders/issues/the-solid-south

[839]   Carl H. Moneyhon, *The Impact of The Civil War and Reconstruction on Arkansas* (Fayetteville, AR: The University of Arkansas Press, 2002), 175–189.

The value of jewelry dropped by over 60 percent. However, the greatest property loss came from emancipation.[840]

The tax records from 1860 showed Arkansas with 60,799 slaves with a value of over $45 million, by far the most valuable property in the state. Over 110,000 slaves were actually counted in the 1860 census, and using the average value above, these were worth over $100 million. The accompanying loss of labor also caused land values to decline by another $34 million.[841]

Such was not the case in Ohio. Even though over 35,000 Ohio soldiers lost their lives in the war, Ohio's overall population actually increased by almost 14 percent between 1860 and 1870. By 1865, most of the state had been cleared for farming, except for the Great Black Swamp area of Northwest Ohio.[842] Since agriculture in Ohio was based on a free market economy, emancipation did not cause the massive property losses and labor shortages that occurred in the Southern states. Unlike the Southern states, where sharecropping replaced the antebellum plantation economy, in Ohio most of the farmers worked their own land.[843]

The Morrill Act, passed in 1862, granted federal land to the states to establish colleges to teach agriculture and mechanical arts. The General Assembly accepted the federal allocation, and in 1870 Ohio chartered the Ohio Mechanical and Agricultural College, to be located on the Neil farm north of Columbus. In 1878 the college was renamed as the Ohio State University.[844]

Cincinnati was the center of Ohio manufacturing before the war, and it became a major port for transporting men and materials to the Union armies farther south. By the end of the war, the steel industry was getting started. Cleveland mills were smelting steel using Lake Superior iron ore, Pennsylvania coal, and Ohio limestone.[845] In 1870 Dr. B.F. Goodrich relocated his rubber factory to Akron, in an area where the automobile industry would later get its start. The oil industry set up its early refineries in the Cleveland area, midway between the oil fields in western

---

[840]   Ibid., 176.

[841]   Ibid.

[842]   Knepper, *supra* note 27, 276.

[843]   Ibid., 276.

[844]   Ibid., 277.

[845]   Ibid., 279.

Pennsylvania and those in northwest Ohio.[846] By the 1880s, Toledo had become a major port and refining center, and Findlay became the center of a natural gas boom.[847] Edwin Libbey relocated his glass factory to Toledo, which soon became a major glass-producing center.[848]

At first glance, it might seem like the Republicans controlled Ohio politics during this era. Ohio elected the first Republican governor, Salmon P. Chase, in 1856, and except for 1874–76, Republican or Union party governors controlled the governor's mansion throughout Reconstruction.[849] More importantly, Republicans dominated Ohio's delegations to the Thirty-Ninth and the Fortieth Congresses. Because of the exclusion of Southern Congressmen from the House, Ohio's delegation made up almost one-eighth of the Republican Congressional Caucus, and one-eighth of the entire House.[850]

By 1867, Ohioans had grown tired of the Radical agenda. Politicians promised that Reconstruction would end once the former Confederate states ratified the Fourteenth Amendment. When the Southern states rejected the amendment, Reconstruction began anew, with far more stringent terms than before. Ohioans then grudgingly lent their support to the new congressional policy.[851]

Ohio Republicans nominated Rutherford B. Hayes for governor, and he prevailed by less than three thousand votes statewide. However, a provision to remove the word *white* from the state constitution[852] was defeated by fifty thousand votes, and

---

[846] Ibid.,

[847] Ibid., 280.

[848] Ibid., 281.

[849] National Governor's Association. Ohio: Past Governor's Bios. Available at: http://www.nga.org/cms/home/governors/past-governors-bios/page_ohio.default.html?begin25341aeb-2c72-425f-902c-d68a3c60362c=25&end25341aeb-2c72-425f-902c-d68a3c60362c=49&pagesize25341aeb-2c72-425f-902c-d68a3c60362c=25&

[850] Kern & Wilson, *supra* note 161, 234.

[851] Sawrey, *supra* note 656, 97–98.

[852] Article V, Section 1 of Ohio's 1851 Constitution provides: "Every white male citizen of the United States, of the age of twenty-one years, who shall have been a resident of the State one year next preceding the election, and of the county, township or ward, in which he resides, such time as may be provided by law, shall have the qualifications of an elector, and be entitled to vote in all elections."

Democrats won control of the General Assembly. The General Assembly quickly rescinded its earlier ratification of the Fourteenth Amendment[853] and replaced Radical Republican Senator Benjamin Wade with Democrat Allen G. Thurman, who served until 1881.[854]

H. A New Constitution? .

In 1873, the Ohio Republicans were damaged by the Panic of 1873. As a result, former Peace Democrat William Allen was elected as governor, and Democrats again gained control of the General Assembly.[855] By this time most Ohioans had grown weary of Reconstruction and African American rights, and economic issues, industrialization, and immigration became more important.[856]

Ohio's 1851 Constitution contained a provision to put a question before the voters every twenty years whether to hold a constitutional convention.[857] By 1871, several groups with mostly unrelated interests endorsed a constitutional convention. By this time Ohio's growing population caused a spike in legal issues, and Ohio courts were overwhelmed. The economy was changing from an economy based on agriculture to one based on industry, and women were demanding the right to vote. The issues discussed by the delegates included:

- the court system, including the Supreme Court, which was four years behind on its docket;
- more legislative control over corporations, including railroads;

---

[853] Nelson, *supra* note 656, 59–60. Congress refused to recognize this action, and the amendment became part of the Constitution on July 28, 1868. Ibid.

[854] Knepper, *supra* note 27, 250. Thurman served as one of the seven Democrats on the Electoral Commission, which selected Hayes as President in 1877. Harpweek. Hayes vs. Tilden: The Electoral Controversy of 1876–1877. Available at: http://elections.harpweek.com/09Ver2Controversy/Overview-3.htm

[855] Kern & Wilson, *supra* note 161, 245.

[856] Ibid., 245.

[857] Ohio Const., art. XVI, § 3

- alcohol issues, both pro and con; and
- women's suffrage.[858]

The delegates assembled in Columbus in May 1873. The members included fifty Republicans, forty-six Democrats, and nine Independents. The convention deliberated until August, then reconvened in Cincinnati in December, and adjourned in May 1874.[859]

The product provided for extensive changes to the judiciary, including ten-year terms for Supreme Court justices as well as intermediate appellate courts, called Circuit Courts, to hear appeals from Courts of Common Pleas. The alcohol issue was discussed, and the delegates decided to place this issue before the voters as a separate amendment.

The governor was granted the veto, subject to a three-fifths override by the General Assembly. Elections would be every two years instead of annually, and fixed salaries for legislators and county officials were adopted. The women's suffrage issue failed to gain a majority of the delegates' votes.[860]

Although the proposed Constitution had bipartisan political support, voters rejected it by a vote of 250,169 to 102,885. Temperance advocates turned out in high numbers to vote down the alcohol amendment. Most of these voters believed that the new constitution related to the alcohol amendment and defeated both.[861]

I. Other Issues

During the conflict, the federal courts in Ohio dealt with issues such as the naval blockade, libel and revenue issues, and treason and confiscation cases, among others. Judge Leavitt dealt with five cases involving treason or disobedience of orders, including Ex parte Vallandigham.[862] After the war's end, the court's docket actually increased because of two major factors.

First, the Reconstruction Congress passed several bills, including the Civil

---

[858]   *History of Ohio Law*, supra note 42, 60.

[859]   Ohio History Central: Ohio Constitutional Convention of 1874. Available at: http://ohiohistorycentral.org/w/Ohio_Constitutional_Convention_of_1873_-_1874?rec=525

[860]   *History of Ohio Law*, supra note 42, 61–62.

[861]   Ibid., 62–63.

[862]   Ibid., 279–280.

Rights Acts of 1866[863] and 1875,[864] the Bankruptcy Act of 1867,[865] the Habeas Corpus Act of 1867[866] and the Jurisdiction and Removal Act of 1875.[867] This legislation served to shift power from the states to the federal government in order to enforce federally mandated rights, including civil and political rights for the freedmen.[868] Second, the increasing levels of business and commerce in the post-war years also served to significantly increase the court's docket.[869]

Congressman Bingham, who Justice Hugo Black referred to as "the Madison of the Fourteenth Amendment,"[870] like Douglas MacArthur's old soldier, didn't die; he just faded away. Bingham was reelected to his seat in 1868 and 1870, but by 1872 local forces had aligned against him. The congressional redistricting occasioned by the census of 1870 moved Bingham's base of power, Tuscarawas County to another district, and his home, Cadiz, was a political backwater. As a result, Bingham was defeated for reelection in the primary.[871]

Before leaving office, Bingham was cleared of any wrongdoing in the Credit Mobilier Scandal, but his reputation was dealt a major blow when he voted for a retroactive congressional pay raise that was quickly rescinded by the next Congress.[872] However, in June 1873 President Grant nominated Bingham to serve as the first American minister plenipotentiary to Japan, and he served in this role for the next twelve years, effectively removing him from the national political scene.[873] It is easy to speculate that the Supreme Court's interpretation of the Fourteenth Amendment in cases such as the

---

[863]   14 Stat. 27–30, 1866.

[864]   18 Stat. 335–337, 1875.

[865]   14 Stat. 517, 1867.

[866]   14 Stat. 385, 1867.

[867]   18 Stat. 470, 1875.

[868]   18 Stat. 470, 1875.

[869]   18 Stat. 470, 1875.

[870]   Richard L. Aynes. *The Continuing Importance of Congressman John A. Bingham and the Fourteenth Amendment.* U. 36 Akron L. Rev. 589, 590.

[871]   Magliocca, *supra* note 661, 164–165.

[872]   Ibid., 166.

[873]   Ibid., 167.

Slaughterhouse Cases,[874] *United States v Cruikshank,*[875] or the *Civil Rights Cases*[876] might have been different had Bingham been present to lend his voice to the debate.

Summary

The Thirty-Ninth Congress played a major role in the Reconstruction Era by using the Fourteenth Amendment to place protection of individual rights in the hands of the federal government, to establish a foundation to eliminate future conflict based on civil war issues, and to reunite the Union and rebel states. Ohio's contribution came from Bingham and the Thirty-Ninth Congress as part of the Committee of Fifteen and from President Grant. Because of need for the army on the frontier, scandals, and the economic Panic of 1873 among other things, Grant's administration still managed to generate peace between the legislative and executive branches and oversee the ratification of the Fifteenth Amendment.

The effects of Reconstruction on Ohio were not as devastating as other areas but still meaningful. Thirty-five thousand soldiers lost their lives. Most of Ohio was farm land but was transitioning to an industry-based economy. In the years immediately after the war, Ohio became a manufacturing hub of steel, iron ore, limestone, rubber, natural gas, glass, and oil. But only about 36,700 African-Americans resided in Ohio in 1860, and presumably most of these had jobs and homes. The end of the war did not result in thousands of homeless and jobless former slaves, as in the Southern states.[877] Finally, a new constitution was proposed to work on issues with the court system, legislative control over corporations, alcohol issues, and women's suffrage. This Constitution was overwhelmingly rejected. All in all, Ohio saw many changes during the Reconstruction Era but was able to sustain growth without the same economic issues most southern states had to deal with.

---

[874]   83 U.S. 36 (1873). (Privileges and Immunities clause only forbids the states from withholding the privileges and immunities of American citizenship, not state citizenship.)

[875]   92 U.S. 542 (1875). (Due process and equal protection clauses apply only to state action, not the actions of private citizens.)

[876]   109 U.S. 3 (1883). (Discrimination by private organizations or individuals does not offend the Constitution.)

[877]   Ohio History Central, African Americans. Available at: http://www.ohiohistorycentral. org/w/African_Americans

Chapter 9

Observations and Conclusions

Reconstruction upon a loyal basis is a success and though the Democracy and the rebels may gnash their teeth, the great majority of the people of the country will rejoice that the vexed question of reconstruction will soon be among the things of the past.

—Marion (Ohio) Independent, 1868

I. Lessons from Reconstruction

Regardless of whether the Reconstruction Era was a success or a failure, a combination of factors, including a temporary congressional Republican "supermajority," the requirement that the former Confederate states ratify the Fourteenth and Fifteenth Amendments to regain full status in the Union, and a group of right-minded representatives like Bingham, ensured that the Fourteenth and Fifteenth Amendments would be approved and ratified. Opposed by the Radicals, who demanded a more punitive policy, and President Johnson, who thought no reconstruction policy was necessary, Bingham and his colleagues crafted these two amendments in a way to ensure ratification by states that had grown weary of war and Reconstruction policies, like Ohio.[878]

An essential element of the amendments was the ability to enforce their provisions. Bingham had argued for years that one of the failings of the original

---

[878] Both amendments were somewhat limited in scope. The Fourteenth did not grant suffrage to the freedmen. The Fifteenth did not grant anything, it just prohibited voter discrimination based on race, color, or previous condition of servitude.

Bill of Rights was that it lacked the ability to enforce its provisions. With the two amendments, Bingham and the other proponents ensured that the appropriate enabling clauses were included in the text of the amendments. These clauses would be an essential element of the "Second Reconstruction" in the next century.

Of the authors relied upon heavily in this work, Foner believed that Reconstruction was a failure. Edwards and Hyman believed that the lofty goals of Reconstruction were left largely unfinished, or unfulfilled. Kern and Wilson call Reconstruction "a significant episode in Ohio and National history."[879] Knepper called Reconstruction a watershed in Ohio and national politics, with uneven pace and mixed results.[880] DuBois, by contrast, highlighted the accomplishments, rather than the failures, of Reconstruction.[881] As for Sawrey, the title of his work (Dubious Victory) says it all.[882] Former Indiana Governor Oliver Morton opined in 1877 that if Reconstruction was a failure, it was because it had been "resisted by armed and murderous organizations, by terrorism and proscription the most wicked and cruel of the age."[883] However, once loyal governments were installed in the seceding states, the slaves freed, and some nominal rights secured for the freedmen, the goals of Reconstruction for moderate states like Ohio were met.

Hyman even went so far as to speculate that no great change in the relationships of the citizens to their government occurred during this era. Hyman quoted former Wisconsin Senator James B. Doolittle, who in 1879 estimated that 90 percent of a citizen's contact with the government was with the states and their political subdivisions. Only those few who traveled overseas, paid federal income taxes, or held national offices were touched by the national government, as was the case before the war.

Professor Bruce Ackerman[884] argues that today's Constitution is the product of three great constitutional moments: The Founding, Reconstruction, and the New Deal. Ackerman then calls for constitutional interpretation that "synthesizes"

---

[879] Kern & Wilson, *supra* note 161, 245–246.

[880] Knepper, *supra* note 27, 251–252.

[881] Egerton, supra note 759, 337–338.

[882] Sawrey, supra note 656, 640.

[883] Egerton, *supra* note 759, 347–348.

[884] Ackerman is Sterling Professor of Law and Political Science at Yale.

the founders' intent at each of these moments. Amar concurs with Ackerman's first two moments; he calls it the "Founding–Reconstruction" synthesis but is less enthusiastic about the third moment, the New Deal. Amar suggests that perhaps the progressive amendments,[885] ratified in the 1910s, served to enlarge federal power at the expense of the states in a more profound way than the unwritten changes which occurred during the 1930s.[886]

II. Ohio and Reconstruction

The state of Ohio was a primary component of this constitutional revolution. Ohio's soldiers and military leaders played a primary role in winning the war, and its political leaders played a leading role in securing the peace. The Reconstruction policies of this era were designed to ensure the support of moderate states, like Ohio.

In the previous seven chapters, we have presented a thumbnail sketch of Ohio's history, laws, politics, and culture. In the seventy years preceding the Civil War, Ohio was transformed from a wilderness populated by a few Native Americans into a vibrant and bustling state with a population of 2 million citizens, a developed agriculture, and a developing industrial base.

Ohioans have always been an independent group. When it came to removing the threat from indigenous Native Americans, or building roads, canals, railroads, and other infrastructure, Ohioans have generally agreed with national policies. Ohioans had enthusiastically supported the war and almost as enthusiastically supported emancipation and the early goals of (presidential) Reconstruction.

On the other hand, Ohioans had on more than one occasion demonstrated a contentious streak. Ohio's first constitution stressed local control. Its legislature held almost all the governmental power, and at various times it declared war on the other branches. Ohio helped pioneer the concept of nullification that led to the

---

[885]   The Sixteenth Amendment, ratified February 3, 1913, authorized a national income tax. The 17th Amendment, ratified April 8, 1913, mandated popular election of US senators, and the 19th amendment, ratified August 18, 1920, mandated women's suffrage, even in state elections.

[886]   One could also argue that the court's opinion in *West Coast Hotel v. Parrish,* 300 U.S. 379 (1937) called "the Court's surrender to the New Deal," and which overturned 30 years of constitutional jurisprudence centered around the "Liberty of Contract" analysis first proposed in *Lochner v. New York,* 198 U.S. 45 (1905), was the pivotal moment to which Ackerman alluded.

Civil War less than four decades later. Ohio flexed its political muscles to wrest the Toledo Strip away from Michigan, and it placed all sorts of procedural obstacles in the way of enforcing the Fugitive Slave Act.

Ohioans considered the Fourteenth Amendment an outline of the final terms of the peace treaty to end the Civil War. Congress directed the first four sections of the Fourteenth Amendment specifically toward the former Confederate states, and the fifth section empowered Congress to enforce the other four. However, Bingham and the other authors must have realized that this amendment would profoundly affect their states as well. Because of these concerns, because of Ohio's prominence in the Union, and because Ohio then, as now, was a political "swing" state, the Republican Congress crafted the amendment in moderate terms with states like Ohio in mind.

Southern states almost immediately rejected the Fourteenth Amendment, supposedly to get a "better deal" if Democrats took over the presidency and Congress in 1868. Ohioans did not take rejection lightly, and they lent their support to Radical Reconstruction. Their enthusiasm waned quickly, and by the time Ulysses S. Grant took office in March 1869, most Ohioans considered Reconstruction to be at an end. By this time, African American suffrage was a vote killer, and the Republicans tried to avoid this issue at all costs. The General Assembly ratified the Fifteenth Amendment the next year, only because Independents joined Republicans in voting for the measure. The scandals that occurred during the Grant administration and the Panic of 1873 diverted Ohioans' attention away from the issue of Reconstruction, and by the time Rutherford B. Hayes took office in 1877, Reconstruction, as a practical matter, was long gone.

III. Transformation

In the years before the war, courts interpreted the first ten amendments in a way that emphasized protecting states' rights. Amar cites two cases that affirmed *Barron* in support of his argument. In *Fox v. Ohio*[887] the court addressed an Ohio law forbidding the passing of counterfeit coin. In its opinion, the court upheld the statute as not repugnant to the Constitution, but the court further held that "the prohibitions contained in the amendments to the Constitution were intended to be restrictions upon the federal government, and not upon the authority of the

---

[887] *Fox v. State of Ohio*, 46 U.S. 410 (1847).

states."[888] In *Withers v. Buckley*,[889] the court held that "the Fifth Amendment must be understood as restraining the power of the general government, not as applicable to the states."[890] Amar contrasted the first ten amendments, which originally served to protect states' rights, with state bills of rights (like Ohio's) designed to protect the rights of citizens.[891]

Bingham is clearly the protagonist/hero in Amar's tale. After all, Madison proposed a "No state shall …" amendment in the 1790s and failed, whereas Bingham proposed his "No state shall" amendment in the 1860s and succeeded. Thanks to Bingham, the first ten (or eight or nine) amendments are set apart from the rest. Finally, Bingham began referring to the first ten amendments as a "Bill of Rights" in the 1850s, and in the next decade he set forth to make it into one. His efforts also helped to remove the taint of slavery from the original document.[892]

Incorporation, Amar writes, allowed federal judges to strike state and local laws. However, the courts did not begin the process of First Amendment incorporation until the 1920s[893] and did not strike down an act of Congress in this area until 1965.[894] It became a simple task to incorporate First Amendment rights (speech, religion, assembly, and press) against the states via the Fourteenth Amendment.[895] Federal judges, rather than local juries, became the guardians of free speech.[896]

Amar writes that the original intent of the Second Amendment was to provide for state—organized militias in lieu of a standing federal army. Bearing arms at that time was a political right equivalent to voting, jury service, or holding office. Reconstruction redefined bearing arms as a core civil right. The purpose

---

[888]   Ibid., 411.

[889]   61 U.S. 84 (1857).

[890]   Ibid., 91.

[891]   Amar, *supra* note 14, 286.

[892]   Amar, *supra* note 14, 293–294.

[893]   *See*, Gitlow v. New York, 268 U.S. 652 (1925).

[894]   Lamont v. Postmaster General, 381 U.S. 301 (1965).

[895]   Amar, *supra* note 14, 234.

[896]   Ibid., 242.

of bearing arms was now to protect one's home and not because the owner served in the militia.[897] Bearing arms thus became an individual, rather than a collective right.

The Third Amendment was not a good candidate for mechanical incorporation. Its original purpose reflected the founders' disdain for standing armies. By Reconstruction, this disdain had largely faded. The Third Amendment became the foundation for a right of privacy in the home that the Supreme Court had formulated in *Griswold v. Connecticut*.[898] By contrast, the Fourth Amendment had from the beginning protected private persons, and their private papers in their private homes.[899]

Reconstructing the Fifth Amendment was easy; Bingham wrote the first section of the Fourteenth Amendment specifically to overrule *Barron*, a property rights case. Even before the war, judges in nearly every state enforced a just compensation rule if one existed in the state Constitution or inferred it if such a clause did not exist.[900] This theme continued after the war, but was now sanctioned by federal legislation.

The founders had considered the jury—grand, petit, and civil—as the foundation of local control. Juries could refuse to enforce acts they consider unconstitutional, and they could easily decide cases in favor of local litigants and against the "Big Brother" that was the federal government.[901] Even before the war, abolitionist lawyers like Salmon P. Chase argued that a free black woman was entitled to a trial by jury before freedom could be taken away. However, the Fugitive Slave Act of 1850 laid the issue of a fugitive's freedom in the hands of a commissioner instead of a jury.[902]

The Reconstruction Congress noted the paradox in this right. Would an African American criminal defendant benefit from a local jury in which all African

---

[897]   Ibid., 258–259.

[898]   381 U.S. 479 (1965).

[899]   Amar, *supra* note 14, 267.

[900]   Ibid., 269.

[901]   Ibid., 98, 103–104.

[902]   Ibid., 270.

Americans were excluded? Similarly, would African Americans in the South benefit if an all-white grand jury refused to indict whites who terrorized them?

Eventually it became clear that southern jury review and jury nullification could be countered by reconstructing juries that impaneled both African-Americans and white citizens. Removal of cases to the federal court system helped accomplish this purpose.[903] Once the Fifteenth Amendment was ratified, African Americans would have the right to vote not only for representatives, but also in juries and in legislatures.

---

[903]   Ibid., 272–273.

Conclusion

It is quite clear that the Civil War and Reconstruction Era (1861–1877) had a profound effect on Ohio and its laws. Ohioans enthusiastically supported the War; over three hundred thousand Ohioans served the Union cause, and over thirty-five thousand died. Ohio citizens endured abuses of their rights of speech and press, as well as arrests of its citizens without trials, suspension of habeas corpus, and trials of civilians by military commissions. During the Reconstruction Era, Ohioans saw the enactment of the Fourteenth and Fifteenth Amendments by the barest of margins, and the General Assembly later repudiated their ratification of the Fourteenth Amendment. The enabling legislation that was a part of the Reconstruction Amendments allowed Congress to expand the jurisdiction of the federal courts, and to remove some cases from local juries and transfer the issues to the federal courts.

However, it is equally evident that Ohio and its citizens had an even more profound effect on the Civil War and Reconstruction. Ohio's citizens responded to the call to arms in record numbers. Its military leaders commanded and served in every major theater of the war. Ohio's farms and factories fueled the Union war machine, and its transportation and logistics facilities helped transport war materials to the troops at the front. Only one military campaign touched Ohio, Morgan's Raid in July 1863, and that was but a small affair.

In addition, Ohio's political leaders helped to secure the peace, and its military leaders enforced Reconstruction in the former Confederate states. Two of its citizens (Grant and Sherman) commanded the army during the Reconstruction era, two served as president of the United States (Grant and Hayes), and another (Wade) would have succeeded to the presidency had the Senate removed Andrew Johnson from the presidency. Another Ohioan (Chase) served as chief justice and presided over the first presidential impeachment trial in the country's history. Even more importantly, one of its citizens, whose name is largely lost to history (John Bingham), took advantage of a temporary congressional Republican "supermajority" to craft and enact the Fourteenth Amendment. This omnibus amendment served not only to answer all the questions left unanswered at the end of the conflict, but it gave a new definition to the term "citizenship" and spelled out the rights of every citizen and every person living in this country.

Bingham and the other "Reconstructors" crafted both the Fourteenth and Fifteenth Amendments with moderate states like Ohio in mind. Once the seceding states pledged their loyalty to the union, renounced slavery, and ratified the Fourteenth Amendment, the goals of Reconstruction were fulfilled for most Ohioans. The Removal legislation did increase the jurisdiction and the docket of the federal courts in Ohio, but the increase in commerce and business transactions in this era had much more impact on the courts. While the Radicals in Congress supported a more punitive Reconstruction policy and more expansive Fourteenth and Fifteenth Amendments, Bingham and his moderate colleagues realized that such policies and the amendments that resulted would never be approved by his constituents. If Ohioans had rejected the Fourteenth and Fifteenth Amendments, it is unlikely that these amendments would have been ratified.

It is also clear that Ohio Congressman John Armor Bingham, the man Magliocca calls "America's Founding Son," is the protagonist/hero in this story as well.

Bibliography

Official Records, Legal Codes and Statutes:

1. An Ordinance for the government of the Territory of the United States Northwest of the River Ohio. § 14, Art. V.
2. Northwest Ordinance of 1789.
3. Judiciary Act of 1789, 1 Stat. 73 (1789).
4. An Act to provide for the more convenient organization of the Courts of the United States. 2 Stat. 89 (1801).
5. Ohio Constitution of 1802.
6. An Act to regulate black and mulatto persons, 2 Laws of Ohio 63 (1804);
7. An Act to amend the act, entitled 'An Act Regulating black mulatto persons', Laws of Ohio 53 (1807) (Act of 1807).
8. An Act establishing Circuit Courts, and abridging the jurisdiction of the district courts in the districts of Kentucky, Tennessee, and Ohio. 2 Stat. 420 (1807).
9. An Act relating to Fugitives from labor or service from other states, 37 Laws of Ohio (1839).
10. Bankruptcy Act, 5 Stat. 440 (1841).
11. Judiciary Act of 1842. Stat. 516, 517 (1842).
12. An Act to authorize the establishment of separate schools for the education of colored children, and for other purposes, 47 Laws of Ohio 17 (1849).
13. Fugitive Slave Act, 9 Stat. 462 (1850).
14. Ohio Constitution of 1851.
15. An Act to Organize the Territories of Nebraska and Kansas. 10 Stat. 277 (1854).
16. An Act to Divide the State Ohio into two Judicial Districts. 10 Stat. 605 (1855).
17. An Act To prohibit the confinement of fugitives from slavery in the jails of Ohio, 54 Laws of Ohio 170 (1857).

18. An Act To prevent kidnapping, 54 Laws of Ohio 221 (1857).

19. An Act To repeal an act entitled 'An act to prohibit the confinement of fugitives from slavery in the jails of Ohio,' 55 Laws of Ohio 10 (1858).

20. An Act To repeal an act therein named, 55 Laws of Ohio 19 (1858).

21. An Act To amend section one of an act for the confinement of persons under the authority of the United States in the jails of this state, passed December 20, 1806, and to repeal section two of said act, 56 Laws of Ohio 158 (1859).

22. Ohio State Reports, Vols. 12–16, Crutchfield, 1861–66.

23. 4 James D. Richardson, *A Compilation of the Messages and Papers of the Presidents*, 1789–1897, (Published by Authority of Congress, 1900).

Newspapers and Periodicals:

1. *About Anti-Slavery Bugle* (New Lisbon, Ohio). 1845–1861. Library of Congress. Available at: http://www.chroniclingamerica.loc.gov/lccn/sn83035487 last visited July 27, 2013.

2. About.com Military History. *American Revolution: Brigadier General George Rogers Clark*. Located at: http://militaryhistory.about.com/od/americanrevolutio1/p/American-Revolution-Brigadier-General-George-Rogers-Clark.htm

3. Bateman and Selby, *Historical Encyclopedia of Illinois and History of St. Clair County* 698–701, found in: http://archive.org/stream/lawsofnorthwestt17nort/lawsofnorthwestt17nort_djvu.txt

4. *Biographical Directory of the United States Congress*. Edward Tiffin, (1766–1829). Available at: http://bioguide.congress.gov/scripts/biodisplay.pl?index=T000268

5. Bureau of the Public Debt. *Our Country: The 19ᵗʰ Century*. Located at: http://www.publicdebt.treas.gov/history/1800.htm

6. Concurring Opinions. The Northwest Ordinance Of 1787 And the Bill of Rights. Available at: http://concurringopinions.com/archives/2011/11/the-northwest-ordinance-of-1787-and-the-bill-of-rights.html

7. *Cong. Globe*, Thirty-Fifth Cong., Second Sess. 982 (1859).

8. Department of the Army: Lineage and Honors. Available at: http://www.history.army.mil/html/forcestruc/lineages/branches/inf/0003in.htm

9. <u>Docsnews.com-the magazine: Rebel Soldiers Lived and Died in Johnson's Island Prison on Lake Erie. Available at:</u> http://www.docsnews.com/johnsons.html

10. *Encyclopedia of Alabama*. Winthrop Sargent. Located at: http://www.encyclopediaofalabama.org/face/Article.jsp?id=h-2371

11. Justin Ewers. *Revoking Civil Liberties: Lincoln's Constitutional Dilemma*. U.S. News and World Report, February 10, 2009, available at: http://www.usnews.com/news/history/articles/2009/02/10/revoking-civil-liberties-lincolns-constitutional-dilemma

12. *Full Text of the Laws of the Northwest Territory*. Available at: <u>http://archive.org/stream/lawsofnorthwestt17nort/lawsofnorthwestt17nort_djvu.txt</u>

13. ExplorePAhistory.com: George Washington, Covenanter squatters Historical Marker. Located at: http://explorepahistorry.com/hmarker.php?markerId+1-A-28F See, also, Charles H. Ambler, George Washington and the West (Chapel Hill: University of North Carolina Press, 1936).

14. Tommy Griffiths. Book Review: *'Team of Rivals'—it's nothing like 'Lincoln.'* WTOP Entertainment News, December 26, 2012, available at www.wtop.com/541/3171891/Book-Review-Team-of-Rivals——its-nothing-like-Lincoln

15. Charles S. Hall, *Life and Letters of Samuel Holden Parsons: Major General in the Continental Army and Chief Judge of the Northwestern Territory, 1737–1789* (Otseningo Publishing Co., 1905). Available at: https://archive.org/details/lifelettersofsam00hall

16. Rutherford B. Hayes, diary entry, September 24, 1852, in *Diary and Letters of Rutherford Birchard Hayes, 19th President of the United States* (Charles Richard Williams ed., Columbus: Ohio Archaeological and Historical Society, Iss. 422, 1922).

17. hermitsdoor. Great American Documents: The Harrison Land Act of 1800. Available at: http://hermitsdoor.wordpress.com/2012/05/16/great-american-documents-the-harrison-land-act-of-1800/

18. Bernard Hibbitts. *Law Professor prompts Ohio to ratify 14th Amendment*. Jurist: Paper Chase Newsburst, March 17, 2003, available at: http://jurist.org/paperchase/2003/03/law-professor-prompts-ohio-to ratify.php

19. History Center Notes & Queries. *Our Stories* from Ft. Wayne & Allen County, Indiana. Located at: http://historycenterfw.blogspot.com/2012/07/remembering-little-turtle.html

20. W.H. Hunter, *Pathfinders of Jefferson County, Ohio.* Ohio Archaeological and Historical Society Publications, VIII (1900) at 195–96.

21. Indiana Commission on Public Records. *The Judicial Structure in Indiana: Northwest Territory Period, 1787–1800.* Available at: http://www.in.gov/icpr/2750.htm.

22. *Thomas Jefferson, James Madison, John Caldwell Calhoun. The Virginia and Kentucky Resolutions of 1798 and '99: With Jefferson's Original Draught Thereof. Also, Madison's Report, Calhoun's Address, Resolutions of the Several States in Relation to State Rights. With Other Documents in Support of the Jeffersonian Doctrines of '98*, Volume 265. Available at: http://books.google.com/books?id=c1c-AAAAYAAJ&dq=thomas+jefferson+quotes+federalists+judiciary&source=gbs_navlinks_s

23. *Journal of the Abraham Lincoln Association. Lincoln's Constitutional Dilemma: Emancipation and Black Suffrage. Available at:* http://quod.lib.umich.edu/j/jala/2629860.0005.104?rgn=main;view=fulltext

24. Justia U.S. Supreme Court: Scott v. Sandford. Available at: https://supreme.justia.com/cases/federal/us/60/393/case.html

25. James Madison, Alexander Hamilton, John Jay. *The Federalist Papers. The Classic Original Edition.* SoHo Books, Paperback edition. ISBN 978-1441413048.

26. Gerard N. Magliocca. *The Father of the 14th Amendment.* The New York Times Opinionator, September 17, 2013. available at: http://opinionator.blogs.nytimes.com/2013/09/17/the-father-of-the-14th-amendment/?_r=0

27. *Maxwell's Code*, available at www.ohiohistorycentral.org/w/Maxwell's_Code?rec=1470

28. Michigan.gov. Important Dates in Michigan's Quest for Statehood. Available at: https://www.michigan.gov/formergovernors/0,4584,7-212—79532—,00.html

29. National Center for Public Policy Research: The Fugitive Slave Act of 1850. Available at: http://www.nationalcenter.org/FugitiveSlaveAct.html

30. Ohio History 79–104 (R. Douglas Hurt, ed.) (quoting Kevin M. Gannon, *The Political Economy of Nullification: Ohio and the Bank of the United States, 1818–1824*, 81–82).

31. Ohio History Central, Ohio's State Tourism Slogans. Available at: http://ohiohistorycentral.org/w/Ohio's_State_Tourism_Slogans

32. Ohio History Central. Enabling Act of 1802. Available at: http://www.ohiohistorycentral.org/w/Enabling_Act_of_1802_(Transcript)

33. Ohio History Central: Charles Hammond. Available at: http://www.ohiohistorycentral.org/w/Charles_Hammond.

34. Ohio History Central. Ohio Constitutional Convention of 1802. Available at: http://www.ohiohistorycentral.org/w/Ohio_Constitutional_Convention_of_1802?rec=523

35. Ohio History Central. Ohio's State Tourism Slogans. available at: http://ohiohistorycentral.org/w/Ohio's_State_Tourism_Slogans

36. Ohio History Central: *Osborn v. Bank of the United States.* Available at: http://www.ohiohistorycentral.org/w/Osborn_v._Bank_of_the_United_States.

37. Ohio History Central. Arthur St. Clair. Located at: http://www.ohiohistorycentral.org/w/Arthur_St._Clair

38. Ohio History Central: Squatters. Located at: http://www.ohiohistorycentral.org/w/Squatters

39. Ohio History Central. John C. Symmes. Available at: http://www.ohiohistorycentral.org/w/John_C._Symmes

40. Ohio Legislative Service Commission, Issue 8. Municipal Home Rule. January 26, 2010. Available at: http://www.lsc.state.oh.us/membersonly/128municipalhomerule.pdf

41. Theodore Calvin Pease, The Laws of the Northwest Territory, 1788–1800 (Springfield, Illinois: Trustees of the Illinois State Historical Library, 1925). Available at: http://www.historykat.com/TNWRO/statutes/theodore-calvin-pease-laws-northwest-territory-1788-1800-springfield-ill-trustees-illinois.html

42. Staff (May 29, 2012). "The Public Land Survey System (PLSS)." National Atlas of the United States. U.S. Department of the Interior. Retrieved April 9, 2014.

43. Harriet Beecher Stowe. *Uncle Tom's Cabin.* SparkNotes.com Available at: http://www.sparknotes.com/lit/uncletom/context.html

44. Tennessee Constitution of 1796 is available at: http://www.tn.gov/tsla/founding_docs/33633_Transcript.pdf

45. *The Judicial Structure in Indiana: Northwest Territory Period, 1787–1800.* Available at: http://www.in.gov/icpr/2750.htm.

46. John Turley. 10 Reasons the US Is No Longer the Land of the Free. *The Wash. Post*, Jan. 13, 2012, *available at* http://www.washingtonpost.com/opinions/is-the-united-states-still-the-land-of-the-free/2012/01/04/gIQAvcD1wP_print.html

47. University of Akron, Thirty-Ninth Congress Project. Available at: http://www.uakron.edu/law/constitutionallaw/39th-congress-project/

48. U.S. Department of State, Office of The Historian. Milestones 1784–1800. Available at: http://history.state.gov/milestones/1784-1800/jay-treaty

49. U.S. HISTORY.com Panic of 1819. Available at: http://www.u-s-history.com/pages/h277.html

50. James Mitchell Varnum, *A Sketch of the Life and Public Services of James Mitchell Varnum of Rhode Island, Brigadier-General of the Continental Army; Member of the Continental Congress; Judge U.S. Supreme Court, N. W. Territory; Major-General Rhode Island Volunteer Militia* (Boston: David Clapp &, Son, Printers, 1906). Available at: https://archive.org/stream/sketchoflifepubl00varn#page/n9/mode/2up

51. Ted Widmer. The Age of Jackson. The Gilder Lehrman Institute of American History. Available at: http://www.gilderlehrman.org/history-by-era/jackson-lincoln/essays/age-jackson

52. Carl Wittke, *The Ohio-Michigan Boundary Dispute Re-examined,* Ohio State Archeological and Historical Quarterly (October, 1936).

Cases:

1. *Trevett v. Weeden,* (1786).

2. *Marbury v. Madison,* 5 U.S. 137 (1803).

3. *Ex parte Bollman,* 8 U.S. 75 (1807).

4. *Martin v. Hunter's Lessee,* 14 U.S. 304 (1816).

5. *State v. Carneal* (1817).

6. *McCulloch v. Maryland,* 17 U.S. 316 (1819).

7. *Cohens v. Virginia,* 19 U.S. 264 (1821).

8. *Osborn v. Bank of the United States,* 22 U.S. 9 Wheat. 738 (1824).

9. *Planter's Bank v. Georgia,* 22 U.S. 904 (1824).

10. *Barron v. Baltimore,* 32 U.S. (7 Pet.) 243 (1833).

11. *Lessee of Livingston v. Moore,* 32 U.S. (7 Pet.) 469 (1833).

12. *Louise v. Marot,* 9 Louisiana Rep. 476, 1836.

13. *Prigg v. Pennsylvania,* 41 U.S. 539 (1842).

14. *Jones v. Van Zandt,* 46 U.S. 215, How. 215 215 (1847).

15. *Fox v. State of Ohio,* 46 U.S. 410 (1847).

16. *Ex Parte Robinson,* 6 McLean 355, 20 F.Cas. 969 (S.D. Ohio, 1855).

17. *Anderson v. Poindexter,* 6 Ohio St. 622 (1856).

18. *Scott v. Sandford,* 60 US 393 (1857).

19. *Withers v. Buckley, 61 U.S. 84 (1857).*

20. *Abelman v. Booth,* 62 U.S. 506 (1859).

21. *Ex Parte Bushnell,* 9 Ohio St. 77 (1859).

22. *Commonwealth of Kentucky v. Dennison,* 65 U.S. 66 (1860).

23. *Ex Parte Merryman,* 17 F. Cas. 144 (C.C.D. Md. 1861)

24. *Ex Parte Vallandigham,* 68 U.S. (1 Wall.) 243 (1864).

25. Ex Parte McCardle, 74 U.S. (7 Wall.) 506.

26. *Ex Parte Milligan,* 71 U.S. (4 Wall.) 2 (1866).

27. *Slaughterhouse Cases,* 83 U.S. 36 (1873).

28. *The Civil Rights Cases,* 109 U.S. 3, (1883).

29. *Plessy v. Ferguson,* 163 U.S. 537 (1896).

30. *Lochner v. New York,* 198 U.S. 45 (1905).

31. Gitlow v. New York, 268 U.S. 652 (1925).

32. *West Coast Hotel v. Parrish,* 300 U.S. 379 (1937).

33. *Adamson v. California,* 322 U.S. 46 (1947).

34. *Brown v. Board of Education of Topeka,* 347 U.S 483 (1954).

35. Lamont v. Postmaster General, 381 U.S. 301 (1965).

36. *Griswold v. Connecticut,* 381 U.S. 479 (1965).

37. *Preterm Cleveland v. Voinovich* (1993), 89 Ohio App.3d 684, 627 N.E. 2d 570.

38. *Hamdi v. Rumsfeld,* 542 US 507 (2004).

Books:

1. Kenneth Ackerman. *The Gold Ring: Jim Fisk, Jay Gould and Black Friday 1869.* Lebanon, IN: De Capo Press, 2005.

2. Akhil Reed Amar. *The Bill of Rights: Creation and Reconstruction.* New Haven, CT: Yale University Press, 2000.

3. Charles H. Ambler, *George Washington and the West*. Chapel Hill, NC: University of North Carolina Press, 1936.

4. Debby Applegate, *The Most Famous Man in America: The Biography of Henry Ward Beeche*r. Image; Reprint edition. 2007

5. Caleb Atwater, *A History of the State of Ohio: Natural and Civil*. Nabu Press, 2010.

6. William Horatio Barnes, *History of the Thirty-Ninth Congress of the United States*. New York: Harper and Brothers Publishers, 1868.

7. John Spencer Bassett, *The Life of Andrew Jackson*. New York: MacMillan, 1931.

8. Michael Les Benedict. *A Compromise of Principle: Congressional Republicans and Reconstruction, 1863–1869*. Norton, 1974.

9. *The History of Ohio Law*. Michael Les Benedict & John F. Winkler eds., Ohio University Press, 2003.

10. *Black's Law Dictionary*. Ninth ed. 2009.

11. Nat Brandt, *The Town that Started the Civil War*. Syracuse University Press, 1990.

12. Jeffrey Paul Brown. *The Pursuit of Public Power: Political Culture in Ohio, 1787–1861*. Kent: Kent State University Press, 1994.

13. R. Carlisle Buley. *The Old Northwest: Pioneer Period 1815–1840*, vol. 1. Bloomington, IN: Indiana University Press, 1950.

14. Josiah Bunting III and A.M. Schlesinger Jr., eds. *Ulysses S. Grant*. Times Books, Henry Holt and Company, LLC, 2001.

15. Marvin R. Cain. *Lincoln's Attorney General Edward Bates of Missouri*. Columbia, MO: University of Missouri Press, 1965.

16. John C. Calhoun, *Exposition and Protest, in Union and Liberty: The Political Philosophy of John C. Calhoun*. Ross M. Lence ed., Indianapolis Liberty Fund, 1992.

17. Andrew R. L. Cayton, *Frontier Republic: Ideology and Politics in the Ohio Country, 1780–1825*. Kent State University Press, 1989.

18. Andrew Robert Lee Cayton. *Ohio: A History of a People*. Columbus, OH: Ohio State University Press, 2002.

19. Andrew Robert Lee Cayton. *The Center of a Great Empire: The Ohio Country in the Early Republic*. Athens: Ohio University Press, 2005.

20. 31 Robert E. Chaddock. *Ohio Before 1850: A Study of the Early Influence of Pennsylvania and the Southern Populations in Ohio, Studies in History, Economics and Public Law.* Faculty of Political Science of Columbia University eds., New York: Columbia University Press, 1908.

21. *The Civil War: A Visual History.* DK Publishing, first edition, 2011.

22. *Prestatehood Legal Materials: A Fifty-State Research Guide.* Michael Chiorazzi & Marguerite Most, eds. N-W. Routledge, 2006.

23. Robert L. Clinton. *Marbury V. Madison and Judicial Review.* Lawrence, KS: University Press of Kansas, 1989.

24. Arthur Charles Cole. *Centennial History of Illinois: The Era of the Civil War, 1848–1870.* Springfield, IL: Illinois Centennial Commission, 1919.

25. Archibald Cox. *The Court and the Constitution.* Boston: Houghton Mifflin Company, 1987.

26. Michael Kent Curtis. *No State Shall Abridge: The Fourteenth Amendment and the Bill of Rights.* Durham: Duke University Press 1987.

27. George Dangerfield. *The Awakening of American Nationalism: 1815–1828.* New York: Harper & Rowe, 1965.

28. Jefferson Davis. *The Rise and Fall of the Confederate Government.* Lebanon, IN: De Capo Press, 1990.

29. Christine Dee, ed. *Ohio's War: The Civil War in Documents.* Athens, OH: Ohio University Press, 2007.

30. David Dixon. *Never Come to Peace Again: Pontiac's Uprising and the Fate of the British Empire in North America.* Norman, OK: University of Oklahoma Press, 2005.

31. James Donovan. *A Terrible Glory.* New York: Back Bay Books, 2008.

32. Douglas R. Egerton. *The Wars of Reconstruction: The Brief, Violent History of America's Most Progressive Era.* New York: Bloomsbury Press, 2014.

33. Joseph J. Ellis. *His Excellency: George Washington.* 2004.

34. *Encyclopedia Britannica*: I: A-ak Bayes. Fifteenth ed. 33–34. Dale H. Hoiberg ed., Chicago, IL: Encyclopedia Britannica Inc., 2010.

35. Don Faber, *The Toledo War: The First Michigan–Ohio Rivalry.* The University of Michigan Press, 2008.

36. Don Faber, *The Boy Governor: Stevens T. Mason and the Birth of Michigan Politics.* Ann Arbor, MI: University of Michigan Press/Regional, 2012.

37. Daniel A. Farber, *Lincoln's Constitution.* Chicago: University of Chicago Press, 2004.

38. D.E. Fehrenbacher. *The Dred Scott Case.* New York: Oxford University Press, 1978.

39. Paul Finkelman, *An Imperfect Union: Slavery, Federalism, and Comity.* The Lawbook Exchange, Ltd. Reprint of the first and only edition, 2000.

40. Louis Fisher, *Presidential War Power.* Second ed. 2004

41. Louis Fisher. *Military Tribunals and Presidential Power: American Revolution to the War on Terrorism.* Lawrence, KS: University Press of Kansas, 2005.

42. Eric Foner. *Gateway to Freedom: The Hidden History of the Underground Railroad.* New York: W.W. Norton & Co., Inc., 2015.

43. Eric Foner. *Reconstruction: America's Unfinished Revolution, 1863–1877.* New York: HarperCollins Publishers Inc., 1988.

44. Shelby Foote. *The Civil War: A Narrative, Volume One, Fort Sumter to Perryville.* New York: First Vintage Books Edition, 1986.

45. William Dudley Foulke. *Life of Oliver P. Morton.* Indianapolis, IN: The Bowen-Merrill Company, 1899.

46. Lawrence M. Friedman. *A History of American Law.* Third Edition. New York: Simon and Schuster, 2007.

47. Alan D. Gaff. *Bayonets in the Wilderness: Anthony Wayne's Legion in the Old Northwest.* Norman, OK: University of Oklahoma Press, 2004.

48. Robert D. Geise. *American History to 1877.* Barron's EZ 101 Study Keys. Barron's Educational Series, February 19, 1992.

49. Alec R. Gilpin. *The Territory of Michigan, 1805–1837.* Lansing, MI: Michigan State University Press, 2002.

50. Doris Kerns Goodwin, *Team of Rivals: The Political Genius of Abraham Lincoln.* New York: Simon & Schuster Paperbacks, 2005.

51. Lawrence Goldstone. *Inherently Unequal: The Betrayal of Equal Rights by the Supreme Court, 1865–1903.* Walker & Company, 2011.

52. Wood Gray. *The Hidden Civil War: The Story of the Copperheads.* Viking, 1942.

53. *A Companion to the American Revolution.* Jack P. Greene & J.R. Pole, eds. Wiley-Blackwell, 2003.

54. Donald Greer. *The Incidence of the Terror during the French Revolution: A Statistical Interpretation.* 1935.

55. Michael Grossberg & Christopher Tomlins eds. *The Cambridge History of Law in America: Volume II, The Long Nineteenth Century (1789–1920).*

56. Sally E. Hadden and Alfred L. Brophy, eds. *A Companion to American Legal History.* Blackwell Publishing, 2013.

57. Daniel W. Hamilton. *Debating the Fourteenth Amendment: The Promise and Perils of Using Congressional Sources,* in Daniel J. Hulsebosch and R.B. Bernstein, eds., *Making Legal History: Essays in Honor of William E. Nelson.* New York: New York University Press, 2013.

58. Holman Hamilton. *Prologue to Conflict, the Crisis and Compromise of 1850.* Lexington, KY: University of Kentucky Press, 1964.

59. Walter Havinghurst. *Ohio: A Bicentennial History.* New York: W.W. Norton & Co., Inc., 1976.

60. Walter Havingshurst, *Ohio: A History.* New York: W.W. Norton, 1976; repr. Urbana: University of Illinois Press, 2001.

61. Michael F. Holt. *The Political Crisis of the 1850s.* New York: Norton, 1983.

62. Lester V. Horwitz. *The Longest Raid of the Civil War.* Cincinnati, OH: Farmcourt Publishing, Inc., 2001.

63. Martin Horwitz. *The Transformation of American Law, 1836–1874.* Cambridge, MA: Harvard University Press, 1977.

64. Charles Clifford Huntington, *A History of Banking and Currency in Ohio Before the Civil War.* BiblioBazaar, 2009.

65. R. Douglas Hurt. *The Ohio Frontier: Crucible of the Old Northwest, 1720–1830.* Bloomington, IN: Indiana University Press, 1998.

66. Harold M. Hyman. *A More Perfect Union. The Impact of the Civil War and Reconstruction on the Constitution.* New York: Alfred A. Knopf Inc., 1973.

67. Joseph B. James. *The Ratification of the Fourteenth Amendment.* Macon, GA: Mercer University Press, 1984.

68. Joseph B. James. *The Framing of the Fourteenth Amendment.* Champaign, IL: University of Illinois Press, 1996.

69. Kevin F. Kern & Gregory S. Wilson. *Ohio: A History of the Buckeye State.* New York: John Wiley & Sons, Inc., 2014.

70. Ralph Kirschner. *The Class of 1861: Custer, Ames, and Their Classmates After West Point.* Carbondale, IL: Southern Illinois University Press, 1999.

71. Frank L. Klement. *The Limits of Dissent: Clement L. Vallandigham and the Civil War*. New York: Fordham University Press, 1998.

72. George W. Knepper. *Ohio and Its People*. Kent State University Press, 1989.

73. A.J. Langguth. *Union 1812: The Americans Who Fought in the Second War of Independence*. New York: Simon & Schuster, 2006.

74. Thomas S. Mach. *"Gentleman George" Pendleton: Party Politics and Ideological Identity in Nineteenth-Century America*. Kent: Kent State University Press, 2007.

75. Gerard N. Magliocca. *American Founding Son: John Bingham and the Invention of the Fourteenth Amendment*. New York: NYU Press, 2013.

76. Earl M. Maltz, *Dred Scott and the Politics of Slavery (Landmark Law Cases & American Society*. University Press of Kansas, 2007.

77. Clement L. Martzolff, *The Autobiography of Thomas Ewing*, Ohio Archaeological and Historical Society Publications 22 (1913): 171–72.

78. Scott M. Matheson, Jr., *Presidential Constitutionalism in Perilous Times*. 2009.

79. William S. McFeeley. *Grant: A Biography*. New York: W.W. Norton & Company, 1981.

80. James M. McPherson. *Battle Cry of Freedom*. New York: Oxford University Press, 1988.

81. Donald F. Melhorn Jr., *Lest We Be Marshall'd: Judicial Powers and Politics in Ohio, 1806–1812*. Akron, OH: The University of Akron Press, 2003.

82. Allen R. Millett and Peter Maslowski. *For the Common Defense: A Military History of the United States of America*. New York: The Free Press, 1994.

83. Fred Milligan, *Ohio's Founding Fathers*. Bloomington, IN: iUniverse.com, 2003.

84. Carl H. Moneyhon. *The Impact of the Civil War and Reconstruction on Arkansas*. Fayetteville, AR: University of Arkansas Press, 2002.

85. Richard B. Morris, *The Forging of the Union, 1781–1789*. New York: Harper and Row, 1987.

86. Mark E. Neeley Jr. *The Fate of Liberty: Abraham Lincoln and Civil Liberties*. New York: Oxford University Press, 1991.

87. William E. Nelson. *Americanization of the Common Law: The Impact of Legal Change on Massachusetts Society, 1760–1830*. Cambridge, MA: Harvard University Press, 1975.

88. William E. Nelson. *Marbury V. Madison: The Origins and Legacy of Judicial Review*. University Press of Kansas, 2000.

89. William E. Nelson. *The 14th Amendment: From Political Principle to Judicial Doctrine*. Cambridge, MA: Harvard University Press, 1988.

90. Allen Nevins, *The American States During and After the Revolution, 1775–1789*. New York: Macmillan, 1924; repr. New York: Augustus M. Kelly, 1969.

91. Richard S. Newman. *The Transformation of American Abolitionism: Fighting Slavery in the Early Republic*. Chapel Hill, NC: University of North Carolina Press, 2002.

92. William J. Novak. *The People's Welfare: Law and Regulation in Nineteenth Century America*. Chapel Hill: Univ. of North Carolina Press, 1996.

93. *Ohio Authors and Their Books*. William Coyle ed. Cleveland, OH: The World Publishing Company, 1962.

94. Peter S. Onuf. *Statehood and Union: A History of the Northwest Ordinance*. Bloomington, IN: Indiana University Press, 1987.

95. Allen Peskin. *Garfield: A Biography*. Kent State University Press, 1978.

96. David M. Potter. *The Impending Crisis: America before the Civil War, 1848–1861*. New York: Harper Perennial, 2011.

97. J.G. Randall. *Constitutional Problems Under Lincoln*. Nabu Press, 2011.

98. Ervin H. Pollack, *Ohio Unreported Decisions*.

99. Whitelaw Reed. *Ohio in the War: Her Statesmen, Her Generals and Soldiers*. Cincinnati, OH: Clarke, 1895.

100. William H. Rehnquist. *All the Laws but One: Civil Liberties in Wartime*. New York: First Vintage Books Edition, 2000.

101. William H. Rehnquist. *Centennial Crisis: The Disputed Election of 1876*. New York: Vintage Books, 2004.

102. Robert C. Remini. *Andrew Jackson and the Course of American Empire, 1767–1821*. New York: Harper and Row, 1977.

103. David S. Reynolds. *Waking Giant: America in the Age of Jackson*. New York: Harper Collins Publishers, 2008.

104. James D. Richardson, *A Compilation of the Messages and Papers of the Presidents, 1789–1897*. Published by Authority of Congress, 1900.

105. Eugene H. Roseboom. *The Civil War Era: 1850–1873*. Columbus, OH: Ohio State Archeological and Historical Society, 1944.

106. Gerald N. Rosenberg. *The Hollow Hope: Can Courts Bring About Social Change?* Second Edition. Chicago: University of Chicago Press, 2008.

107. Carl Sandburg, *Abraham Lincoln: The War Years.* New York: Harcourt, Brace and Company, 1939.

108. Robert D. Sawrey. *Dubious Victory: The Reconstruction Debate in Ohio.* Lexington, KY: University of Kentucky Press, 1992.

109. David Schoenbrun. *Triumph in Paris: The Exploits of Benjamin Franklin.* New York: Harper & Row, 1976.

110. Charles Sellers. *The Market Evolution: Jacksonian America, 1815–1846.* New York: Oxford University Press, 1991.

111. Phillip R. Shriver & Clarence E. Wunderlin Jr., *Documentary Heritage of Ohio. Ohio Bicentennial Series.* Ohio University Press, 2001.

112. *The Sixty Years' War for the Great Lakes, 1754–1814.* David Curtis Skaggs & Larry L. Nelson eds. East Lansing, MI: Michigan State University Press, 2001.

113. Carl E. Skeen, *John Armstrong, Jr., 1758–1843: A Biography.* Syracuse University Press, 1982.

114. Jean Edward Smith. *Grant.* New York: Simon and Schuster, 2001.

115. *The Life and Public Services of Arthur St. Clair.* William Henry Smith ed. Robert Clarke & Company, 1882.

116. Steven H. Steinglass & Gino J. Scarselli. *The Ohio State Constitution.* Oxford University Press, 2011.

117. Geoffrey R. Stone. *Perilous Times: Free Speech in Wartime.* New York: W. W. Norton & Co., first ed. 2004.

118. Joseph Story, *Commentaries on the Constitution of the United States.* 1833.

119. Wiley Sword. *President Washington's Indian War: The Struggle for the Old Northwest, 1790–1795.* University of Oklahoma Press, 1985.

120. *The Civil War: A Visual History.* DK Publishing. First edition. 2011.

121. 1 & 2 *The Life and Public Services of Arthur St. Clair.* William Henry Smith ed. Robert Clarke & Company, 1882.

122. *The Sixty Years' War for the Great Lakes, 1754–1814.* David Curtis Skaggs & Larry L. Nelson eds. East Lansing, MI: Michigan State University Press, 2001.

123. Benjamin P. Thomas and Harold M. Hyman. *Stanton: The Life and Times of Lincoln's Secretary of War.* Greenwood Press reprint, 1980.

124. Gilbert Treadway, *Democratic Opposition to the Lincoln Administration in Indiana*. Indianapolis, IN: Indiana Historical Bureau, 1973

125. Hans L. Trefousse. *Andrew Johnson: A Biography*. New York: W.W. Norton, 1989.

126. Logan Douglas Trent. *The Credit Mobilier*. New York: Arno Press, Inc., 1981.

127. Robert M. Utley. *Frontier Regulars: The United States Army and the Indian, 1866–1891*. Lincoln, NE: University of Nebraska Press, 1973.

128. William T. Utter, *The Frontier State: 1803–1825*. Ohio Historical Society, 1968.

129. David Von Drehle. *Rise to Greatness: Abraham Lincoln and America's Most Perilous Year*. New York: Henry Holt and Company, first edition, 2012.

130. John Waugh. *On the Brink of Civil War: The Compromise of 1850 and How It Changed the Course of American History*. Wilmington, DE: Scholarly Resources, 2003.

131. Jennifer L. Weber. *Copperheads: The Rise and Fall of Lincoln's Opponents in the North*. New York: Oxford University Press, 2006.

132. Joseph Wheelan. *Terrible Swift Sword: The Life of General Phillip H. Sheridan*. De Capo Press, 2012.

133. C. Albert White, *A History of the Rectangular Survey System*. Bureau of Land Management, 1983.

134. Jonathan W. White. *Abraham Lincoln and Treason in the Civil War: The Trials of John Merryman*. Baton Rouge, LA: Louisiana State University Press, 2011.

135. Frank J. Williams. *Judging Lincoln*. Southern Illinois Press, first edition, 2002.

136. John F. Winkler, *Fallen Timbers 1794: The US Army's First Victory. Campaign*. Osprey Publishing, first ed., 2013.

137. Calvin M Young, *Little Turtle. Me-she-kin-no-quah: The Great Chief of the Miami Indian Nation; Being a Sketch of His Life, Together with that of William Wells and Some Noted Descendants*. Sentinel Ptg. Company, 1917.

138. Arthur Zilversmit, *The First Emancipation: The Abolition of Slavery in the North*. Chicago: University of Chicago Press, 1967

Articles:

1. Jason A. Adkins, *Lincoln's Constitution Revisited*, 36 N. Ky. L. Rev. 211, (2009).

2. Richard L. Aynes. *Unintended Consequences of the Fourteenth Amendment and What They Tell Us About Its Interpretation*, 39 Akron L.Rev. 289 (2006).

3. Richard L. Aynes, *The Thirty-Ninth Congress (1865–1867) and the 14th Amendment: Some Preliminary Perspectives.* 42 Akron Law Rev. 1019 (2009).

4. Michael Les Benedict, *Lincoln and Constitutional Politics*, 93 Marq. L. Rev. 1333 (2010).

5. James Bond. *The Original Understanding of the Fourteenth Amendment in Illinois, Ohio, and Pennsylvania.* Akron L.Rev. 18 (Winter 1985).

6. Robert G. Bracknell, Book Review, 47 Naval L. Rev. 208, (2000) (Reviewing William H. Rehnquist, All the Laws but One: Civil Liberties in Wartime (1998)).

7. Michael B. Brennan, Book Review, 83 Marq. L. Rev. 221, (1999) (Reviewing William H. Rehnquist, All the Laws but One: Civil Liberties in Wartime (1998)).

8. Burrus M. Carnahan. *Lincoln, Lieber, and the Laws of War: The Origins and Limits of the Principle of Military Necessity.* 92 American Journal of International Law 213 (1988).

9. Carol Chomsky. *The United States–Dakota War Trials: A Study in Military Injustice*, 43 Stanford Law Review (1990).

10. Frank Theodore Cole. *Thomas Worthington.* Ohio Archaeological and Historical Quarterly (October 1903).

11. Edwin S. Corwin, *The Rise and Establishment of Judicial Review*," parts 1 and 2, Mich. L. Rev. 9 (December 1910): 102–25; (February 1911): 283 – 316.

12. Steven P. Crowley. *The Majoritarian Difficulty: Elected Judiciaries and the Rule of Law*, 62 U. Chi. L. Rev. 689, 714 716 (Spring 1995)

13. Michael Kent Curtis. *Lincoln, Vallandigham, and Anti-War Speech in the Civil War*, 7 William and Mary Bill of Rights Journal 105 (1998).

14. Paul Finkelman, *Scott v. Sandford: The Court's Most Dreadful Case and How It Changed History*, 82 Chi.-Kent L. Rev. 3, 3–48 (2007).

15. Sydney G. Fisher. *The Suspension of Habeas Corpus During the War of the Rebellion*, 3 Political Science Quarterly 454 (1888).

16. Margaret A. Garvin, *All the Laws but One: Civil Liberties in Wartime*, 16 Const. Comment 691, (1999).

17. Timothy S. Huebner, *Lincoln's Legacy: Enduring Lessons of Executive Power*, 3 Alb. Gov't L. Rev. 615, 621 (2010).

18. Robert H. Jackson, *Wartime Security and Liberty Under Law*, 55 Buff. L. Rev. 1089, (2008).

19. Thomas Jefferson. Notes on the State of Virginia.

20. Robert A. Kagan, Bliss Cartwright, Lawrence M. Friedman, and Stanton Wheeler, *The Business of State Supreme Courts, 1870–1970, 30 Stanford L. Rev.* 121 (1977).

21. Craig S. Lerner, *Saving the Constitution: Lincoln, Secession, and the Price of Union*, 102 Mich. L. Rev. 1263, (2004).

22. Clement L. Martzolff, *The Autobiography of Thomas Ewing*, Ohio Archaeological and Historical Society Publications 22 (1913).

23. Eli Palomares, *Illegal Confinement: Presidential Authority to Suspend the Privilege of the Writ of Habeas Corpus During Times of Emergency*, 12 S. Cal. Interdisc. L.J. 101, 105 (2002).

24. Michael Stokes Paulsen, *The Constitution of Necessity*, 79 Notre Dame L. Rev. 1257, (2004).

25. Saikrishna Bangalore Prakash, *The Great Suspender's Unconstitutional Suspension of the Great Writ*, 3 Alb. Gov't L. Rev. 575, (2010).

26. William H. Rehnquist, *Civil Liberty and the Civil War: The Indianapolis Treason Trials*, 72 Ind. L.J. 927, 927 (1997).

27. William J. Rich. *Why Privileges and Immunities? An Explanation of the Framers Intent. 42 Akron L. Rev.* 1113 (2009).

28. Irwin S Rhodes, *The History of the United States District Court for the Southern District of Ohio.* U. Cin. L. Rev. 24 (Summer 1955)

29. Francis P. Sempa, *The Wartime Constitution: The Charging Balance of Power Among the Three Branches of Government in Wartime*, 26 T.M. Cooley L. Rev. 25, (2009).

30. Geoffrey R. Stone, *Abraham Lincoln's First Amendment*, 78 N.Y.U. L. Rev. 1, 22 (2003).

31. Barbara A. Terzian, *Symposium: The Ohio Constitution—Then and Now: An Examination of the Law and History of the Ohio Constitution on the Occasion of Its Bicentennial: Ohio's Constitutions: An Historical Perspective,* 51 Clev. St. L. Rev. 357 (2004).

32. Amanda L. Tyler, *The Forgotten Core Meaning of the Suspension Clause,* 125 Harv. L. Rev. 901, (2012).

33. Frank J. Williams, *Abraham Lincoln, Civil Liberties and the Croning Letter,* 5 Roger Williams U. L. Rev. 319, (2000).

34. John F. Winkler. *The Probate Courts of Ohio.* 28 U. Tol. L. Rev. 563.

Printed in the United States
By Bookmasters